CREATIVE HOMEOWNER®

ULTIMATE GUIDE

Cabinets, Shelves,
and Home Storage Solutions

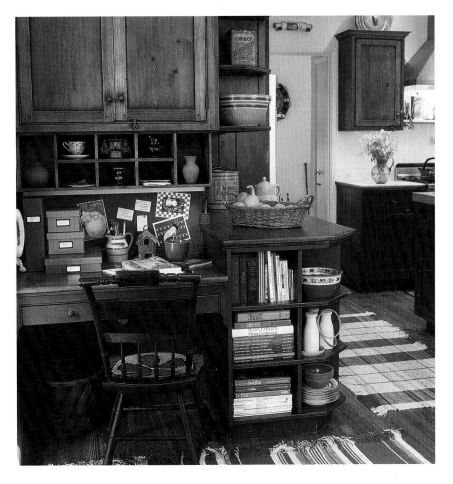

36 STORAGE PROJECTS
Plus Ideas for Organizing Your Home

CREATIVE HOMEOWNER®, Upper Saddle River, New Jersey

CRE ATIVE
HOMEOWNER®

A Division of Federal Marketing Corp.
Upper Saddle River, NJ

ULTIMATE GUIDE CABINETS, SHELVES, AND HOME STORAGE SOLUTIONS, Second Edition

WRITERS	Herb Hughes, Ken OBerrect, Bob Flexner (Wood Finishing), Neal Barrett
MANAGING EDITOR	Fran Donegan
JUNIOR EDITOR	Jennifer Calvert
PHOTO COORDINATOR	Mary Dolan
DIGITAL IMAGING SPECIALIST	Frank Dyer
INDEXER	Schroeder Indexing Services
ILLUSTRATIONS	Frank Rohrbach, Paul M. Schumm, Tom Klenck
COVER DESIGN	Glee Barre
LAYOUT	David Geer
COVER PHOTOGRAPHY	(front) Olson Photographic, LLC (back) courtesy of Ikea

CREATIVE HOMEOWNER

VICE PRESIDENT AND PUBLISHER	Timothy O. Bakke
MANAGING EDITOR	Fran J. Donegan
ART DIRECTOR	David Geer
PRODUCTION COORDINATOR	Sara M. Markowitz

Current Printing (last digit)
10 9 8 7 6 5 4 3 2 1

Manufactured in the United States of America

Ultimate Guide to Cabinets, Shelves, and Home Storage Solutions, Second Edition
First edition published as *Cabinets, Shelves & Home Storage Solutions*
Library of Congress Control Number: 2008934550
ISBN-10: 1-58011-436-9
ISBN-13: 978-1-58011-436-3

CREATIVE HOMEOWNER®
A Division of Federal Marketing Corp.
24 Park Way
Upper Saddle River, NJ 07458
www.creativehomeowner.com

safety

Although the methods in this book have been reviewed for safety, it is not possible to overstate the importance of using the safest methods you can. What follows are reminders—some do's and don'ts of work safety—to use along with your common sense.

- Always use caution, care, and good judgment when following the procedures described in this book.
- Always be sure that the electrical setup is safe, that no circuit is overloaded, and that all power tools and outlets are properly grounded. Do not use power tools in wet locations.
- Always read container labels on paints, solvents, and other products; provide ventilation; and observe all other warnings.
- Always read the manufacturer's instructions for using a tool, especially the warnings.
- Use hold-downs and push sticks whenever possible when working on a table saw. Avoid working short pieces if you can.
- Always remove the key from any drill chuck (portable or press) before starting the drill.
- Always pay deliberate attention to how a tool works so that you can avoid being injured.
- Always know the limitations of your tools. Do not try to force them to do what they were not designed to do.
- Always make sure that any adjustment is locked before proceeding. For example, always check the rip fence on a table saw or the bevel adjustment on a portable saw before starting to work.
- Always clamp small pieces to a bench or other work surface when using a power tool.
- Always wear the appropriate rubber gloves or work gloves when handling chemicals, moving or stacking lumber, working with concrete, or doing heavy construction.
- Always wear a disposable face mask when you create dust by sawing or sanding. Use a special filtering respirator when working with toxic substances and solvents.
- Always wear eye protection, especially when using power tools or striking metal on metal or concrete; a chip can fly off, for example, when chiseling concrete.
- Never work while wearing loose clothing, open cuffs, or jewelry; tie back long hair.
- Always be aware that there is seldom enough time for your body's reflexes to save you from injury from a power tool in a dangerous situation; everything happens too fast. Be alert!
- Always keep your hands away from the business ends of blades, cutters, and bits.
- Always hold a circular saw firmly, usually with both hands.
- Always use a drill with an auxiliary handle to control the torque when using large-size bits.
- Always check your local building codes when planning new construction. The codes are intended to protect public safety and should be observed to the letter.
- Never work with power tools when you are tired or when under the influence of alcohol or drugs.
- Never cut tiny pieces of wood or pipe using a power saw. When you need a small piece, saw it from a securely clamped longer piece.
- Never change a saw blade or a drill or router bit unless the power cord is unplugged. Do not depend on the switch being off. You might accidentally hit it.
- Never work in insufficient lighting.
- Never work with dull tools. Have them sharpened, or learn how to sharpen them yourself.
- Never use a power tool on a workpiece—large or small—that is not firmly supported.
- Never saw a workpiece that spans a large distance between horses without close support on each side of the cut; the piece can bend, closing on and jamming the blade, causing saw kickback.
- When sawing, never support a workpiece from underneath with your leg or other part of your body.
- Never carry sharp or pointed tools, such as utility knives, awls, or chisels, in your pocket. If you want to carry any of these tools, use a special-purpose tool belt that has leather pockets and holders.

contents

storage solutions

IDEAS FOR CUTTING THE CLUTTER IN YOUR HOME

MANY HOMEOWNERS complain that they do not have enough storage space in their homes. But in some cases, it isn't the square footage that is lacking but how the space is organized. In other homes, valuable storage areas are overlooked entirely. The ideas presented throughout this book will help in both situations. We will show you how to maximize storage and provide ideas for squeezing out of your home the most available storage space possible.

The first step to conquering your storage problem is to determine just what it is that needs to be stored. For example, requirements for kitchen storage differ from your storage needs in the bedroom or bath. Go through each room in the house, and list the storage requirements. Sometimes the list alone will give you ideas as to where and how to store specific items. Then turn to the projects in this book. They will provide practical solutions to your storage problems.

Lofts and sloping ceilings present unusual storage situations. These owners turned a loft into a private reading area with simple built-in shelves and floor-level windows.

Consider every available space for storage or display. These shallow under-stair shelves hold collectibles.

Clockwise (from above) This built-in displays an owner's collection of rare books while keeping the more pedestrian TV behind a panel door. A landing spot for keys, cell phones, and family messages makes getting in and out of the house easy. Baskets can hold gloves, hats, and scarves when placed near a back door or in a mudroom. Kitchen storage is always at a premium, but don't forget a place for recyclables—or often-used small appliances.

Closed cabinets keep gardening supplies hidden while cabinets with glass doors display vases.

Clockwise (from above) Units like this come in handy when placed near the entrance that the family uses. Small bathrooms often require tall, narrow cabinets for toiletries and beauty supplies. Wall-mounted files keep the home office neat, and they put often-used materials where you can reach them easily. Keep sports gear accessible with custom-closet units.

Clockwise (from top right) When life gives you a window, make a window seat and add matching cabinets—note the heating vents near the floor. This reading nook is surrounded by cabinet storage in this kitchen. When planning storage units for your mudroom, be sure to provide space for everyone in the family, including the pets. A refurbished hutch can provide valuable storage space and become a design focal point.

1 techniques

The real mark of an experienced wood-worker is not the number of tools that he or she owns or the square footage of his shop, but rather the techniques he has developed over the years. An accomplished craftsperson will have a few well rehearsed ways of completing a given task. In comparison, a less experienced person may waste time and materials trying to figure out how to perform the same operation. For the most part, technique is something refined over time, but mastering a few techniques now will prevent you from wasting time and effort.

The techniques explained here are widely applicable for the projects in this book. Some techniques, such as those for building drawers and doors, appear in this chapter so that they needn't be repeated with each project. Wherever necessary, these techniques have been conveniently cross-referenced throughout the book.

WORKING WITH PLYWOOD

Plywood is the material of choice for most of these projects. Plywood cabinets are easier to build because you are starting with large panels that, unlike solid wood, will not shrink or swell with changes in humidity. Building with plywood is less expensive than using solid wood. However, the 4x8-foot panels are awkward to handle.

FINISHING EDGES

ONE OF THE PROBLEMS WITH PLYWOOD is the appearance of its edges. Unless you are working with a premium plywood material, such as Baltic birch ply, most plywoods have voids within their laminations, leaving unsightly gaps visible along the edges. Many of the joinery techniques used in cabinetmaking conceal most of the plywood edges, but there will be those occasions when you will have to take measures to conceal an ugly edge. If the plywood will be painted, you can fill the rough edge and sand it smooth. Otherwise, you can conceal the edge with wood tape or solid-wood edge banding.

Filling an Edge. Thin down latex wood putty with water until it is easily spreadable, and apply it along the edge with a putty knife. After the putty has dried completely, lightly sand the edge with 150-grit sandpaper.

Wood Tape. Most home centers now stock wood tape to match commonly sold plywood panels. Some kinds of wood tape come with pressure-sensitive or heat-activated adhesive so the tape can simply be pressed or ironed onto the edge of the plywood. After the tape is firmly attached to the plywood, lightly sand the edges with 150-grit sandpaper. Installing wood tape to cover a plywood edge is fast, easy, and economical, but it isn't the most durable edge treatment.

Molding and Solid Wood. You can get a more durable edge that's almost as easy to apply as wood tape simply by gluing solid wood directly onto the edge of the plywood. Screen and half-round molding are both good choices; wider trim will give the appearance of a more substantial panel. You can use masking tape to hold the molding in place while the glue dries. After the glue dries, you can sand or plane the edge flush with the plywood, but it's easier to use a piloted flush-trimming bit in your router.

WOOD TAPE

MOLDING AND SOLID WOOD

Masking Tape

CUTTING AND TRIMMING PLYWOOD

BECAUSE A FULL PLYWOOD PANEL is large and heavy, it is usually easier and safer to cut the panel using a portable saw or router instead of trying to maneuver the panel over a table saw or router table.

One way to break panels down to a manageable size is to make freehand cuts using a portable circular saw, running the saw along a layout line. However, freehand cuts are not accurate enough for most cabinet work. So begin by using a portable circular saw to rip panels about ¼ inch oversize. Then rip them to final width on the table saw, guiding the factory edges against the rip fence.

Even after panels are ripped to width, many are too long and wide to crosscut to length on the table saw. Instead, make your crosscuts with the portable circular saw, guiding the saw against a straightedge, or better yet, make a straight-cutting jig.

Making the Straight-Cutting Jig. Guiding a circular saw along a simple straightedge is a bit tricky because the straightedge must be offset from the cut line by a distance that is exactly equal to the distance between the edge of the saw base and the blade. The straight-cutting jig is custom-cut to your saw and blade so you can set the edge of the jig right on the cut line without worrying about an offset.

The jig is simply a straight-edged board that is glued to a hardboard base. For your straightedge, use any length of plywood or solid lumber that has two straight edges and is at least 2 inches wide. Glue the straightedge to a length of ⅛-inch-thick tempered hardboard, allowing about 8 inches of hardboard on both sides.

Fasten the straightedge onto the hardboard with glue and screws. Screw through the hardboard into the straightedge, and countersink the screws slightly.

Once the glue has dried, trim off one side of the base. To do this, square the blade to the base of the saw; adjust the depth of cut to ¼ inch; and place the jig on a scrap of plywood. When you make the cut, run the edge of the circular saw's base against the straightedge. This will create a straight base edge that shows the saw's exact cutting line.

To use the jig, clamp it onto the workpiece, and align the edge of the base along the cutting line. Place the clamps along the extra hardboard on the untrimmed side of the jig so that the saw's motor won't run into clamps during the cut. When you get a new saw blade, retrim one side of the jig so you know the cut line will coincide precisely with the edge of the jig.

MAKING THE STRAIGHT-CUTTING JIG

Guide

Tempered Hardboard Base

Countersunk Screws

pro tip

SPLINTER-FREE PLYWOOD CUTS

WHEN MARKING PLYWOOD, SCORE THE LAYOUT LINES WITH A UTILITY KNIFE INSTEAD OF DRAWING A PENCIL LINE. SCORING HAS TWO ADVANTAGES OVER DRAWING LINES. FIRST, YOUR KNIFE IS A MORE ACCURATE MARKING TOOL THAN A PENCIL. THE SECOND ADVANTAGE IS THAT BY CUTTING THROUGH THE VENEER, THE KNIFE LINE WILL HELP PREVENT CHIPPING AND TEAR-OUT WHEN YOU MAKE THE CUT.

● EDGE-GLUING STOCK

SOMETIMES YOU NEED A PANEL for a project, and plywood just won't do. You want the look of solid wood, but today's lumberyards rarely have solid wood in wide panels. The solution is to edge-glue smaller boards to make a wider panel. If you are careful to match grain, it will be hard to tell that the panel is not one wide board.

1 Cut stock and joint edges. The key to successful edge-gluing is perfectly straight glue surfaces on the edges. The easiest way to achieve such edges is with a jointer, but if you don't have one, you can carefully plane the edges square and flat with a hand plane. Use the largest plane you have for the flattest edge.

2 Arrange the boards. Check the ends of the boards for the direction of the annual growth rings in the wood. Orient all the boards in the same direction. This way, if the panel has any tendency to warp, the boards will all move in the same direction, and fas-

teners will more readily control the warping. If you alternate the growth rings up and down as some books recommend, the panel will turn into a washboard.

3 Glue and clamp the panel. Apply glue to all the edges to be glued. Using as many bar or pipe clamps as necessary, clamp the panel together. Make sure you alternate the clamps above and below the panel for even clamping pressure. Check that all the boards are aligned with no edges sticking up.

4 Finish the panel. Don't wait until the glue dries hard to clean up the squeeze-out. It's easier to scrape off the excess glue if you do so when it has reached a rubbery consistency; then it just peels off cleanly. In any case, make sure you get all the glue off before you plane. Glue will quickly dull the plane's blade. Once the glue is cured, plane or sand the panel smooth.

1. CUT STOCK AND JOINT EDGES

Hand Plane

2. ARRANGE THE BOARDS

Orient growth rings in the same direction.

3. GLUE AND CLAMP THE PANEL

Hardwood cauls help evenly distribute clamping pressure.

Alternate clamps above and below.

4. FINISH THE PANEL

Stop

● JOINERY

You can join wood in a variety of ways, ranging from the simple butt joint, to the stronger, more sophisticated dovetail joint, to a whole range of other types of joints that vary in strength and complexity. However, only a few simple joints are called for in the projects in this book. The cabinet carcases are assembled with butt, rabbet, dado, and miter joints. For the frame and panel doors, you will also need to learn how to make simple mortise-and-tenon joints.

Butt Joint

A butt joint is simply two pieces of wood butted together. It is typically secured with glue and some other type of fastener. Although it's a weak joint, it can be easily reinforced. Butt joints are commonly used in face frames where strength is not important because the face-frame members are usually glued to the cabinet. However, face-frame butt joints are often reinforced with dowels or biscuits, which not only add strength but help align the pieces during glue-up.

Miter Joint

A miter joint is essentially an angled butt joint. Like the butt joint, the miter joint requires additional reinforcement with fasteners. Use a miter joint where two pieces of trim or molding meet at a corner. You can also use a miter joint on a plywood carcase so that none of the unsightly plywood edge shows along the joint line.

BUTT JOINT

MITER JOINT

Reinforcing Joints with Dowels

Wood dowels can increase the strength and improve the accuracy of butt joints. In face-frame construction, the joint usually includes two dowels glued into each end of a rail (the horizontal member) and then into corresponding holes in the stiles (the vertical members).

1 **Locate the dowel holes.** To locate dowel holes accurately, temporarily position the two mating pieces in place. Strike a line on both members indicating the dowel locations. Transfer that mark onto the edge of each piece with a square.

2 **Drill the holes.** Use a doweling jig to ensure that the dowel holes are drilled exactly equidistant from the two faces of the piece. Use a stop collar or a piece of tape on the bit to indicate when you have drilled to the correct depth.

3 **Assemble the parts.** Apply glue to the dowels, and insert them in the holes in one of the parts to be joined. Attach the mating part, and clamp the assembly until the glue has set.

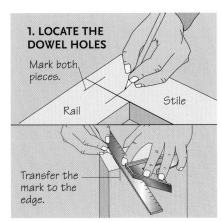

1. LOCATE THE DOWEL HOLES

Mark both pieces.

Rail

Stile

Transfer the mark to the edge.

2. DRILL THE HOLES

Doweling Jig

Stop Collar

Stile

3. ASSEMBLE THE PARTS

Dowels

Reinforcing Joints with Biscuits

Biscuit joinery is quickly replacing dowel joinery because these strong joints can be made more quickly. Biscuit joinery uses wooden biscuits that are pieces of pressed wood shaped like flat footballs. The biscuit joining machine or plate joiner cuts slots in the pieces to be joined. The slots are perfectly aligned from top to bottom. The biscuits are slightly shorter than the slots to allow a bit of lateral adjustment during glue-up. This is very handy because face surfaces are automatically flush but you can move pieces back and forth a bit during glue-up to make sure ends are absolutely flush and square.

Making Biscuit Joints

1 **Locate biscuit slots.** Mark the locations of biscuit slots on the faces of parts to be joined just as you would dowel holes, but you don't have to extend the lines to the edges. Make sure that the workpieces are thick enough or wide enough to accept the elliptically-shaped biscuits without having them stick through the sides. Also make sure you use the right size biscuit for the job and that the plate joiner is set to the correct depth of cut for the biscuit size you are using. The three most common biscuit sizes are 0 (smallest), 10 (medium), and 20 (largest and most commonly used in ¾-inch sheet stock).

2 **Make the cuts.** Clamp the workpiece to a stable work surface. Align the biscuit joiner with the marks you made, and move the cutter into the wood. Make sure you hold the machine firmly and properly aligned during the cut.

3 **Apply glue and assemble the parts.** Spread glue in the slots and along the edges of the parts to be joined. Don't put glue on the biscuits. One of the major reasons why biscuits are so strong is that they expand when they come in contact with the glue. If you put glue on them first, the biscuits won't fit in their slots. Once you've spread the glue, tap the biscuits into their slots. Clamp the parts until the glue is dry.

1. LOCATE BISCUIT SLOTS

Mark biscuit location on both pieces.

2. MARK THE CUTS

Biscuits

3. APPLY GLUE AND ASSEMBLE THE PARTS

DADOES, GROOVES, AND RABBETS

DADOES AND GROOVES are identical except for their relationship in respect to the wood's grain: dadoes are actually a type of groove that runs across the grain; grooves that run with the grain are not dadoes. For the sake of clarity, we'll use the term groove to describe only grooves that run with the grain. A rabbet is like a ledge cut along one edge of a piece. Dadoes are commonly used for fitting shelves and partitions into cabinet panels. Grooves are commonly used for fitting partitions and insetting shelf standards, while rabbets most often are used for joining cabinet panels and insetting cabinet backs.

Making Dadoes and Grooves with a Table Saw

Use a rip fence when making dadoes and grooves on a table saw. As a result, this method is most suited to making long grooves. For example, this is a very handy setup for making grooves for insetting shelf standards.

You can use the table saw to make dadoes as well, but the longer the panel is, the more awkward this operation will be. You will find that the router is usually the better tool for making dadoes in large cabinet sides.

1 Make a test cut. Unplug the saw, and replace your regular saw blade with a dado cutter. Use either the wobble-style or stacked cutter setup for the desired cut. Adjust the cutter for the proper depth of cut, and set the fence to the desired distance from the cutter.

2 Make the final cut. To cut the groove or dado in your panel, simply run the panel over the blade, and make the cut. Always use push blocks and hold-downs where appropriate to keep the workpiece from lifting off the saw table or kicking back.

You can make a featherboard hold-down simply by kerfing the end of a small board that has had its ends cut on the diagonal.

Note: When working with a stacked or wobble-type dado blade, you may need a different throat plate with a wider opening than the one used with an ordinary blade. Install the dado head, and turn the blade by hand to test its clearance. If it makes contact with the throat plate, you will have to make a replacement wooden throat plate. Refer to your saw's owner's manual for instructions.

1. MAKE A TEST CUT

Rip Fence

End View

Workpiece

Table Insert

Dado Cutter Set to Width and Depth of Dado

Saw Table

2. MAKE THE FINAL CUT

Featherboard Hold-Down Clamped to Fence

Rubber-Bottom Push Block

Making Rabbets with a Table Saw

Cutting rabbets on the table saw is similar to cutting grooves and dadoes, but you will need to equip your saw with an auxiliary wood fence so that the blade can run right up against the edge. Again because the rip fence is used, this operation is more suitable for cutting rabbets along the edges of long panels than it is for cutting rabbets along the top or bottom of long panels.

1 **Make and mount the auxiliary fence.** Make the auxiliary fence from ¾-inch plywood. Make the auxil-

iary fence the same length as the rip fence and a couple of inches higher than the rip fence. Screw the auxiliary fence onto your rip fence (refer to your owner's manual for specific directions). Install the cutter in your saw, and drop the blade below the saw-table surface.

2 **Cut a blade cove.** To make the dado cutter easy to adjust, cut a blade cove into the auxiliary fence. With the dado cutter lowered beneath the saw's table, move the fence so that it extends over the blade by approximately ⅝ inch, and lock it in place. Make a pencil mark on the left

face of the auxiliary fence 1 inch above the saw table. Turn on the saw, and slowly raise the dado cutter until it hits the pencil mark.

3 **Install and adjust the cutter.** After mounting a dado cutter to the saw arbor, set the cutter to the proper blade height, and adjust the auxiliary fence to the desired rabbet width.

4 **Make the cut.** Make a sample cut on a piece of scrap to check your measurements and saw settings. When the setting is perfect, put the workpiece on the table, and run the piece over the blade.

1. MAKE AND MOUNT THE AUXILIARY FENCE

Rip Fence

Screws Through Rip Fence into ¾" Thick Plywood Auxiliary Fence

2. CUT A BLADE COVE

⅝" Deep x 1" High Cove

Plywood Auxiliary Fence

Pencil Mark

Rip Fence

3. INSTALL AND ADJUST THE CUTTER

Set blade height and adjust fence.

4. MAKE THE CUT

Featherboard Hold-Down Clamped to Fence

MAKING DADOES AND RABBETS WITHOUT A DADO BLADE

IT IS POSSIBLE TO MAKE DADOES AND RABBETS WITHOUT A SPECIAL DADO BLADE. SET UP YOUR REGULAR SAW BLADE JUST AS YOU WOULD A DADO HEAD, AND RUN THE PANEL OVER THE BLADE. AFTER THE FIRST PASS, SHUT OFF THE SAW, AND MOVE THE FENCE ABOUT ⅛ INCH FROM THE BLADE FOR THE SECOND PASS. CONTINUE MAKING PASSES IN ⅛-INCH INCREMENTS UNTIL THE DADO OR GROOVE IS CUT TO THE DESIRED WIDTH.

Making Dadoes with the Router

In cabinetmaking, if you are making a dado in a panel, chances are you'll be making a matching dado in an opposing panel. The easiest way to make sure opposing dadoes are perfectly aligned is to cut them both in the same pass. You can do this by using a simple straightedge as a guide, but you will find it is really worth your while to make a T-square router guide. When cutting dadoes with a router, it is very tricky to get the cutting edge of the bit exactly the right distance away from the straightedge guide. With the T-square guide, you cut a dado into the crosspiece, then simply align the dado to your layout line on the workpiece. The other advantage is, of course, that the T-square makes sure your dadoes are perfectly square to the edges of the workpiece. By routing one dado on each side of the crosspiece, you can use the guide for dadoes of two different widths.

1 **Make the T-square router guide.** Construct this guide from two pieces of ¾-inch-thick plywood. Make the crossbar about 3 x 14 inches long. Make the guide 3 inches wide and about 3 inches longer than the width of your workbench. Assemble the guide with three screws positioned as shown in the illustration *Make the T-Square Router Guide*. When the glue has dried, fit your router with a straight bit whose diameter matches the dado

width you want to cut. Set the bit to the desired dado depth. Guiding the router against the guide, cut a dado in one side of the crossbar. Later, when you need a dado of a different width, you can make a cut in the other side of the crossbar.

2 **Cut the dadoes.** To use the cutting guide, align the dado in the crossbar to the dado layout on the workpiece. Clamp the workpiece to a stable work surface. Clamp both ends of the jig to the work surface. Or if the workpiece is narrower than the work surface, clamp one end of the guide to the work surface, and insert a clamping block that is the same thickness as the workpiece between the table and the other end of the jig, as shown.

When using a router, work from left to right when the router is between you and the guide.

1. MAKE THE T-SQUARE ROUTER GUIDE

Guide

Crossbar

Dadoes of Two Different Widths

2. CUT THE DADOES

Align dado in crosspiece to dado layout in workpiece.

Guide

Clamping Block

C-Clamp

"X" marks cutting side of layout line.

MAKING RABBETS WITH A ROUTER

YOU CAN MAKE RABBETS using your router, a straight bit, and a straightedge guide. Another option is to purchase special bits specifically designed for cutting rabbets. The best rabbeting bits have ball-bearing tips that roll easily along the workpiece and prevent burning the edges of the wood. You can buy the bits in different sizes or in a kit that includes a carbide-tipped bit with interchangeable bearings for making rabbets of different dimensions.

Regardless of which technique you use, remember always to run the router through the stock against the rotation of the router bit. This will keep the bit from skating dangerously along the stock.

RABBETING WITH A ROUTER AND A STRAIGHTEDGE

Edge Guide Clamped to Workpiece

Feed Direction

Rabbets can be cut with a straight bit.

RABBETING WITH A BALL BEARING GUIDE

Router

Rabbeting bits have ball bearing guides, eliminating the need for a straightedge guide.

● SQUARING A CARCASE

ONE OF THE BENEFITS of working with plywood in carcase construction is that you can build a large carcase with just a few panels. However, carcase assembly can still be a real headache. Often, you are working with large, heavy panels, trying to position them exactly in place and long enough to drive a screw, or until the glue has had enough time to adequately set the joint. Once they are in place, it is essential that the corners are perfectly square and that they stay this way.

Always check a carcase for square as soon as it is assembled and before the glue is set. To check for square, measure diagonally from corner to corner. If the measurements match, the carcase is square.

If measurements don't match, you can reposition clamps or apply clamping pressure diagonally to bring the carcase into square before the glue sets.

Using the Back to Square a Carcase

It's possible to square up your cabinet accurately without ever reaching for a measuring tape or framing square. As long as at least one corner of the back panel was cut with a square corner (that is, the corner is made of two factory-cut edges), it will true up the rest of the carcase as it is installed. The key to this procedure is to install the back immediately after assembling the carcase, while the glue is still wet and will allow you to shift things around a bit.

1 Install the back. Apply glue to the back edges, and drop the back into position. Align the square corner with one top corner of your carcase, and secure it using an appropriate screw or finishing nail.

2 Align the carcase. Next, shift the carcase so that it is flush along the bottom edge of the carcase, and drive one fastener through the bottom corner opposing the fastened top corner. Shift the carcase as necessary until the sides are aligned. Secure the remaining corners; then drive fasteners as necessary along the perimeter to clamp the back panel until the glue sets.

SQUARING A CARCASE

Measurements across both diagonals should be the same.

USING THE BACK TO SQUARE A CARCASE

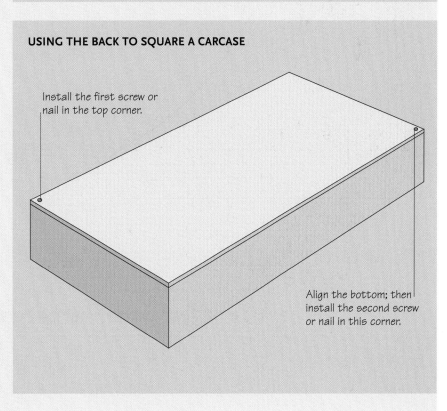

Install the first screw or nail in the top corner.

Align the bottom; then install the second screw or nail in this corner.

● MAKING CABINET DOORS

Slab Doors

This type of door can be as simple as a flat piece of wood or a panel of plywood, or it can be adorned with trim or faced with veneer for a more elegant effect.

Building a Slab Door

1 **Cut the panels.** Because slab doors are made of plywood, the exposed edges need to be covered with ¼-inch-thick strips of solid wood. So begin by cutting plywood panels that are ½ inch narrower and shorter than the final width and length you need.

2 **Cut the edge strips.** Make the edge strip out of the same species as the face veneer of the plywood. This way, the edging will blend in with the panel. Cut the edging ⅛ inch wider than the panel thickness.

3 **Glue the edging in place.** Cut lengths of edging that are about 1 inch longer than the edges they'll cover. Edge the top and bottom of each door first. Apply

glue to the edge, and then put the edging in place so that it overhangs the panel on all sides. Secure the edging to the panel using masking tape. (See "Molding and Solid Wood," page 12.) After the glue has set, saw each end of the edging flush with the sides of the door. Use a block plane to pare the edging flush with the faces of the door. Now install the edging on the sides of the door the same way.

Frame-and-Panel Doors

These consist of a pair of rails and stiles that frame a center panel. This panel can be as simple as a piece of glass or plywood, or it can have beveled edges that create a raised panel.

Building a Frame-and-Panel Door

1 **Cut the rails and stiles.** Cut the stiles to door height. Cut the rails to door width, plus the length of the two tenons, less the width of the two stiles. For example, if the door is 20 inches wide with 2-inch-wide stiles, and you want 1-inch tenons, you would cut the rails 18 inches long (20 + 2 − 4 = 18). Do this work with the miter gauge on the table saw.

2 **Cut mortises in the stiles.** For doors made of ¾-inch-thick stock, plan on tenons that are ¼ inch thick, usually the same thickness as the door panels. Place marks on the edges of the stiles to indicate the ends of each mortise. Use a doweling jig to guide the drill as you bore slightly overlapping holes to remove the waste from the mortise. Note that the mortise is slightly deeper than the tenon length to allow space for any extra glue that might prevent the joint from closing.

Use a ¼-inch chisel to square the ends of each mortise; then use a wide chisel to pare the mortise walls smooth, removing any waste that is left from drilling.

3 **Groove the stiles and the rails.** Adjust the dado cutter in your saw to a width that matches the thickness of your door panels. Position the rip fence to guide the frame member sides when milling the panel grooves. It's important that the grooves are centered on the frame edges. To test your fence position, turn on the saw, and guide a scrap cutoff against the fence and

BUILDING A SLAB DOOR

Draw molding lines on panel.

¼" Edge Strips

Attach optional molding with glue and brads.

through the cut. Now, turn the piece around, and with the groove facing down, guide its opposite face against the fence to make a second pass. The groove shouldn't increase in width with the second pass.

4 Cut the tenons. When working with ³/₄-inch-thick material, each rail tenon is ¹/₄ inch thick and 1 inch long. Lay out a sample tenon on an extra piece of rail stock. Adjust the dado cutter's height to ¹/₄ inch. Screw a wooden auxiliary fence to your miter gauge so it will support stock close to the blade. Clamp a stop block to the rip fence ahead of the blade. Because most dado blades will only cut a maximum width of ³/₄ inch with one pass, you will need to make at least two passes. Adjust the fence and stop block for the first pass, allowing the blade to remove about one half of the waste from the tenon face. Clamp the rail securely to the miter gauge, and slide it past the stop block and over the dado cutter. This eliminates the danger of pinching the work between the cutter and the rip fence. Flip the rail over, and cut the opposite side of the tenon. The fit should be snug.

When satisfied, make the first pass for all tenons. Next, readjust the position of the rip fence and block to yield 1-inch-long tenons; then make these cuts. Finally, readjust the blade height and position of the stop block to cut the notch at the outside edge of the tenons. This notch yields a "haunched" tenon that fills the exposed end of the panel groove in the stiles. Hold the rail on edge against the miter gauge for these cuts.

Note: For panel grooves that are less than ¹/₄ inch wide, use a chisel to adjust the groove width at the stile ends to accommodate the tenon "haunch."

DRILLING OUT THE MORTISES

Stop Collar on Bit

Drilling Jig

Stile

GROOVING THE STILES AND RAILS

End View

Rip Fence

Stile or Rail

Adjust the dado cutter and fence to cut a groove in the center of the frame member.

Saw Table

CUTTING THE TENONS

Miter Gauge Extension

Stop Block Clamped to Rip Fence

First Cut   **End View**

Dado Cutter

Dado Cutter

BUILDING A FRAME-AND-PANEL DOOR

Tenon with Haunch

Top Rail

³/₄"

2"

2"

2"

¹/₄" x ³/₈" Groove

Raised Panel

2"

Bottom Rail

Install overlay hinges 2" from stile ends.

Making a Raised Panel

A raised panel is a board with beveled or tapered ends and edges so the stock is thicker in the center than at its perimeter. The center, unbeveled part of the panel is called the field. The panel is usually mounted in a frame that allows it to expand and contract without otherwise stressing the rest of the project. The easiest way to bevel the ends and edges is with your table saw.

The raised panel bevels can run directly to the field as shown in *Raised Panel Styles*, or for a more formal look, you can add a shallow step between the bevel and the field. In either case, the bevel must be angled to fit within its groove without splitting the sides of the groove or being too loose in its frame. For the projects in this book, a 15-degree angle will fit nicely as long as you use $\frac{3}{8}$ x $\frac{3}{8}$-inch grooves in the door stiles and rails.

With the directions presented here, you can make raised panels in $\frac{5}{8}$-inch-thick stock or $\frac{3}{4}$-inch stock, with or without steps for either thickness.

1 **Install an auxiliary fence.** You'll need an auxiliary fence tall enough to support the wide panel. Make the fence from a piece of $\frac{3}{4}$-inch plywood or a straight 1x6 or wider board, and bolt it onto your saw's fence according to your saw's instructions.

2 **Raise the panel.** For $\frac{3}{4}$-inch panels that will have a step, or for $\frac{5}{8}$-inch-thick panels without a step, raise the blade to 1$\frac{1}{2}$ inches. For $\frac{3}{4}$-inch panels without a step, raise the blade to about 2 inches. For $\frac{5}{8}$-inch panels that will have a step, raise the blade to 1 inch. Tilt the blade away from the fence 15 degrees from vertical. Set the fence $\frac{1}{4}$ inch from the blade's near teeth. Back the panel against the auxiliary fence. Select a scrap of 1x3 or 1x4 that is a little longer than the panel.

Place this scrap guide board on top of the auxiliary fence and clamp it to the panel as shown in *Raise the Panel*. Press firmly on the guide board as you run the panel through the saw. Cut the two bevels that go across the grain first. That way, any tear-out will be eliminated when you cut the bevels that run with the grain.

3 **Square the step.** To square the step, raise the blade to the step depth, as shown. Then set the rip fence to the edge of the panel. Cut the step square on all four sides.

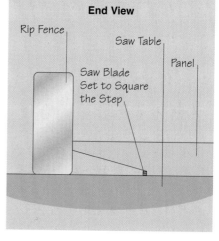

INSTALLING DOORS AND HINGES

THREE TYPES OF HINGED DOORS are used in cabinets: flush-fit, overlay (also called surface mounted), and inset (sometimes called lipped). Overlay doors are the easiest to fit because the door overlaps the face frame of the cabinet rather than fitting into an opening. Inset doors have a rabbet around the inside face so that the doors fit into the opening but have a lip that closes over the face frame. Inset doors must be fit more exactly than overlay doors, but the lip does provide a little margin of error. Inset doors fit into the opening so that they are flush with the face frame. They require the most exacting fit because the gap between door and cabinet must be even all around. Each door type has different hinging requirements. A wide variety of hinges are available to meet the requirements of each door type. *Types of Hinged Doors* shows the most common method for hinging each door type.

TYPES OF HINGED DOORS

Cabinet — Flush-Fit Door — Butt Hinge

Cabinet — Overlay Door — Overlay Hinge

Cabinet — Inset Door — Inset Hinge

Installing Flush-Fit Doors

It is always a good idea to make flush-fitting doors after you make the cabinets, so you fit them to the actual size of the cabinet. If the cabinet will be built-in, install it before you install the door. After installing the cabinet, make sure that the frame is plumb and level before hanging the doors. Doors hung before cabinet installation could bind if the cabinet flexes.

1 Fit the door. Measure the height and width of each door, and allow yourself a 3/32-inch gap on all edges. To make installation a little easier, some cabinetmakers bevel the edges of flush-fit doors 3 to 5 degrees toward the back.

2 Select the hinges. With solid-wood doors or doors with solid-wood frames, you can use butt hinges. Or for a more Colonial look, you can use fully exposed hinges as shown in the illustration *Select the Hinges*. Butt hinges are unsuitable for plywood or particleboard doors because these materials aren't strong enough to support fasteners in their edges. You can use fully exposed hinges for plywood or particleboard, but flat panel doors such as these usually look better with a concealed wraparound hinge, as shown. Attach whichever hinges you choose to the door. The position of the hinges along the length of the door is mostly an aesthetic decision, but you usually want to stay between 2 and 5 inches from the top and bottom of the door.

1. FIT THE DOOR   3/32" Gap

Flush-Fit Door

2. SELECT THE HINGES

Fully Exposed Hinges

Concealed Wraparound Hinges

CONTINUED ON NEXT PAGE.

CONTINUED FROM PREVIOUS PAGE.

3 Score the hinge mortises. If the hinges you choose must be mortised into the door, start by clamping the door in a bench vise with the edge to be mortised facing up. Position the hinge on the door, and score the perimeter with a knife. Remove the hinge, and carefully deepen the score cuts to the depth of the hinge. Then use the thickness of one hinge leaf to set the ruler on a combination square. Use the square and a knife as shown in *Score the Hinge Mortises* to score the hinge depth on the face of the door.

4 Cut the mortises and install the hinges. Cut the mortises using a chisel. First, use a hammer and chisel to chop the waste areas into sections as shown in the illustration. Then use the chisel to pare out the waste. Mark the locations of screw holes, and drill pilot holes. Install the hinges on the door.

5 Install the hinges on the cabinet. Hold the door in position using shims. Then mark the hinge locations with a pencil. If you need to mortise the hinges into the cabinet, cut the outlines of the mortise with a knife. Cut the mortise with a chisel. Mark the screw holes, and drill pilot holes. Install the hinges and door.

3. SCORE THE HINGE MORTISES

Panel Face

4. CUT THE MORTISES AND INSTALL THE HINGES

Chisel chops break up waste.

5. INSTALL THE HINGES ON THE CABINET

Use a pencil to mark the hinge locations.

Shims hold the door in position.

INSTALLING OVERLAY DOORS

1 Install the hinges on the doors. You'll find overlay hinges available in a variety of styles and finishes. Mark the hinge locations, and drill pilot holes for hinge screws. Install the hinges in the door.

2 Install the hinges on the cabinet. After the cabinet has been installed, set the doors in place with the hinges already attached. With the doors correctly positioned, mark the face frame for the hinge-screw pilot holes. Drill the holes in the face frame; attach the door pulls; and hang the door.

INSTALLING INSET DOORS

1 Measure for door size. After the cabinet has been installed, measure the door opening, and add $\frac{1}{2}$ inch to the height and $\frac{1}{2}$ inch to the width. This will give you a $\frac{3}{8}$-inch-wide lip, while giving the inset portion of the door $\frac{1}{8}$ inch of clearance all around.

2 Cut the rabbets and round-overs. Use a router and a $\frac{3}{8}$-inch rabbeting bit to mill a $\frac{3}{8}$-deep rabbet along all four sides of the back of the door. Then if you like, use a $\frac{3}{8}$-inch roundover bit to round over the front edges of the door.

3 Install the hinges on the door. Mark the locations of screw holes, and drill pilot holes. Install the hinges in the door.

4 Hang the door. Hold the door in position in the cabinet, and mark the locations of the hinges and screw holes. Drill pilot holes, and hang the door.

MEASURING FOR DOOR SIZE

Cabinet

Inset Door

$\frac{3}{8}$" Wide Lip $\frac{1}{8}$" Gap Between Inset and Cabinet

CUTTING THE RABBETS AND ROUNDOVERS

Hinges

Use a $\frac{1}{4}$" or $\frac{3}{8}$" roundover bit to ease the front edges.

Use a $\frac{3}{8}$" rabbeting bit on the back of the door.

ADJUSTABLE CABINET SHELVES

If you want to make cabinet shelves that are adjustable for height, there are two common ways to do it. One way is to use pins in holes drilled inside the cabinet; the other is to use metal shelf standards. Both are easy to use and install. Whichever you choose, check the hardware before you build your shelves. Different shelf-support hardware may require different clearances that may affect the size of the shelf.

Installing Metal Standards

Cut shelf standards to length with a hacksaw, cutting them all off at the top end so they will align to each other when registered to the bottom of the cabinet. Shelf standards can simply be screwed to the inside of the cabinet, but it is much more elegant to inset them into grooves. Cut the grooves on the table saw as described in "Making Dadoes and Grooves with a Table Saw," page 17.

SHELF STANDARDS

Recessed

Surface Mounted

INSTALLING SHELF PINS

SHELF PINS come in a variety of styles. Some include brass insets that you tap into the holes, dressing them up a bit and making them more durable. Most shelf pins require a ¼-inch-diameter hole, but this varies.

1 Make a shelf-pin hole template. The trick to drilling holes for shelf pins is making sure every set of four holes is in perfect horizontal alignment. If they aren't aligned horizontally, the shelves will rock. If the holes are slightly misaligned to the front and back of the cabinet, it won't affect their function.

To ensure perfect horizontal alignment, make a simple drilling template from a scrap of ¼-inch-thick plywood. Rip the scrap to about 5 or 6 inches wide, and make it about 5 inches shorter than the inside height of the cabinet. Mark one long edge of the template as the "register edge." On this template, lay out the hole spacing you want. A good spacing is to make the holes two inches from the register edge. Lay out the first hole about 8 inches from the bottom of the template; then lay out a hole about every 1½ inches from the bottom of the template. Stop about 3 inches from the top of the template.

2 Drill the holes. Use a stop collar or a piece of tape on the drill bit to mark the depth you want to drill. Align the register edge of the template to the front edge of the cabinet. Make sure the bottom of the template rests on the bottom of the cabinet. Clamp the template in place, and drill the holes. Now flip the template over so you will be drilling through the other side. Push the register edge against the back of the cabinet. Drill the holes. Repeat this process for the holes in the opposing panel.

1. MAKE A SHELF-PIN HOLE TEMPLATE

3"

Register Edge

1½"

8"

2"

2. DRILL THE HOLES

Register Edge

After drilling the front holes, flip the template and place the register edge against the back.

BUILDING DRAWERS

The most important rule in drawer construction is squareness: if the drawer is not square, it will not function, period.

Bigger drawers require thicker stock. For the projects in this book, drawer sides and end panels can be ¾-inch-thick solid wood or ⅜- to ¾-inch plywood. Use plywood for drawer bottoms. For light-duty drawers, you can get away with ¼-inch drawer bottoms, but ⅜-inch bottoms are recommended for larger drawers or cabinets that you expect to receive heavy-duty use.

There are many different joints for attaching drawer fronts to sides, but for the purposes of this book, you will do quite well with a few simple options. Butt joints are the least glamorous, but they are the simplest to master, and when reinforced with nails or dowels and glue, they are more than adequate for the applications in this book. Rabbet and dado joints are also used in this book for added strength and better appearance.

Size the drawer to fit the opening and the hardware you are going to use. What follows is a common method for making drawers, using primarily plywood.

Drawer Construction

The instructions and drawings here assume your drawers will overlay the face frame. Cut the parts for each project according to the dimensions in the Materials List accompanying the project.

1 Groove the side and front panels. Set the table-saw blade ¼ inch above the table and ¼ inch away from the fence. Run the front

pro tip

SHORTENING THE BOTTOM FOR A SQUARE DRAWER

You might find it a little difficult to square up a drawer after the bottom is installed. Some cabinetmakers recommend making the drawer bottom $\frac{1}{32}$ inch shorter in length and width to allow some room for adjustment.

Test-fit the bottom before permanently installing it. Clamp the panel in place, and check for square. If you find that you cannot coax the drawer square, plane or sand the edges off the bottom panel to provide a little more leeway.

Drawer Bottom

Palm Sander

panel and each side panel over the blade to create a $\frac{1}{8}$-inch-wide by $\frac{1}{4}$-inch-deep groove in each panel. Move the fence $\frac{1}{8}$ inch further from the blade, and run each piece through again to widen the groove to $\frac{1}{4}$ inch. Leave the fence set as it is for the next step.

Note: If you are using $\frac{3}{8}$-inch-thick wood for a heavy-duty drawer bottom, then you will have to make a third run over the table-saw blade to make a $\frac{3}{8}$-inch groove. Also, if you are using bottom-mounted drawer slides, you may need to raise the bottom panel to $\frac{3}{8}$ inch or $\frac{1}{2}$ inch from the bottom edge of the sides. Always purchase the hardware you will use before making drawers.

CONTINUED ON NEXT PAGE.

DRAWER CONSTRUCTION

Front Installation Screws

Drawer Front

Side

False Front

Drawer Opening Height Plus $\frac{3}{4}$"

Back

Bottom

Drawer Opening Height Minus 1"

1. GROOVE THE SIDE AND FRONT PANELS, (End Views)

Rip Fence

First Pass

Side

$\frac{1}{4}$"

$\frac{1}{4}$"

Rip Fence

Second Pass

Side

$\frac{3}{8}$"

CONTINUED FROM PREVIOUS PAGE.

2 Trim the rear panel. Don't move the rip fence, but raise the blade about $\frac{1}{2}$ inch. Rip $\frac{1}{2}$ inch off the rear panel. (Be sure to use a push stick, not your hand, to move this narrow piece between the fence and blade.) Now the rear panel will be precisely the right height to fit above the drawer bottom.

3 Rabbet the sides. Set the dado cutter for a width that matches the thickness of your back pieces. Raise the cutter to $\frac{1}{4}$ inch above the table saw. Remove the fence from the saw. Use the miter gauge to mill a $\frac{1}{4}$-inch-deep rabbet that has a width that matches your wood. Rabbet each end of each side panel. In the absence of a dado cutter, make each rabbet with multiple passes over the saw blade.

4 Assemble the drawer box. Apply glue to the front rabbets in the side panels and the ends of the front panel, and attach the side panels to the front panel using three 3d finishing nails on each side. Slide the bottom panel into position, all the way forward. Apply glue to the

rear rabbets in the side panels and to the ends and bottom edge of the rear panel. Put the rear panel in place, flush with the top of the side panels, and nail on the sides. Check the drawer for square; then secure the bottom to the rear panels with $\frac{3}{4}$-inch brads.

5 Attach the drawer front. If your project has inset doors and you want your drawers to match, rout a $\frac{3}{8}$ x $\frac{3}{8}$-inch rabbet all the way around the inside face of the false front. (Keep in mind, this will make the drawer travel $\frac{3}{8}$ inch further into the opening, so you may have to shorten the drawer sides accordingly.) After the false front has been raised, routed, or otherwise readied for finishing, attach it to the front end panel using four #6 x 1$\frac{1}{4}$-inch wood screws driven through countersunk pilot holes near each front inside corner of the drawer.

If your project doesn't have inset doors, there is no need to rout. Attach the false front using four #6 x 1$\frac{1}{4}$-inch wood screws as described above.

2. TRIM THE REAR PANEL

End View

Raise the blade to cut through the back.

$\frac{3}{8}$"

Back

$\frac{1}{2}$"

3. RABBET THE SIDES

4. ASSEMBLE THE DRAWER BOX

3d Finishing Nails

Back Panel

Side Panels

Apply carpenter's glue.

$\frac{3}{4}$" Brads

3d Finishing Nails

5. ATTACH THE DRAWER FRONT

Drawer Front

#6 x 1$\frac{1}{4}$" Wood Screws

Portion in shaded area can be rabbeted out to match inset doors.

● DRAWER SLIDES

THERE ARE SEVERAL OPTIONS for drawer slides depending on how you build the cabinet. The simplest drawer slide system is the drawer that just fits inside its drawer opening and is supported on wooden runners. However, this system does not work well for drawers that will carry heavy loads, such as kitchen drawers. It's also not recommended for drawers with plywood sides because the plywood edges won't hold up.

Another option is wooden slides which can be built in several ways. But the problem with all wooden slides is that they change dimensions with changes in humidity, causing drawers to bind or be sloppy in their openings. Wood drawer slides also wear out faster when subjected to heavy use.

For heavy use and guaranteed smooth operation, metal slide hardware is the way to go. There are commercial slides for every need, and some models can even handle loads from 75 to 100 pounds. For the projects in this book, side-mounted and bottom-mounted slides are used. In general, follow the manufacturer's instructions for installation. Here are some basic instructions for installing the most common side-mounted drawer slides.

Installing Drawer Slide Hardware

1 Install the drawer slides. Use the screws supplied to attach the drawer slides to the bottoms of the sides, locating the rollers at the rear of the drawer. The nonroller end should touch the back of the drawer front.

2 Install the drawer guides in the cabinet. Align the drawer guide perpendicular to the cabinet front and resting on the bottom of the cabinet opening with the wheel at the front of the opening. Most slides have both oblong and round holes for mounting screws. If you first mount the guides to the sides of the cabinet using the oblong holes, you can make fine adjustments before permanently positioning the guides using the round holes.

1. INSTALL THE DRAWER SLIDES

Drawer Slide

2. INSTALL THE DRAWER GUIDES IN THE CABINET

Drawer Guide

● COUNTERTOPS

YOU'LL NEED TO CONSIDER countertop options for the cabinets that you will install in the kitchen, bathroom, or utility room.

Plastic laminate is a durable, stain-resistant material that has many applications. Laminate comes in various lengths, widths, textures, and colors to match just about any job and to fit into any project budget. You will find that the 0.05-inch general-purpose grade is the most common laminate for countertops, cabinets, and furniture.

Be extra careful when working with sheets of laminate. The sheets can crack or chip quite easily before you attach them to a substrate. If you can, have large sheets cut to size at a home center or a cabinet shop.

You can build plastic laminate countertops in your own shop, or you can purchase factory-made countertops, which are available in several standard sizes in most home centers. Some stores can even cut panels to order. These post-formed counters feature integral backsplashes and curved front edges or no-drip bullnose profiles.

Cutting Plastic Laminate

While it is possible to cut plastic laminate using a saber saw and a special laminate-cutting blade, it's slow work.

The best tool for cutting plastic laminates is your router and a ¼-inch straight-cutting bit. Use a carbide-tipped bit; plastic laminate will dull a steel-tipped bit in seconds. To guide the router when cutting laminate, make a jig similar to the straight-cutting jig on page 13. In fact, if you have made the straight-cutting jig, you can use it as a laminate-cutting jig simply by routing a ¼-inch slot in the side of the jig you are not using to guide the circular saw.

When you use the laminate-cutting jig (above center), set the laminate on top of a sacrificial piece of plywood. Align the cutting slot to your cutting layout line. Clamp the laminate and the jig to the plywood. Set the router cutting depth to go through the laminate and slightly into the plywood.

Cut edge strips for any project about ¼ inch wider than you need. (You will trim the excess off with a router and a flush-trimming bit after installation.) Cut countertops, coverings for doors and drawer faces, and other flat surfaces about ½ inch larger on all dimensions.

COUNTERTOP OPTIONS, (Cross-Section Details)

Integral Backsplash
Post-Formed Plastic Laminate

Integral Backsplash
Post-Formed Plastic Laminate
No-Drip Bullnose

Laminate-Covered Backsplash
Laminate-Covered Top
Laminate-Covered Front Edge

Hardwood Backsplash
Laminate-Covered Top
Hardwood Front Edge

PLASTIC-LAMINATE-CUTTING JIG

¾" Plywood or Solid Wood Guide

Tempered Hardboard Base

¼" Wide Slot

Fasten hardboard to the straightedge using glue and screws.

CUTTING PLASTIC LAMINATE

Router

Plastic Laminate

¼" Straight Bit

Guide   Base   Sacrificial Plywood

Gluing Laminate to Substrate

Use contact cement to attach plastic laminate to plywood or particleboard substrate. Make sure you have plenty of ventilation, and stay away from any source of flame.

1 Apply adhesive to the edges and edge strips. Using a brush or small roller, coat the edges of the substrate and the back of the laminate with contact cement. In most cases, this includes the edges of the countertop and the edges of doors and drawers. For these smaller areas, use a brush or smaller roller. Allow the adhesive to dry at least as long as recommended on the can. (It should be dry to the touch.)

2 Install and trim the edge strips. Install the edge strips, making sure they overhang both sides of the surface. Use a laminate roller to firmly seat the piece. (A rolling pin also works well in a pinch.) Trim both sides of the laminate using a flush-trimming bit in the router.

3 Laminate the countertop. Next, apply contact cement to the horizontal surfaces and the bottom of the laminate. The easiest way to do this is to pour some cement right on the surface and spread it out using a short-napped paint roller, a large brush, or even a scrap of laminate. When the cement is dry to the touch, cover the substrate with plain brown wrapping paper or small strips of lath. Leave about 1/2 inch of exposed surface along one edge of the substrate. Carefully lay the laminate on the paper or lath. Do not allow it to touch the substrate yet or it will tack immediately.

Align the laminate, and press it in place where you left the exposed cement. Gradually remove the paper or lath, and press the laminate in place to work out any bubbles. Use a laminate roller or a rolling pin to ensure that the laminate is properly seated. Use a router and flush-trimming bit to trim the overhanging edges of laminate flush with the surface.

1. APPLY ADHESIVE TO THE EDGES AND EDGE STRIPS

Cross-Section Detail

Top

Laminate

Edge Strip

Carcase

2. INSTALL AND TRIM THE EDGE STRIPS

Flush-Trimming Bit

Plastic Laminate

Lath

3. LAMINATE THE COUNTERTOP

INSTALLING CABINETS AND BUILT-INS

Installing cabinets and other built-in projects is not difficult, but it can be an exercise in patience. Your cabinets must be installed plumb and vertical, which can be a challenge if your wall or floor is out of whack. If you find installation to be a sometimes slow but always methodical job, you're probably doing it right.

You might have to remove some molding before installation. (See "Removing Trim," page 37, for more details.)

Finding Studs

Wall materials such as plaster and drywall don't have the strength to support heavy cabinets or built-ins. Cabinets should be supported by framing inside the wall, which usually means screwing through the wall surface into studs. Studs are typically installed on 16-inch centers, so once you've located one, you can measure along the wall to find other fastening points.

A magnetic stud finder is one of the simplest and least expensive ways to find studs. These nifty gadgets detect the nails or screws used to attach the wallboard to the wood. A bit more expensive but even better than the magnetic stud finders are the electronic stud finders now available in home centers and hardware stores.

In the absence of a stud finder, you can probe the wall with a small nail or a small-diameter bit as long as you are sure that the holes you are making will be covered by the cabinet after installation.

REMOVING WALLBOARD

SOME OF THE PROJECTS in this book require you to remove wallboard so the cabinet can be installed inside the wall. Before planning such a project, make sure there will be no plumbing or electrical wiring where you want to install the cabinet, otherwise you will have to plan to relocate pipes or wiring.

Even if you think that there are no wires in the wall you wish to remove, go to the circuit box and switch off power to that portion of the house to be safe.

Use a reciprocating saw or drywall saw to cut through the wallboard and remove the material. Be warned that this will be a dusty operation, so cover adjacent areas and be sure to wear a dust mask and safety glasses.

REMOVING WALLBOARD

Stud

Drywall Saw

REMOVING CARPET

IF YOU ARE PLANNING to install your project over preexisting hard floor coverings, such as wood, tile, or vinyl, just install the project right over it, there's no need to remove anything. However, if the room is carpeted, you will need to remove the carpet before installation.

Before you cut the carpet, measure the base of your project without baseboard or trim molding. Transfer those measurements to the floor, exactly where the project will be installed. Use a straightedge and a carpet knife or utility knife to remove both the carpet and the pad.

MEASURING THE CABINET

CUTTING THE CARPET

INSTALLING BASE CABINETS

THERE IS NO SUCH THING as a perfectly level floor or plumb wall. Even the best walls have a slight ripple; the best laid floor may slope away from the wall imperceptibly. These minor imperfections can ruin a perfectly good finish. Fortunately, it's easy to adjust for these imperfections during installation.

1 Find the floor's high point. Use a level to find the high spot in the floor where you are installing the cabinet. To do this, set a level on the floor, and check if the floor is level. If it isn't, slide the level along to the high side until the bubble shifts to the other side of the vial. Mark that spot as the high point of your floor.

2 Scribe a level line. Measure up the wall from the floor's high point, and make a mark at cabinet height. Use the level to scribe a level line along the wall for the full length of the cabinet.

3 Install the cabinet. Slide the cabinet against the wall, and check it against the level line. Use wood shims at the back of the cabinet to level it from front to back. Use shims under the cabinet to level it from side to side. Once the cabinet is level and plumb, attach it to the studs using 3½-inch screws. Trim the shims using a utility knife or chisel.

4 Finish the kickplates. There are at least three ways to cover the gaps caused by shimming. An easy and ideal solution for kitchens and baths where floors will get wet is to use vinyl base molding. You can attach vinyl molding with construction adhesive or contact cement. It is flexible enough to allow you to press it into place and then trim it at the top with a utility knife.

For dry areas, such as the living room, where vinyl molding might not look appropriate, you can face the kickplate with strips of ¼-inch-thick plywood. Or you can add a run of quarter-round molding. The quarter-round looks particularly appropriate if it has been used as a shoe molding on the baseboard in the room.

Wood Shims

Reference Line

LEVELING A BASE CABINET

Reference Line

Wood Shims

COVERING THE SHIM GAPS

Kickplate

Shim Space

Vinyl Base Molding, Installed with Adhesive

Kickplate

Shim Space

Quarter-Round Molding

SCRIBING A LEVEL LINE

Level Line

35

INSTALLING WALL CABINETS

WALL CABINETS are a little more difficult to install than base cabinets because they must be hung. Even positioning small units in place can be exhausting, unless you have a means of supporting them. One of the most basic ways of doing this is to screw a temporary rail, or ledge, along the bottom line of the cabinets. Not only will the rail ensure that the cabinet is hung level, but you never have to worry about your arms getting tired.

1 Install the ledger. Using a level, draw a line along the wall indicating the bottom of the wall cabinets. Using 2-inch screws, secure a temporary ledger along that line. Make sure that you've screwed into studs and that the board is perfectly level before continuing to the next step.

2 Hang the cabinets. Lift the cabinet onto the ledge, and position it as close to the wall as possible. Drive two 3-inch screws through the upper hanging cleat just tight enough to hold the cabinet in place. Check for level from front to back. You may have to do a little shimming to get the cabinet completely level. Secure the bottom of the cabinet to the wall by driving two 3-inch screws through the lower hanging cleat and into the studs. At this point you can remove the ledger by unscrewing the ledger. You may need to patch the holes left by the screws.

3 Apply molding. Depending on how flat and plumb the walls are, there will probably be gaps between the walls and the cabinet. These can be easily concealed by installing quarter-round or other molding along the back edge of the cabinet.

INSTALLING A TEMPORARY LEDGER

Level Line

HANGING THE CABINETS

Upper Hanging Cleat

Lower Hanging Cleat

Temporary Ledger

TRIM AND MOLDING

Besides adding another level of decor to your project, molding can be used to conceal screw holes, nailholes, and other blemishes that are inevitable in construction. Molding serves as a transition piece to cover up the gap between a cabinet and a wall or a cabinet and a cabinet.

Replacing Trim

Replace any molding and trim you removed earlier, and add new matching trim and molding as required. Wherever possible, use the existing nailholes. Nail removal will have enlarged the holes, so use larger nails during replacement. Fill the nailholes, and do any necessary touch up.

When replacing molding, you'll have to fit pieces together around corners. Miter joints are the way to go for outside corners. But for inside corners, use cope joints. Done properly, a coped joint looks seamless, allowing the profile to continue smoothly around the corner. Coped joints are less likely to open up than inside miter joints.

NAIL SAFETY

FOR SAFETY, REMOVE NAILS FROM TRIM AS SOON AS YOU REMOVE THE TRIM FROM THE WALL. THE BEST WAY TO PULL FINISHING NAILS FROM TRIM WITHOUT DAMAGING THE FACE OF THE TRIM WOOD IS TO PULL THE NAILS COMPLETELY THROUGH THE BACK OF THE PIECE. USE SLIP-JOINT PLIERS OR NAIL NIPPERS TO GRAB THE POINT OF THE FINISHING NAIL AND LEVER THE NAIL OUT BY ROCKING THE TOOL. IF THE MOLDING IS DAMAGED, OR IF YOU ARE NOT PLANNING TO REUSE A PIECE, BEND THE NAILS OVER WITH A HAMMER.

Nippers

Countersunk Nail

REMOVING TRIM

YOU WILL HAVE TO REMOVE any baseboard or crown molding before you can install the built-in units. Work carefully and you can reinstall them later.

   The best place to start removing trim and molding is where it begins—at a door or corner. If the joint at the corner is coped, remove the coped piece first, then the butted piece. Starting at the end, coax the molding away from the wall with a pry bar. Pry as near the nails as possible, and use a thin scrap of wood behind the pry bar to protect the wall.

   If a strip of molding won't come loose, drive the nails through the piece using a nail set. It's much easier to patch these holes later than to fix broken trim.

Scrap protects wall.

Baseboard

Door Casing

MAKING A COPED JOINT

1 Miter the molding to be coped. To make a coped joint, first miter the piece of molding as if you were fitting an inside miter. Pencil a 90-degree angle at the top edge of the molding. Then run the pencil along the profile revealed by the miter cut.

2 Cope the joint. Using a coping saw, back-cut the molding by following the line where the miter meets the front of the molding. If the molding has curves across its entire face, cope all the way across. If it is a molding such as a baseboard with a large, flat field, you may want to complete the cut with a miter saw. Test-fit your coped piece, and fine tune it using a chisel or small file.

3 Finish the installation. Once the coped joint is in position, butt the cope against the existing baseboard molding and allow the opposite end to run long. Mark the back of the long end, and square-cut it to the correct length.

90°

45°

90°

MITERING THE MOLDING

90°

COPING THE JOINT

CUTTING CROWN MOLDING

WHETHER YOU'RE ADDING NEW MOLDING to a project or recutting and replacing molding you removed for cabinet installation, you should have no trouble making the simple cuts using a miter box and backsaw or power miter saw. One type of molding that might give you some trouble, however, is crown molding. Because of its design, it gets installed differently and must be cut differently.

   Crown molding leans at a 45-degree angle from the vertical surface where it's attached—whether the surface is a wall where it meets the ceiling, or at the top of a cabinet or bookcase. The trick to cutting crown molding is to lean it in the miter box at that same angle. The easiest way to do this is to turn the molding upside down when it's in the miter box or miter saw. To keep the molding in place when you lean it, attach a stop block to the fence or table. Use a strip of ¾-inch-square stock, and screw or clamp it in place.

CUTTING CROWN MOLDING

Wooden Stop Screwed to Fence

Top of molding is at the base of the saw or miter box during the cut.

Crown Ready for Cutting

2 tools

GETTING STARTED

Many people new to woodworking and do-it-yourself projects are surprised to learn how much they can accomplish with simple hand tools and a few portable power tools. It doesn't take a shop full of expensive machinery to build practical and attractive furnishings. What's more, as your skills develop, you'll be able to build pieces by hand that are in many ways superior to those that roll off an assembly line.

If you've tackled other do-it-yourself projects, or have done home repairs, you may already own most of the hand and power tools necessary to build the projects in this book. There are many other sophisticated tools that can simplify tasks, but there is no need to run out and buy them all at once. It makes sense to start slowly, adding tools as the need arises. This way, you'll be sure to purchase only what you really need.

ESSENTIAL HAND TOOLS

Here's a list of the hand tools you'll need for the projects in this book. Below this list, you'll find a list of tools that aren't essential, but will help you work more efficiently.

Hammers and Related Tools

Every woodworker should be armed with at least three basic hammers: a claw

---

MEASURING TOOLS AND SQUARES

Measuring Tools

Steel Tape Measure. Tape measures commonly come in lengths from 6 to 50 feet. A 16-footer will serve fine for any project in this book. If you want to use the tape measure for carpentry work as well, choose a 25-footer. Good quality tapes have ¾-inch-wide blades that can stay rigid up to about 7 feet.

Folding Rule. Sometimes a tape measure just won't do—as in measuring in tight spots—or isn't accurate enough. In these cases a traditional folding wooden rule is the answer.

Squares

They're used for measuring, marking, and checking the inside and outside squareness of right angles.

Framing Square. This square is available in a few sizes. The larger version has a 24-inch-long blade and 16-inch-long tongue, and is the tool of choice for house framing work. You may find one of the smaller models,

measuring 8 x 6 or 12 x 8 inches, more convenient for smaller projects.

Try Square. This square has a broad blade attached to a stock at a right angle. The blade, which may be graduated for measurement, is available in lengths from 2 to 12 inches. Use a try square to test, or try, the squareness of right angles, to scribe lines, and to calibrate tools. One type, called a try-and-miter square or just a miter square, has a 45-degree angle built into the handle so that it can also try and scribe miters.

Tape Measure

Try Square

Folding Rule

Framing Square

Combination Square

Sliding Adjustable Bevel Gauge

Small Square

hammer, a tack hammer, and a mallet. Each is indispensable for its own specific task. A claw hammer is the first choice for driving and removing nails and brads. But when it's necessary to drive tacks or brads that are too tiny to grip, you'll appreciate the magnetic head on your tack hammer. A wooden mallet or soft-faced hammer should be used whenever a metal hammer might damage a surface, as when tapping in wood plugs, a tight-fitting tenon, or when working with wooden-handled chisels and gouges.

Nail Sets and Center Punches. A nail set is used to drive finishing nails below the work surface without dent-

ing the surface, so the holes can be easily filled. A set rests on top of a nail or brad, enabling you to safely sink the nail without damaging the surrounding wood. The standard three-piece set—consisting of $\frac{1}{32}$-, $\frac{1}{16}$-, and $\frac{3}{32}$-inch nail sets—will handle most of the jobs for the home workshop.

A center punch looks like a nail set, except that its sharp, conical point tends to stick into wood. You'll need one for locating and punching starter holes for twist-drill bits to keep them from "walking" off their mark during the initial drilling. Starter holes are also handy when hand-driving screws.

Mallet
Tack Hammer
Mallet
Mallet
Mallet
Nail Sets
Claw Hammer

Combination Square. This tool consists of a 6-, 12-, or 16-inch graduated steel blade with a sliding handle that can be tightened at any position. Most come equipped with a spirit level and scratch awl built into the handle.

The combination square is one of the most useful tools in any woodworker's shop. You can use it to check for level or plumb, or diagonally as a miter square. It serves as a try square depth gauge, marking gauge, and straightedge. It's also the ideal tool for locating and centering screw holes and scribing layout lines.

Sliding Adjustable Bevel Gauge. This simple tool consists of a handle or stock attached to a 6- or 8-inch slotted blade. It is commonly used in the workshop for duplicating angles other than 90 degrees. Set the tool and transfer exact angles from place to place.

SAFETY EQUIPMENT

COMMON SENSE SHOULD TELL YOU NOT TO ATTEMPT ANY PROJECT WITHOUT ADEQUATE EYE AND EAR PROTECTION. WEAR SAFETY GOGGLES OR PLASTIC GLASSES WHENEVER YOU ARE WORKING WITH TOOLS OR CHEMICALS ... PERIOD. MAKE SURE THAT YOUR EYE PROTECTION CONFORMS TO THOSE REQUIREMENTS SET BY EITHER THE AMERICAN NATIONAL STANDARDS INSTITUTE (ANSI) OR CANADIAN STANDARDS ASSOCIATION (CSA).

THE U.S. OCCUPATIONAL SAFETY AND HEALTH ADMINISTRATION (OSHA) RECOMMENDS THAT HEARING PROTECTION BE WORN WHENEVER THE NOISE LEVEL EXCEEDS 85 DECIBELS (DB) FOR AN 8-HOUR WORKDAY. CONSIDERING THAT A CIRCULAR SAW EMITS 110 DB, EVEN SHORTER EXPOSURE TIMES ARE DANGEROUS. INSERT AND MUFF-TYPE PROTECTORS ARE AVAILABLE; MAKE SURE THAT YOU CHOOSE MODELS WITH A NOISE REDUCTION RATING (NNR) OF AT LEAST 20 DB.

BECAUSE SAWDUST IS A BY-PRODUCT OF ANY PROJECT, IT'S A GOOD IDEA TO WEAR A DUST MASK. TWO TYPES OF MASKS ARE AVAILABLE: DISPOSABLE DUST MASKS AND CARTRIDGE-TYPE RESPIRATORS. A DUST MASK IS GOOD FOR PROTECTING YOU FROM MOST FINE PARTICLES. RESPIRATORS GENERALLY OFFER SUPERIOR PROTECTION, BUT ALSO HAVE CERTAIN DISADVANTAGES. WITH A RESPIRATOR, BREATHING IS MORE LABORED AND IT CAN GET WARM INSIDE THE MASK. WHICHEVER YOU PURCHASE, BE SURE THAT IT HAS BEEN STAMPED BY THE NATIONAL INSTITUTE FOR OCCUPATIONAL SAFETY & HEALTH/MINE SAFETY AND HEALTH ADMINISTRATION (NIOSH/MSHA) AND IS APPROVED FOR YOUR SPECIFIC OPERATION. IF YOU CAN TASTE OR SMELL THE CONTAMINATE, OR IF THE MASK STARTS TO INTERFERE WITH NORMAL BREATHING, IT'S TIME FOR A REPLACEMENT.

Levels

Levels are made of wood, metal, or plastic. They are used to determine whether a surface is horizontal (level) or vertical (plumb). New electronic digital levels are also capable of checking other angles. Levels come in lengths from 9 inches to more than 72 inches. Pick up a 2-footer to start with; it is small enough for working in tight quarters, yet long enough to provide an accurate reading.

Planes

Although you could build every project in this book without ever having to reach for one, few tools can remove paper-thin shavings of wood or smooth a rough board as quickly or precisely as an old-fashioned hand plane.

If you have to do without a hand plane, don't despair. Since the development of efficient power tools that can make short work of most trimming and smoothing chores, as well as the widespread availability of surfaced lumber, hand planes aren't as much of a necessity in the typical home workshop as

they once were. But once you get the hang of using such basic planes as the block plane, smooth plane, and jack plane, you'll find them a valuable addition to your toolbox.

The block plane is the most versatile plane in the home workshop. Designed for trimming end grain, called blocking or blocking in, this little plane can also be useful for other small trimming jobs, such as easing the backs of mitered joints or planing down edging flush with a plywood panel.

Jack planes and smooth planes are types of bench plane. They look very similar to each other, with both having blades about $1\frac{3}{4}$ to 2 inches wide, but they differ in length. Jack planes are between 11 and 14 inches long. Smooth planes range from 6 to 10 inches long.

Wood Chisels

Designed for removing wood in chips, chunks, and shavings, wood chisels can be driven with a mallet or manipulated by hand for precise paring. They are particularly handy for making quick work of hinge mortises. A four-

Bench Plane

Block Plane

Chisels

chisel set including $\frac{1}{4}$-, $\frac{1}{2}$-, $\frac{3}{4}$-, and 1-inch chisels will see to most needs in the home workshop.

An old shop rule warns against striking a chisel with anything but a wooden or leather mallet. This rule still holds with wooden chisels; the blade tangs can split the handle if the tool is used improperly. Modern plastic-handled chisels, however, are much more durable and can be used with ordinary steel hammers.

Other Helpful Hand Tools

You'll need some other tools to help with the projects.

Utility Knife. Always make sure the blade is sharp because dull blades aren't as precise and may slip off the mark.

Screwdrivers. Although they may rank as one of the simplest tools found in any toolbox, a good set of screwdrivers is essential for the do-it-yourselfer. The two most common types of screwdrivers are the slotted and the Phillips head. The best way to avoid stripping screw heads is to have a good selection of different size screwdrivers to properly fit the different size screws.

SAWS

YOU'LL NEED A HANDSAW for cutting wood and wood products and a hacksaw for cutting metal. For some of the decorative curves, you may find a need for a coping saw. For other chores, you might want to buy special dovetail and veneer saws.

Handsaw

Backsaw

Dovetail Saw

Veneer Saw

Hack Saw

Coping Saw

CLAMPS AND VISES

No shop ever has enough clamps, vises, or handscrews, yet these essential tools are most often overlooked by beginning do-it-yourselfers. Clamps are designed for such jobs as edge-gluing boards and attaching trim to plywood edges. It won't take long for you to discover how valuable they can be throughout your shop. Use clamps to secure workpieces for sawing, routing, drilling, or sanding. A good basic starter set consists of a pair or two of 4-inch C-clamps, at least one pair of pipe clamps, and some spring clamps.

Bar Clamps and Pipe Clamps. Bar clamps provide greater reach than most other clamps and are ideal for drawing frame members and cabinet panels together. They range in size from about 1 to 8 feet. Bar clamps of 24 to 36 inches will see to many chores in the home workshop and aren't prohibitively expensive. Big bar clamps, however, might prove too costly for the do-it-yourselfer on a tight budget.

Pipe clamps offer a less-expensive alternative, especially for big clamping tasks. These clamps, consisting of cast-iron fixtures that you thread onto lengths of separately purchased black-iron pipe, are available from home centers, hardware stores, and mail-order sources. You should be able to buy threaded pipe at a home center, otherwise you may have to go to a store that specializes in plumbing supplies. A pair of 48-inch pipe clamps will take care of most jobs. When you need something bigger, you can simply join two pieces of pipe with a pipe coupler.

Strap Clamps. These clamps consist of a fabric strap that fits around the work. The clamp has hardware that lets you tighten the tension on the strap as if you were tightening a seat belt. Strap clamps work best on unusually shaped surfaces.

Handscrew

Handscrew

Vises

Bar Clamp

Strap Clamp

C-Clamp

Spring Clamp

Pipe Clamp

Bar Clamps

POWER TOOLS

To build the projects in this book, you'll need an electric drill, saber saw, circular saw, router, and an electric sander. You can get by without any stationary power tools, but a table saw can save a lot of time when you need to cut sheet stock, mill grooves or rabbets, and tackle a great variety of other sawing chores.

Drills, Bits, and Accessories

Look for a $\frac{3}{8}$-inch, variable-speed, reversible drill for everyday use. Cordless drills may be more expensive, but they are the most convenient because they can be used anywhere without an extension cord. Today there are 12-volt cordless drill/drivers powerful enough to handle most tasks. Many come with keyless chucks, adjustable clutches, and driver-bit storage. If you decide to purchase one, consider buying an extra battery so you will always have a backup power supply.

Basic Bits. Invest in a set of twist-drill or brad-point bits with sizes from $\frac{1}{16}$ to $\frac{1}{4}$ inch; you can always buy the larger sizes as they are needed. Brad-point bits cost a little more, but are better for drilling wood. Their pointed tips are less apt to skid across your work, and they generally bore cleaner holes. For most larger wood-boring chores, you can get by with inexpensive spade bits for holes up to $1\frac{1}{2}$ inches in diameter and hole saws for boring holes up to $2\frac{1}{2}$ inches in diameter.

You'll also want screwdriver bits, which you can buy individually or in sets for standard slotted, Phillips, and other types of screws.

Countersink and Counterbore Bits. You'll want to invest in a set of inexpensive countersink bits for drilling and countersinking holes for screws in sizes from #4 to #12. Although you can drill, countersink, and counterbore screw holes with ordinary drill bits, counterboring bits can perform all three functions in one step.

Doweling Jig. For assembling furniture and cabinets with dowels, you'll need a doweling jig. It will enable you to drill perfectly aligned holes in parts to be joined.

Doweling Jig

Charger

Drill

Sanding Attachments

Drill Bits and Accessories

PORTABLE POWER SAWS

Saber Saw. Use a saber saw with a saw guide to cut straight lines or freehand to make pocket cuts, circular cuts, and other cuts of unusual shape. A saber saw is excellent for cutting and trimming panel stock, back-cutting large moldings, and making cut-outs in countertops. With the right blade you can use a saber saw to cut metal, plastic pipe, laminates, or Plexiglass. Look for a saw that has orbital action (which advances the blade on the cutting stroke), for faster cutting speeds and longer-lasting blades.

Circular Saw. This workhorse is as indispensable in the home workshop as it is on a commercial construction site. The standard saw uses a 7¼-inch blade that can crosscut or rip stock up to 2½ inches thick, which means this saw will easily handle nominal 1-inch and 2-inch lumber and all sheet stock.

There are various blades available for the circular saw designed for crosscutting, ripping, and other specific chores and materials, as well as general-purpose combination blades that will do several jobs fairly well. Generally, the more teeth a blade has, the finer it will cut; a 7¼-inch circular blade with 36 to 40 carbide-tipped teeth will provide a reasonably splinter-free cut.

Circular Saw and Router Guides. Without any kind of guide, a circular saw can make cuts that are straight enough for carpentry work. However, to make cuts straight and square enough for cabinet work, you'll need a guide. Router bits designed to shape edges have their own pilots, but a guide is essential to mill dadoes and grooves with the router.

You can buy a guide that attaches to a circular saw and runs along the edge of the board as you make a cut. This kind of guide works only for cuts that are within a few inches of the edge. As a result, it is useful mainly for making rip cuts along the length of a board or panel. This can be handy if you don't have a table saw for ripping. You can buy a similar sort of guide to attach to your router, but you won't need one for the projects in this book.

A more versatile approach to guiding both the circular saw and the router is to use a straightedge guide that you clamp to the work. You can buy metal guides that have clamps built in. Plans for a shop-built guide that works for both the router and circular saw can be found on page 12. On the same page you'll find plans for a T-square guide that ensures that your router cuts are square.

Saber Saw

Circular Saw

ROUTERS, BITS, AND ACCESSORIES

THE ROUTER ranks just behind drills and saws in popularity among woodworkers. This versatile tool deserves its place in the workshop because of its capacity to perform a tremendous variety of tasks, such as making rabbets, dadoes, and grooves; routing decorative edges in wood; making moldings; and cutting plastic laminates.

All routers are basically a motor mounted on a base. The wide range in prices largely reflects differences in power: $\frac{1}{3}$- to $\frac{1}{2}$-horsepower (hp) models are considered light-duty, while heavy-duty models are powered with 2- to 3-hp motors. Also, some routers can plunge the bit into the work, a feature you won't need for the projects in this book. If you are purchasing one router for general purposes, get one with about $1\frac{1}{2}$ horsepower.

Basic Bits. Outfit your router with a set of basic bits including straight, roundover, rabbeting, cove, and chamfering bits. If you plan to laminate your countertops, you'll also need a flush-trimming bit. All of these bits, except the straight bit, are piloted edge-shaping bits. Some bits are piloted by a ball bearing that runs along the edge of the wood. Bits are also available with fixed pilots that spin with the bit. These are cheaper, but the friction of the spinning pilot often burns the edge of the wood.

Router Table. You can buy or build a router table. This accessory lets your router function like a small shaper. A table is ideal for many applications where it's easier or safer to bring the material to the tool, instead of vice versa. This is the preferred way to make your own moldings and to mill decorative edges on panels, such as drawer fronts.

Router

Plunge Router

Sanders

No chore is as tedious as hand sanding. A general-duty electric sander will save untold amounts of time and will help produce a more uniform finish.

Pad Sander. Also known as finishing sanders, pad sanders are available in three popular sizes to accommodate $\frac{1}{4}$, $\frac{1}{3}$, or $\frac{1}{2}$ sheets of sandpaper. The $\frac{1}{3}$-sheet and $\frac{1}{2}$-sheet sanders are designed for two-handed operation, while the $\frac{1}{4}$-sheet models, often called palm sanders, are for one-handed use. Pad sanders sand in an orbital motion for fast material removal or straight-line motion for fine finishing; some can be switched between the two modes.

Pad Sanders

Random-Orbit Sanders

Random-Orbit Disc Sander. This sander is popular with woodworkers because it removes wood faster than a pad sander while its random orbit eliminates the swirls you get with a pad sander.

Plate Joiner

One of the most versatile tools finding its way into home shops is the plate joiner, or biscuit joiner. Once reserved for professionals, this tool has become attractive to do-it-yourselfers because it quickly and precisely makes strong joints to join panels or cabinet parts. The tool cuts a precise semicircular kerf in which a plate or biscuit is inserted. The biscuit is a pressed wafer of wood that expands with the moisture of glue to make for very tight joints.

Table Saws, Blades, and Accessories

By far, the most valuable and versatile tool for any serious home workshop is the table saw. It's available in a wide variety of sizes and prices, ranging from inexpensive 8-inch bench-top models for just over $100 to the 12-inch industrial powerhouses that cost more than $2,000. The saw most popular among woodworkers uses a 10-inch blade.

Blades. The usual rule applies: buy the best you can afford. Carbide blades are initially more expensive than steel blades, and high quality carbide blades cost more than lower quality ones, but the better blades will cut cleaner and stay sharp longer. For general purposes, buy one of the 40- or 50-tooth combination blades. For making clean, splinter-free cuts in plywood and other materials, buy an 80-tooth, carbide-tipped blade designed for such purposes.

Dado Cutters. A table saw equipped with a dado cutter can make short work of cutting dadoes, grooves, and rabbets. Depending on the style of the cutter, most are capable of cutting widths ranging from $1/4$ to $13/16$ inch.

One type of dado cutter blade is often called a wobbler or wobble saw. When this single-blade cutter is installed in the table saw, its offset blade oscillates, or wobbles, creating a kerf that's wider than the usual $1/8$ inch. A problem with this style cutter is that it tends to dish out the bottoms of the grooves.

Another type of cutter is called a stacked dado cutter set or simply dado set. This type consists of two cutters that resemble combination blades and a set of chippers and shims. The width of the cut is determined by installing different shims and chippers between the blades.

MITER SAWS are among the most versatile tools for the home workshop. These tools allow you to make precise straight and angled cuts in wood. The simplest saws cut miter and bevel angles, but you must block up the wood in the correct position. Compound miter saws handle both operations in one pass, with wood lying flat on the table. A sliding compound miter saw has a blade and saw motor that slides on rails for cutting extra-wide stock.

When cutting long boards and strips of molding, be sure to support the stock that extends beyond the miter saw table. You can stack wood scraps and other objects on your workbench or sawhorses, invest in adjustable supports designed for such purposes, or build your own supports.

Extended Work Table

Adjustable Support

Portable Work Station

Table Saw and Accessories

3 materials

Building materials come in a dizzying array of types, species, grades, sizes, finishes, and configurations for an ever-growing variety of applications. There are hardwoods and softwoods, but some softwoods are actually harder than the softer hardwoods. There is some wood that's referred to by its nominal thickness and width instead of its actual dimensions, and other wood that's sold by its actual dimensions, which may or may not turn out to be true sizes. You can buy wood by the lineal or running foot or by the board foot. Hardboard comes tempered or not, perforated or not. There are interior and exterior grades of plywood, yet we often use exterior plywood indoors.

It doesn't take long to gain a basic understanding of, and familiarity with, most of the materials you'll use in woodworking projects.

PLYWOOD

Plywood is made from thin veneers of wood glued together in a sandwich. Each veneer is oriented perpendicularly to the next to make plywood stronger and more resistant to warping than solid wood. Plywood is available with either softwood or hardwood surface veneers and is sold in 4x8-foot sheets, although many home centers also stock half and quarter sheets. Common thicknesses range from $\frac{1}{8}$ to $\frac{3}{4}$ inch. Because of its stability, its availability in wide panels, and because it is generally less expensive than solid-wood panels, plywood is used in all of the projects in this book.

PLYWOOD GRADES

SOFTWOOD PLYWOOD is graded by the APA: The Engineered Wood Association (formerly the American Plywood Association) with a two-letter code. Each letter indicates the quality of one of the veneer faces. The best is "N" which stands for "natural," because the face veneer will look great with a clear finish that shows the grain. The remaining grades are "A" through "D" in descending order of quality. For example, a sheet graded A-A has two good face veneers and is an excellent choice if both sides of a finished project will show. However, A-A is an expensive choice. With one premium face and one utility-grade face, A-C plywood is the most economical option if one side of the panel will be against a wall or another cabinet.

Hardwood plywood is available with many different species of face veneers, such as red oak, white oak, mahogany, birch, and cherry. Most of the hardwood plywood sold in the United States is imported, and as a result, grading isn't as standardized as it is for domestic softwood plywood. In general though, Grade A has clear wood surfaces with no visible defects and is well-matched in terms of grain patterns and color. Grade B also has clear surfaces free of defects, although its grain patterns won't be matched as well. Grade 2 is similar to A and B in wood quality, but is not well-matched in color and grain: it's fine for painting but not for clear finishes. Grade 3 will exhibit small knotholes, discoloration, spaces between veneer joints, and other minor defects easily hidden with a little filler and paint. Grade 4 is pretty rough, with splits up to an inch wide and knotholes up to 2 inches in diameter. Special A-quality sheets exhibiting unusual grain patterns, such as bird's eye or fiddleback, are graded SP.

As with softwood plywood, you can save money by buying hardwood plywood, which is a better grade on one side than the other if only one side will show in the finished project.

TYPICAL BACKSTAMP

Grade of Veneer on Panel Face

Grade of Veneer on Panel Back

Grading Agency

Species Group Number

Designates the Type of Plywood

Product Standard Governing Manufacture

Mill Number

A-C

GROUP 2
EXTERIOR
PS 1-74 000

APA
THE ENGINEERED
WOOD ASSOCIATION

PLYWOOD VENEER FACE GRADES

N- Smooth surface "natural finish" veneer is select, all heartwood or all sapwood. It is free of open defects and allows not more than six repairs, wood only, per 4 x 8-foot panel, made parallel to the grain and well-matched for grain and color.

A- This smooth paintable veneer allows not more than 18 neatly made repairs, parallel with the grain. It may be used as a natural finish in less demanding situations.

B- Solid-surface veneer permits shims, circular repair plugs, tight knots to 1 inch across the grain, and minor splits.

C-Plugged- Improved C veneer has splits limited to $\frac{1}{8}$ inch wide and knotholes and borer holes limited to $\frac{1}{4}$ x $\frac{1}{2}$ inch. It permits some broken grain. Synthetic repairs also are permitted.

C- This veneer has tight knots to $1\frac{1}{2}$ inches. It has knotholes to 1 inch across the grain with some to $1\frac{1}{2}$ inches if the total width of knots and knotholes is within specified limits. Repairs are synthetic or wood. Discoloration and sanding defects that do not impair the strength are permitted. Limited splits and stitching are allowed.

D- Knots and knotholes to $2\frac{1}{2}$ inches wide across the grain and $\frac{1}{2}$ inch larger within specified limits are allowed. Limited splits are permitted.

Plywood Buying Tips. If you are planning to cover the edges of plywood with a matching solid wood, buy the plywood before the solid wood. This is the best way to ensure a match because in most areas, hardwood plywood is readily available only in a few commonly used domestic species. Of course, edging plywood with a contrasting wood is an excellent design option, too.

Plywood that's damaged at the mill, en route, or at the lumberyard gets downgraded and sold at sale prices that are often drastically reduced. Ask your supplier about shop-grade plywood and blows. Most people are surprised to learn how much they can save on expensive plywood that exhibits only minor defects. A small dent on one side, or a little damage to one corner can save you 30 to 50 percent.

PARTICLEBOARD

Particleboard is a term used to describe several different types of sheet materials made from ground-up bits of wood and glue. Admittedly, it's not much to look at, but because it is very stable and considerably cheaper than plywood, particleboard is typically used as an underlayment for a number of projects.

Some of the benefits of working with particleboard are that it doesn't warp, shrink, or swell with changes in humidity. On the downside, particleboard is heavy and tends to sag under a load more than plywood or solid wood, and interior grades of particleboard can disintegrate if placed in direct contact with water unless properly sealed. In addition, particleboard chips easily, and it doesn't hold fasteners well; it's best to use special particleboard fasteners instead of wood screws. Always cut using carbide-tipped blades because it will dull other blades in a few passes.

Particleboard, like plywood, is available in 4 x 8-foot sheets. It also comes in a variety of board and panel widths up to 16 inches that are great for shelving. Thicknesses range from $\frac{1}{4}$ to $\frac{3}{4}$ inch.

HARDBOARD

Hardboard is made from wood fibers bonded with pressure and heat to form a thin, durable panel. It's normally used where it can't be seen, such as for drawer bottoms and rear panels for cabinets. Like particleboard, hardboard will dull your saw blades quickly, so always cut it with a carbide-tipped blade.

Perforated Hardboard. Also known as pegboard, perforated hardboard is often used as wall material in workshops and garages where it serves as a place to hang tools and other items. It also serves the same purpose in some specialized closets and cabinets. Because of its perforations, it's a good choice of back-panel material for hampers and other projects requiring ventilation.

Tempered Hardboard. Both plain and perforated hardboard are available as tempered products, which are impregnated with resin to make them stronger and more resistant to moisture. Hardboard is highly susceptible to humidity fluctuations, which can cause it to warp and buckle. So always buy tempered hardboard, which costs only a little more than the standard product.

LUMBER

Wood is classified as either softwood or hardwood. Softwoods are usually softer than hardwoods, but that's not always the case. Balsa, for example, is a hardwood, but it's softer than Douglas fir, a softwood. Technically speaking, softwoods come from coniferous or cone-bearing trees, which include pine, redwood, cedar, and spruce. Hardwoods come from deciduous trees, such as oak, walnut, maple, cherry, and birch. Generally speaking, softwoods are less expensive and easier to work with than hardwoods, while hardwoods are more durable and have more attractive grain patterns.

Wood

Category	Grade	Description
Select (Best appearance)	A	Practically flawless—takes any finish
	B	A few small defects—takes any finish
	C	Some defects—paint recommended
	D	More defects, but easily concealed with paint
Common (Lesser quality)	1	Tight knots and limited physical blemishes
	2	No warps or splits. A few checks at ends, knots, and other blemishes
	3	Defects which may cause some waste removal
	4	Numerous defects such as open knotholes
	5 (Rare)	Very low quality. Use as filler only
Structural (Framing lumber 2" or more thick)	Construction	High quality
	Standard	Good quality with some defects
	Utility	Poor structural quality, space more closely
	Economy	Lowest quality structural lumber

Hardwood

Grade	Description
Firsts	$91\frac{2}{3}$% clear on both sides—best material
Seconds	$83\frac{1}{3}$% clear on both sides—very good material
Firsts and Seconds	Mixture of firsts and seconds containing not less than 20% firsts
Selects	90% clear on one side only—can be used for cabinet work but with some waste
No. 1	$66\frac{2}{3}$% clear on one side only—use as inside pieces, paint
No. 2	50% clear on one side only—paint

Air-dried vs. Kiln-dried Wood

How lumber is dried after it is cut is almost as important as what it was cut from. Green, or unseasoned, lumber contains a lot of water—perhaps as much as 80 percent by weight. Drying to lower moisture levels increases the strength and stability of lumber.

Wood is either air-dried or kiln-dried. Air-dried lumber is stacked with spacers to allow air to circulate and is usually marked indicating its maximum moisture content at the time it leaves the mill; 19 percent lumber is stamped "S-dry" (semi-dry), 15 percent is marked "MC-15" (moisture content 15 percent). In a kiln, temperature and humidity can be controlled more carefully; the kiln-dried lumber typically has a moisture content of 10–12 percent. Kiln-dried wood is more expensive, but it has less tendency to shrink after it's been installed.

It is important to realize that no matter how wood is dried, it continues to contract and expand with changes in humidity. Air-dried wood will continue to shrink and dry if placed in a heated room. Likewise, kiln-dried wood will absorb moisture and expand if left outdoors or in a damp garage. It is a good idea to give lumber a sufficient amount of time to acclimate itself to its environment. If possible, you should try to buy wood products several weeks before you need them and store them in a dry (preferably heated) place.

No matter where you store lumber and wood products, or for how long, don't just lean it haphazardly against a wall until you need it. Take measures to protect it from damage and warping. To get an idea of how to store wood at home, pay attention to how it's stored where you buy it. If you bring home kiln-dried lumber that was stored indoors at a home center, stack it neatly indoors to prevent warping. If it's air-dried wood that was stored outdoors at a lumberyard, chances are it was stacked with spacers between the boards, placed about every 12 inches, to facilitate air circulation; do the same at home, using strips of one-by scrap.

Although you'll often find particleboard and lower grades of plywood stacked horizontally in racks, the higher grades are usually stored vertically to protect fine-face veneers. That's the way you should store sheet stock at home, too, with the best veneers protected and out of harm's way. If possible, store it away from high-traffic areas to protect vulnerable edges and corners.

Lumber Grades

In North America, most softwood is sold for construction purposes. It is used by carpenters who will cut it to length and nail it in place. In some carpentry applications, such as trim work, appearance is important. In other applications, such as framing, only structural strength matters. Hardwood, on the other hand, is used mostly by woodworkers who purchase rough-sawn, random-width lumber, which they plane to thickness and cut to width and length. The grading systems for softwood and hardwood reflect the difference in the way the materials are used.

The hardwood grading system emphasizes the percentage of clear wood you can expect to get out of a given piece. This information can be very useful if you choose to use hardwood for the projects in this book. Because the projects are made of plywood, solid wood is used mostly as edging material to hide plywood edges. This calls for narrow pieces. As a result, you can obtain clear stock by purchasing lower grade wood and cutting around the knots.

If you have the ability to plane and joint your own hardwood to thickness and width, you'll find your best price and selection by shopping at a sawmill instead of a lumberyard. Some mills do plane wood to thickness while leaving length and width random. This is known as surfaced two sides (often denoted as S2S). The most common hardwood sold by many lumberyards and home centers that already has been surfaced on both faces and edges is oak. Wood sold this way is called surfaced four sides (S4S).

American Standard Softwood Lumber Sizes*

Item	Thickness Actual Size Minimum Dressed			Face Width Actual Size Minimum Dressed		
	Named Size	Dry	Green	Named Size	Dry	Green
	(in.)	(in.)	(in.)	(in.)	(in.)	(in.)
Board	1	$3/4$	$25/32$	2	$1\frac{1}{2}$	$1\frac{9}{16}$
	$1\frac{1}{4}$	1	$1\frac{1}{32}$	3	$2\frac{1}{2}$	$2\frac{9}{16}$
	$1\frac{1}{2}$	$1\frac{1}{4}$	$1\frac{9}{32}$	4	$3\frac{1}{2}$	$3\frac{9}{16}$
				5	$4\frac{1}{2}$	$4\frac{5}{8}$
				6	$5\frac{1}{2}$	$5\frac{5}{8}$
				7	$6\frac{1}{2}$	$6\frac{5}{8}$
				8	$7\frac{1}{4}$	$7\frac{1}{2}$
				9	$8\frac{1}{4}$	$8\frac{1}{2}$
				10	$9\frac{1}{4}$	$9\frac{1}{2}$
				11	$10\frac{1}{4}$	$10\frac{1}{2}$
				12	$11\frac{1}{4}$	$11\frac{1}{2}$
				14	$13\frac{1}{4}$	$13\frac{1}{2}$
				16	$15\frac{1}{4}$	$15\frac{1}{2}$
Dimension	2	$1\frac{1}{2}$	$1\frac{9}{16}$	2	$1\frac{1}{2}$	$1\frac{9}{16}$
	$2\frac{1}{2}$	2	$2\frac{1}{16}$	3	$2\frac{1}{2}$	$2\frac{9}{16}$
	3	$2\frac{1}{2}$	$2\frac{9}{16}$	4	$3\frac{1}{2}$	$3\frac{9}{16}$
	$3\frac{1}{2}$	3	$3\frac{1}{16}$	5	$4\frac{1}{2}$	$4\frac{5}{8}$
	4	$3\frac{1}{2}$	$3\frac{9}{16}$	6	$5\frac{1}{2}$	$5\frac{5}{8}$
	$4\frac{1}{2}$	4	$4\frac{1}{16}$	8	$7\frac{1}{4}$	$7\frac{1}{2}$
				10	$9\frac{1}{4}$	$9\frac{1}{2}$
				12	$11\frac{1}{4}$	$11\frac{1}{2}$
				14	$13\frac{1}{4}$	$13\frac{1}{2}$
				16	$15\frac{1}{4}$	$15\frac{1}{2}$
Timber	5 and greater		$\frac{1}{2}$ less than named size	5 and greater		$\frac{1}{2}$ less than named size

*From American Softwood Lumber Standard PS 20.70.

Lumber Size and Finish. Softwood lumber is available in lengths of 4 to 20 feet in two-foot increments. Most of the softwood lumber you will buy has already been surfaced on both sides and both edges. Softwood lumber is sold according to its nominal size: the dimensions of the board when it was cut at the mill. After surfacing and drying, the wood's actual dimensions are smaller. The chart *American Standard Softwood Lumber Sizes* shows the nominal and actual thicknesses and widths of lumber.

When you buy rough-sawn hardwood in random widths and lengths, the nominal length and the actual length are the same thing. The exception is the planed and jointed oak boards you'll find at the lumberyard or home center. For this material, nominal and actual sizes differ just as they do for softwood.

BUYING LUMBER

Defects. Inspect lumber for any defects. Watch for small cracks, called checks, at the ends of the boards, and large cracks, called splits, that may extend through the entire board. Both are symptoms of uneven drying. The various manifestations of warp, also usually caused by improper drying or storage, include cup, twist, and bow.

END VIEW	LONG VIEW
Bow	
Cup	
Crook	
Twist	
Check	
Split	
Wane	
Knot	
Decay	
Pitch Pocket	

Avoid warped boards because they're extremely difficult to work with. Pitch pockets are cavities in softwood that are filled with resin or pitch, which can ooze from the cavity, even through paint. Also be wary of stained wood where the discoloration penetrates the surface. Insect-damaged wood is obvious and unusable for most purposes.

Most lumber is sold by the board foot, lineal foot, or piece. Although prices on large quantities are usually quoted in board feet, most of the lumber you buy for the home workshop is priced by the lineal foot or by the piece, which eliminates the need for any complicated mathematical exercises. For wood that sells for $1.25 a lineal foot, for example, an 8-footer would cost you eight times $1.25, or $10.

Here is what you need to know to figure your cost with board-foot pricing. A board foot is simply one square foot of lumber, one (nominal) inch thick. An 8-foot 1x12 contains 8 board feet. The same size 2x12 contains 16 board feet. Other dimensions, however, don't translate so easily; for that operation you need a formula: thickness (nominal inches) times width (nominal inches) times length (actual feet) divided by 12 equals board feet. To determine how many board feet are in a 16-foot 2x8, for example, multiply 2 (thickness) times 8 (width) times 16 (length) for a product of 256. Dividing 256 by 12 tells you there are 21.333 board feet in that single piece.

It is good practice to buy lumber at least a few inches longer than needed, because the ends often contain flaws and are not squarely cut. If you're looking to salvage clear stock from large pieces of lower grade lumber, count on buying from 25 to 30 percent more stock than you might need for any project.

● MOLDING

MOLDING can dress up many projects. Use it to tie a project in with the rest of the room, or simply to add some interesting detail. Practically speaking, molding is also handy for concealing seams, gaps, plywood edges, and other unsightly necessities of construction and assembly.

Both softwood and hardwood moldings are available. If you plan to finish any project with a clear or semitransparent product, be sure to buy clear molding that matches the wood you're using. For painted projects, use paint-grade stock, sometimes called "finger-jointed" molding, which consists of short pieces of molding joined into longer strips by means of adhesive and interlocking joinery.

Molding is sold in standard lengths up to 16 feet, sometimes in increments of 2 feet. Most lumberyards will cut strips for you to specified lengths. Try to buy all the molding for any single project from the same mill run. Even within the same design, width and thickness

can vary minutely, but nevertheless disastrously, if you end up with two sizes on the same project.

Most moldings are available only in softwood, usually pine. Hardwood moldings are also available, most commonly in oak. If you need another type of hardwood molding to match your project, you can always make it yourself with a router or with a table saw equipped with a molding head.

GRADES OF MOLDING

Clear · Paint Grade

TYPES OF MOLDING

Chair Rail · Mullion · Wainscoting Cap · Crown · Cove · Astragal · Outside Corner · Clamshell Casing · Clamshell Baseboard · Base Shoe · Dentil · Colonial Casing · Colonial Baseboard · Quarter Round · Half Round

4 hardware and adhesives

Every home center and hardware store seems to have an endless variety of mechanical fasteners, dozens of different kinds of adhesives, and an overwhelming assortment of hardware for every imaginable purpose. The good news for woodworkers is that less can be more than enough. Two or three different adhesives will see to most of your joining needs; mechanical fasteners are mostly nails and screws; and the rest of the hardware you'll need to complete the projects in this book (knobs, hinges, and latches) is simple to understand and easy to install.

FASTENERS

The basic fasteners for all of the projects in this book are nails or screws, and glue. Although screws are considerably stronger than nails, glue is the most important fastener in any wood joint. A good glue joint can be stronger than the wood itself.

For the projects in this book, nails and screws are most often used as clamps that hold the wood pieces together while the glue cures. There are, of course, instances in which you want to use screws without glue. One obvious instance is when you are fastening cabinets to walls. Another less obvious example is when you need to allow a piece room for humidity changes. For example, the short bookcase project on page 197 is a plywood box with a solid wood top. The solid wood will expand and contract more than the plywood. If you glued it on, the top would crack or the glue joint would fail. Instead, the top is attached with screws through oversized holes in the plywood.

NAILS

NAIL LENGTH is expressed in terms of the penny—at one time the price per hundred. Penny is designated by the small letter "d." A two-penny (2d) nail is 1 inch long. See the chart "Nail Sizes" to convert penny designations into inches. Nails longer than 6 inches are measured by the inch.

The five main types of nails are box nails, common nails, finishing nails, casing nails, and brads. Use box and common nails for rough work, and finishing and casing nails for cabinetry and trim, respectively. Casing nails have a slightly larger diameter than finishing nails and a more tapered head. Both finishing and casing nails come with either dimpled or smooth heads; the dimpled heads are easier to countersink with a nail set. Brads resemble finishing nails, except they are much smaller. Brads are used for attaching small moldings and other thin materials. They're sold in sizes from $3/8$ inch to $1\frac{1}{2}$ inches.

COMMON TYPES OF NAILS

- Box Nail
- Common Nail
- Finishing Nail
- Casing Nail
- Brad

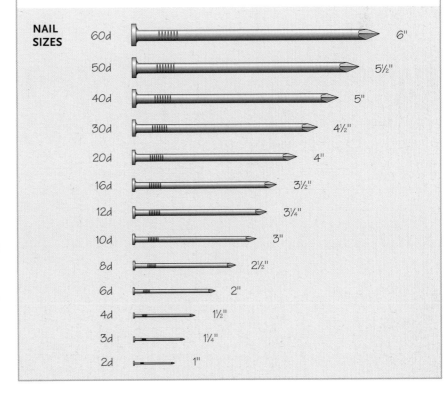

NAIL SIZES

60d	6"
50d	5½"
40d	5"
30d	4½"
20d	4"
16d	3½"
12d	3¼"
10d	3"
8d	2½"
6d	2"
4d	1½"
3d	1¼"
2d	1"

SCREWS

SCREWS come in a great variety of diameter and length combinations. They're identified by the thickness or gauge of their shafts and by their lengths, followed by head type. A flathead screw with a 10-gauge thickness and length of 3½ inches would be labeled as #10 x 3½-inch flathead.

Wood Screws. Wood screws are tapered so the threads bite into the wood, which makes a stronger bond than nails. Screws take longer to install, however, because most installations, especially in hardwood, require a pilot hole for each screw. Most screw holes also must be countersunk or counterbored.

The problem with using wood screws is that their heads remain visible after installation. Round-head screws are the most visible; use them where they won't show. Oval heads are less obvious, and are sometimes used for decorative purposes. Flathead screws are the most common for woodworking projects, because they are designed to be driven flush with the wood's surface. You can also counterbore holes to sink the screw heads beneath the wood's surface, and then conceal them with wood plugs.

Drywall Screws. Also known as the all-purpose, or buglehead screw, these screws do not require a pilot hole in softwoods; their aggressive threads are designed to drive fast and hold tight. In addition, these screws are self-countersinking in most softwoods. The Phillips head is extra deep to prevent stripping and make driving easy with power drivers.

TYPES OF WOOD SCREWS

Flathead   Oval Head   Round Head

DRYWALL SCREW

Buglehead

SPECIALTY FASTENERS

SOME PROJECTS can't be installed with conventional nails and screws. For example, hollow plaster or drywall and solid masonry walls pose special problems that must be solved with specialty fasteners.

Hollow-Wall Fasteners. Toggle bolts and hollow-wall anchors are designed for use in plaster or drywall walls. A toggle bolt has spring-loaded wings that open against the inside of the wall as the bolt is tightened. Instead of wings, a hollow-wall anchor bolt has a sleeve that expands against the inside of the wall.

It's best to attach cabinets and other built-ins to wall studs, even if you can only attach part of the unit to a stud and must use a hollow-wall fastener for a second attachment point. If there's no way to attach to even one stud, make sure you are using a fastener designed to support the weight of the object you are mounting.

Solid-Wall Fasteners. Fasteners for use in brick or concrete walls usually take the form of bolts that fit into expansion shields or anchors of some kind, or plastic anchors used with wood screws. To attach a cabinet to a masonry wall using anchors, drill holes in the wall the same diameter as the anchors. Insert the anchors. Install the cabinet with the anchor bolts or screws, which will cause the anchors to expand as they are tightened.

HOLLOW-WALL FASTENERS

Hollow-Wall Anchor   Toggle Bolt

SOLID-WALL FASTENERS

Plastic Anchor
Cabinet Back
Wood Screw
Solid Masonry Wall

ADHESIVES

Adhesives are available for all kinds of materials, from fabrics to ceramics, plastics to metals, and for porous and nonporous surfaces. For woodworking, you need only two or three adhesives for the bulk of your wood-joining tasks.

Carpenter's Wood Glue. Aliphatic resin glue, commonly called carpenter's glue or yellow glue, is the adhesive of choice for bonding wood to wood. It sets relatively quickly, can be cleaned up with water, and is sandable.

Aliphatic resin glues are available for both interior and exterior uses. Both versions are water soluble when wet, but after it has time to cure, the exterior formula is water resistant. This is the glue to use for outdoor projects and for projects used indoors around water, such as cutting boards and butcher-block countertops.

Contact Cement. This rubber-based liquid glue bonds on contact. Use it to join plastic laminate or other veneers to a wood, plywood, or particleboard underlayment. Apply contact cement to both surfaces, and allow it to dry for approximately 15 minutes before joining the parts. The parts will stick together immediately upon contact. Fumes given off by this adhesive can be dangerous, so look for the nonflammable type, and use it only in a well-ventilated area. Carefully read and follow the manufacturer's directions.

HARDWARE

Although the assortment of hardware available for cabinets and other woodworking projects might seem bewildering at first, much of it is repetitive in design and function. And some is highly specialized and rarely used. Fortunately, most of it is easy to understand and install.

KNOBS AND PULLS

DOOR AND DRAWER KNOBS AND PULLS are made of plastic, metal, ceramic, and wood in hundreds of sizes, colors, and designs to fit any decor and serve any purpose. If your project calls for both knobs and pulls, you can buy matching sets. Most mount with screws driven from the back of the door or drawer front. You'll even find hardwood continuous-pull moldings that you can cut to length and finish to match your doors and drawers.

HINGES

HARDWARE for hanging cabinet doors is available in basic types for overlay, inset, and flush-fit, as well as designs for special purposes, such as concealed mounting and mounting on glass. (See "Installing Doors and Hinges," page 25.) There are plain hinges, and decorative hinges, and hinges that automatically close the door. Several of the projects in this book use piano, or continuous, hinges, which are available in lengths up to 72 inches and can be cut with a hacksaw to any length you need.

Butt Hinge

Decorative T-Hinge

Flush Hinge

Continuous (Piano) Hinge

Semi-Concealed Hinge

Inset Hinge

Flush Butterfly Hinge

Decorative Flush Hinge

CATCHES AND LATCHES

CATCHES and latches, usually made of brass or wrought iron, provide a rustic look. Mechanical or magnetic catches provide a cleaner, modern look. These catches consist of one part that attaches to the inside of the door and another that mounts inside the cabinet. Another choice is called a push latch, or touch latch. It is a spring-loaded magnetic device that holds the door closed and pops it open when the door is pushed.

Roller Catch
Spring-Loaded Catch
Friction-Clamp Catch
Rustic Catch
Spring-Loaded Touch Catch
Roller-Style Friction-Clamp Catch
Magnetic Catches
Cupboard Catch

DRAWER SLIDES

FOR FURNITURE PROJECTS, you'll want to make your own wooden drawer slides. For kitchen and bathroom cabinet drawers, however, you may opt for commercial slides. These metal slides come in dozens of designs for bottom and side mounting. The smoothest operate on ball-bearing wheels or roller-bearing sleeves. For heavy-duty applications, you'll find slides rated for capacities of 75 to 100 pounds.

Bottom-Mounted

Side-Mounted

SHELF STANDARDS AND SUPPORTS

METAL SHELF STANDARDS, also known as pilaster strips, are made of steel or aluminum and come in a variety of finishes. Standard lengths range from 12 to 144 inches, and the standards can be cut with a hacksaw to fit any requirements. They are either surface or flush mounted with screws, nails, or staples. Clip-style shelf supports snap into holes located every $\frac{1}{2}$ inch to allow shelves to be adjusted quickly and easily.

Even simpler are shelf support pins. These merely push into holes bored in pairs in cabinet and bookcase sides. Sometimes brass inserts go into the holes to give them a more finished look.

Shelf Standard

Adjustable Shelf Pins

5 wood finishing

Finishing is a simple craft that anyone can learn. The objective is nothing more complicated than to transfer a liquid stain, finish, or paint from a can, or other container, to the wood. There are only three tools used to do this: a rag, a brush, or a spray gun. Each tool is easy to use. Even a spray gun is no more difficult to use than a router. However, as discussed below, spray equipment is costly and the need for separate spraying space and special ventilation usually precludes its use in a home shop.

Stains, finishes, and paints are also easy to understand. There are only three main ingredients used to make up these products: colorant, binder, and thinner. Stains and paints are colorant, usually pigment, in a binder that is thinned with a thinner. The

STAINS, PAINTS, AND FINISHES (from left) are each made with only three main ingredients. Stains and paints are colorant (usually pigment), binder, and solvent or thinner. Finishes are simply binder, with a solvent or thinner usually added.

principal difference between a stain and a paint is the amount of thinner added. Stain has a lot of thinner; paint has just enough thinner to make it brushable. You want a stain to highlight the grain of the wood, not cover it. You use a paint to hide the wood.

Finishes are binder, usually with some thinner added. You can think of a clear finish as paint without the colorant. Finishes protect the wood, like paint does, but they don't color it.

FINISHING TOOLS

There are four key differences between rags, brushes, and spray guns.

1. Cost. Rags cost very little or nothing, especially if you make an effort to save old, worn-out cotton clothing. Brushes are also inexpensive. In contrast, even the cheapest spray guns cost $200 or more. So if cost is a factor, choose a rag or brush.

2. Speed. You can apply stain, finish, or paint to a larger area faster with a rag or spray gun than you can with a brush. For example, if you want to apply stain to a set of cabinets and get all the excess wiped off before the stain begins to dry, you will be more successful if you use a rag or spray gun to apply the stain than if you use a brush.

3. Film Leveling. In cases where you are not wiping off the excess, leveling is important. The more flawed the film you apply, the less satisfied you will be with your work. It is nearly impossible to apply a stain, finish, or paint with a rag without leaving deep ridges in the film. Brushes perform better, but they leave brush marks. This is true even with sponge brushes which leave ridges at the edges. Spray guns produce the most level surface of the three tools. It is true that most spray guns leave a light pimply surface called "orange peel," but this defect is usually minor compared to ridges and brush marks.

4. Weather. If you live in a cold climate and can't finish outdoors for a large part of the year, you will have problems using a spray gun. Spray guns create a lot of overspray, which floats around the room and lands on everything, including your work. You must exhaust this overspray, and this presents two problems: replacing the exhausted air with warm air, and trapping the overspray before it gets to the fan and builds up on it. In contrast, rags and brushes transfer all the liquid efficiently from the can to the wood. The only leftover is evaporating solvent as the coating cures.

Replacing air with warm air on cold days can be a strain on your heating system. Placing a heater in the room in which you are spraying can be a hazard, especially if there is an open flame in the heater. Never spray in a room where there is an open flame. It can cause an explosion.

5 wood finishing

To trap overspray, arrange a bank of filters between you and the exhaust fan. Don't allow finish or paint to build up on the fan. In addition, don't allow solvents from a solvent-based paint or finish to be drawn across a motor that is not explosion proof.

Rags

There's not much to say about rags except that cotton almost always works best, and rags can be a serious fire hazard when used with oil finishes and not disposed of properly. Oil finishes cure by absorbing oxygen from the air. The by-product of the reaction between the oil and oxygen is heat. If the heat can't dissipate from the rag, it will build up until it reaches the ignition temperature of the rag, and the rag will burst into flame.

The easiest and safest way to dispose of oily rags is to open them to air immediately after use. Spread the rags out on the floor or drape them over the edge of a table or trash can. As long as air can get to all parts of the rags so the heat can dissipate, there is no chance of a fire. When you have time, take the rags outside and hang them over a tree limb or fence. When the rags harden due to the oil curing, they can be safely thrown in the trash. Cured oil in rags is no more of a hazardous waste than cured oil in wood.

BRUSHES

THERE ARE FOUR common types of brushes: natural bristle, synthetic bristle, sponge, and paint pads. All can be used to transfer stain, finish, or paint from the can to the wood.

Natural-bristle brushes are made from animal hair. The best are made from Chinese hog hairs. These hairs are tapered and have split ends which means that the parts of the hairs that are in contact with the wood are extremely thin. The thinner the bristles, or split ends, the more level the applied film. Though China-bristle brushes are a little more expensive, the improved results are usually worth it.

Synthetic-bristle brushes are made from polyester and nylon. These brushes became popular for use with latex paint because natural bristles lose their shape in water. The better synthetic-bristle brushes also have split ends and perform almost as well as natural-bristle brushes. Use synthetic-bristle brushes with all water-based products. Use either type of brush with solvent-based products.

WHEN YOU FINISH cleaning your brush, put it back in the cardboard holder it came in, or wrap it in heavy paper, so the bristles dry straight.

Sponge brushes are cheap and are usually considered to be disposable. They are very effective with all finishing products except lacquer, which dissolves them.

Paint pads are flat sponge material with many tiny fibers attached. The pads are usually held in a plastic handle. Paint pads are effective for applying all finishing products except lacquer to a flat surface.

Cleaning Brushes

If you use a good-quality brush, you will want to clean it after each use. It is wise, in fact, to clean it before using it the first time in order to remove any loose bristles or dirt.

The procedure for cleaning brushes varies a little depending on the finish you are using. In all cases, however, the last step is to wash the brush in soap and water and store it in the cardboard holder it came in, or in a heavy-paper wrapping like that of a grocery-store bag. You can use any mild soap. A convenient one is dish soap. The idea is to wash the brush until it is clean enough so that the soap makes suds. Wrapping the brush is necessary so the bristles dry straight.

Variations in the cleaning procedure occur in the steps getting the brush ready to be washed with soap and water. The variations depend on the paint, stain, or finish you are using. For example, no prior steps are required for cleaning brushes used for latex paint or water-based stains and finishes. Simply rinse the brush, and then wash with soap and water. For brushes used for shellac or lacquer, rinse the brush first in alcohol (for shellac) or lacquer thinner (for lacquer), or in a solu-

56

tion of half-and-half household ammonia and water, and then wash with a mild soap.

The most difficult paints, stains, and finishes to clean are oil-based. The easiest way to prepare a brush for the soap-and-water washing is to rinse it once or twice in paint thinner and then in lacquer thinner. Lacquer thinner removes the oiliness left by the paint thinner so that the soap succeeds in making suds after only one or two washings. Without the lacquer thinner wash, you will have to wash more times in soap and water. You could substitute lacquer thinner for the earlier paint-thinner steps, but lacquer thinner is more expensive.

If you think you may want to use the brush again within a day or two, and you'd rather not go to the trouble of cleaning it, you can store it in a can or jar containing the solvent or thinner for the finish you are using. Alcohol is the solvent for shellac. Lacquer thinner is the solvent for lacquer. Water is the thinner for latex paint and water-based stains and finishes. Paint thinner (mineral spirits) is the thinner for oil paints and stains, varnish, and polyurethane. Hang the brush in the container of liquid so that the liquid comes at least half way up the bristles. Don't let the brush rest on the bottom of the container or it will assume a permanent bent shape.

If you allow paint or finish to harden on the brush, you can often reclaim it by letting it soak in the solvent for the finish (this works with shellac and lacquer) or in paint-stripper for paints.

PREPARING WOOD

Of all the steps in finishing, preparing the wood is the most boring and labor intensive, but it is very important. You cannot achieve quality results if the wood has not been properly prepared.

Preparing wood for painting is easier than for finishing with a clear finish because paint covers flaws while clear finish highlights them. The following steps do not have to be done so well if you intend to paint the wood. There are three steps to preparing wood for accepting a stain or finish:

- Sand the wood smooth.
- Remove all glue seepage.
- Make wood-putty patches blend in.

Sanding Wood

Sanding wood is a lot of work. It may make it easier if you understand why you have to do it. After all, before the invention of machine tools in the mid-nineteenth century, very little if any sanding was required once the boards were shaped and joined. Indeed, there was no sandpaper before the development of machine tools. Wood was smoothed and shaped with hand tools which left the surface of the wood almost perfectly smooth.

It is the machine tools, which you love because they make woodworking so much easier, that cause you to have to work so hard sanding before applying the stain and finish. Machine tools, no matter how sharp and how well tuned, leave marks in the wood that show up under a stain or finish. The price you pay for using machines to do woodworking is that you have to spend a lot of time sanding to remove the marks left by these machines.

The goal when sanding wood is to remove the flaws as quickly and efficiently as possible without leaving excessively deep scratches in the wood. In practice, this usually means beginning with either 80-grit or 100-grit sandpaper. There may be cases, however, when it would be more efficient to use a coarser grit, and there may be cases where you can get by beginning with 120- or 150-grit sandpaper. For paint, sanding to 100 grit usually is enough.

Always sand in the direction of the wood grain no matter which grit sandpaper you use. Sanding across the grain or at diagonals can damage wood fibers in a way that requires a great deal of sanding to remove.

Whichever grit sandpaper you begin with, you need to progressively sand out the scratches until you have all the wood sanded evenly to about 180 grit. There may be cases where you can stop at 150 grit or where you might want to continue to as fine as 220 grit, but until you gain some experience so you begin to notice differences, use 180 grit as your standard.

ALL POWER CUTTING and shaping tools leave marks in the wood that must be sanded out. The "washboarding" shown here is caused by a jointer or planer.

TO SEE IF YOU HAVE SANDED ENOUGH to remove washboarding and coarse sanding scratches, look at the wood in a raking light.

YOU CAN MAKE A CORK BLOCK by gluing ⅛-in.-thick gasket cork to the bottom of a soft-wood block about 2¾ in. x 3⅞ in. Chamfer the top edges.

It is theoretically most efficient to sand through each grit of sandpaper until you reach 180 grit, but most people skip a grit when sanding. In other words, most people find they get good results jumping from, say, 80 grit to 120 grit to 180 grit, thus skipping 100 grit and 150 grit. Decisions like these are very individual because each of us uses varying pressures and sands more-or-less long with more-or-less worn sandpaper.

It's difficult to see what you are accomplishing with sandpaper on bare wood. A trick that will help is to look at the wood in a raking light. That is, arrange your work so there is a light or a window just above the plane of the wood. You will be able to see flaws or deep sanding scratches that you haven't yet removed in the reflection.

If you are hand sanding a flat surface, always back your sandpaper with a soft cork, rubber, or felt block. Otherwise, your fingers will cause the sandpaper to dig out the softer spring-growth wood, creating a rippled effect that you may not notice until you make the surface shiny with a finish. You can make a cork block that fits snugly in your hand by gluing ⅛-inch gasket cork from an auto parts store

to softwood that is chamfered on the top edges.

You can, of course, use hand-held machine sanders to make sanding easier. There are three common hand-held sanding machines: orbital, belt, and random orbit. Orbital or pad sanders are the cheapest and least efficient type. It is very difficult to do serious damage using these sanders, but they are very slow. Belt sanders are more expensive, and they are very efficient at removing a large amount of wood. But belt sanders are difficult to control. It is very difficult to sand with a belt sander without gouging the wood. It is even more risky using a belt sander to sand veneered plywood. You will most likely sand through in places.

The most effective hand-held sanding machine is the random-orbit sander. This sander is also relatively expensive. Random sanders remove a lot of wood without much risk of gouging. Only by setting the sander down on the wood while it is running are you likely to gouge the wood. It's best to place the sander on the wood before you turn it on.

No matter which sander you use, finish sanding by hand using your finest-grit sandpaper (usually 180 grit). Both the orbital and the random-orbit sanders leave squiggly marks in the wood that often show under a stain or finish. A light hand sanding removes these marks.

THERE ARE THREE commonly available hand-held machine sanders. (From left) an orbital sander, a belt sander, and a random-orbit sander.

SANDPAPER

THERE ARE FOUR commonly available types of sandpaper. Two are best for sanding wood, and two are best for sanding finishes. All four types of sandpaper are identified by standard sandpaper grit numbers, which run from a low of 36 grit to a high of 2000 grit. Grits are defined by the number of openings in a 1-inch-square mesh screen through which the abrasive stones are sifted. The smaller the openings, the higher the number describing the sandpaper, and the finer the sandpaper grit.

The sandpapers that are best for sanding wood are made with garnet and aluminum-oxide abrasives. **Garnet sandpaper** is usually orange in color. The abrasives break off at sharp angles, so garnet sandpaper continues to cut well until the abrasives are completely worn down. Garnet sandpaper is the least expensive of the four types and is the most popular sandpaper used for hand sanding wood. Grits range from 36 to 280.

Aluminum-oxide sandpaper is usually tan in color. The abrasives are more durable than garnet, but don't break off as sharply. Aluminum-oxide sandpaper is more expensive than garnet sandpaper, but it lasts longer. Because of this, aluminum-oxide abrasives are almost always used on sanding belts and disks that are expensive to make. Grits range from 36 to 280.

The sandpapers that are best for sanding finishes are made with silicon-carbide abrasives. There are two types. **Black silicon-carbide sandpaper** is made with a water-resistant glue to attach the abrasives to the paper. This sandpaper is often referred to as "wet-or-dry" sandpaper because it can be used with a water or oil lubricant, or no lubricant at all. In almost all cases, you should use this sandpaper together with some type of lubricant. Otherwise, it will clog up fast, which makes sanding very expensive. Grits range up to 2000.

Gray silicone-carbide sandpaper contains a soap-like lubricant, which makes it easier to sand finishes without using an additional lubricant. The lubricant is zinc stearate, the same one that is added to most sanding sealers. This type sandpaper is most often referred to as "lubricated," "no-fill," or "stearated" sandpaper. Grits range up to 400.

Black silicon-carbide sandpaper, used with a water or oil lubricant, is best for sanding after you have applied several coats of finish, enough so that you can be sure that you won't sand through. Gray silicon-carbide sandpaper, used dry, is best when sanding your first and second coats of finish. Damage will not be so great if you sand through in places.

Glue Seepage

Glue seepage at joints, or glue deposited on the wood by unclean hands, seals the wood and prevents the stain or finish from penetrating. The result is a lighter glue blotch. Glue blotching can be very frustrating.

On edge-to-edge glue-ups, whether solid-wood-to-solid-wood or solid-edging-to-veneered-plywood, you want glue seepage because it tells you that you have applied enough glue and enough pressure. You must remove all the seepage, and then sand the wood to below where the glue has penetrated.

There are two ways to remove the glue: wash it off immediately with a wet rag, or let the glue set up to the point where you can lift it off in a strip by getting under it with a putty knife or dull chisel. In both cases, you will have to sand to remove any remaining glue that has soaked into the wood.

AN EASY WAY to remove glue seepage is to lift it off in a strip with the help of a dull chisel or putty knife after the glue has begun to set.

If the glue dries solid before you remove it, you will have to scrape it off. This may tear up some of the wood. For this reason, it is best to remove the glue before it dries solid.

Glue seepage on perpendicular glue-ups, such as stiles and rails and legs and rails, is more difficult to deal with because sanding is more difficult. It is difficult to sand perpendicular joints without sanding cross grain on one of the pieces of wood. It's best, therefore, if you can keep the glue from seeping at all. This means don't apply more glue than necessary to make a strong bond. Unfortunately, this is not easy to do because you are moving too fast.

There is a trick that will help on dowel joints. Drill the dowel holes about 1/8 inch deeper than needed, and use dowels that are chamfered on the ends. This will create pockets at the bottom of the holes for excess glue that is squeezed deeper into the holes to collect. To create pockets for glue that is squeezed out the holes to collect, countersink the top of the dowel holes using a countersink bit.

Of course, you should not apply glue to the end-grain part of the glue-up. Glue in this area adds no permanent strength, and it can't help but squeeze out when you clamp the parts together.

If glue does squeeze out of your cross-grain joints, and you catch it before it dries, wash it off with water. You will then need to sand the wood to remove the raised grain that the water causes. There are two ways to do this without leaving cross-grain scratches. Sand the short butted piece first, crossing over to the crossing piece. Then sand the crossing piece to remove the scratches left by the earlier sanding. Alternatively, place masking

USE MASKING TAPE to protect a stile from cross-grain scratching while you sand the rail.

tape on each piece in turn, while you sand the other.

If the glue dries before you notice it, there are two ways to remove it: dissolve it off, or take it off mechanically by sanding or scraping.

You can dissolve white and yellow glue with water. By heating the water, or adding an acid such as vinegar to the water, you increase the effectiveness. Water raises grain, however, and stain will absorb more into this area, making it darker. To even the stain penetration, you must resand this area to below the water damage after the wood has dried.

Toluene (sometimes called toluol) and xylene (sometimes called xylol) can also be used to remove cured white and yellow glue. These solvents soften the glue enough so it can be scrubbed off with a coarse cloth or soft-bristle brush, and they do this without raising the grain.

You can also sand or scrape off the glue to below where it has penetrated. Then sand the area to the same grit as the rest of the wood so that the stain colors evenly.

If you have already applied stain before you notice the glue seepage, the correction is the same. You still have to dissolve or mechanically remove the glue. The problem you may experience here is that the stain acts as a lubricant for sandpaper, causing the scratching to be a little less than it would be without the stain. The result is that more stain applied to the area you have sanded may not color quite as dark. If this happens, correct the problem by applying stain to the entire part—rail, stile, leg, etc.—and wet-sand this part with the same grit sandpaper or one grit lower than you have used elsewhere. Wipe off the excess stain.

If nothing you do evens the coloring, apply paint stripper to the entire project and strip out as much of the color as possible (paint stripper will also remove white and yellow glue). It's not necessary to remove all the color. Then resand the entire surface with your final grit sandpaper, and restain. The stain should come out evenly as long as it's not the wood that is causing the blotching.

WOOD PUTTY

YOU CAN USE WOOD PUTTY to patch gaps, gouges, large nailholes, and other flaws in your project. If you are going to paint the project, simply sand the putty patch flat. The paint will cover it. If you are going to stain the wood, the patch will show. This is because wood putty doesn't take stain like wood.

To make the wood putty blend in better to the stained wood, use a colored wood putty that matches the wood after it has been stained. You may need to apply a little stain to a piece of scrap to see what this color is.

Most commercial wood putties are made with wood flour (very fine sawdust) and some type of finish that cures and binds the wood flour particles to each other. Most homemade wood putties are made by mixing sawdust with glue, usually white glue or epoxy. Because neither finish nor glue can absorb common stain, it's simply not possible to make a wood putty that takes stain like wood.

There are three common types of commercial wood putties: those based on lacquer, those based on water-based finish, and those based on gypsum (plaster-of-Paris). You can tell which kind you have by the instructions on the container. Lacquer-based wood putties will state that they can be thinned or cleaned up with acetone or lacquer thinner. Water-based wood putties will state that they can be cleaned up with water.

Gypsum-based wood putties come in powder form, which you are instructed to mix with water.

Applying wood putty. Each of these wood putties is applied in a similar manner. Take a little of the putty out of the container or tube with a putty knife (or screwdriver if the hole to be filled is small). Push the putty down in the hole or gouge, and if the depression is not very deep, smooth off the top by pulling the putty knife across the surface towards you. You want the putty to form a very slight mound so that when it shrinks as it dries, it won't leave a depression.

It's best not to manipulate the putty any more than necessary because it becomes increasingly unworkable the longer it's exposed to air. Try to avoid sloppiness. Remember that the binder in the putty is finish, glue, or plaster. It will bond to any part of the wood it comes in contact with, prevent stain penetration, and cause a blotch.

For a nailhole, one or two coats usually does the job. If the depression is deep, it's best to apply several coats to build the putty level with the surface. One thick layer will take a long time to cure throughout and will probably crack due to uneven curing. Let each coat cure hard before applying the next. Once the putty is thoroughly cured, sand it level with the surrounding wood. If you're working on a flat surface, back the sandpaper with a flat cork, felt, or wood block.

WOOD PUTTY doesn't take stain like wood. A wood-putty patch stains a solid color without grain or figure.

TO APPLY WOOD PUTTY, press it into the hole with a putty knife or dull screwdriver, leaving a little excess so a hollow won't occur as the putty dries and shrinks.

Matching Color

There are two ways to match the color of the wood putty to the surrounding wood. The easiest is to color the putty while it is still in paste form, or use an already-colored commercial wood putty. The other is to color the patch after it has cured. You can combine the two by using a colored wood putty to approximate the lightest color in the surrounding wood; then continue coloring the wood putty after it has cured.

You can use universal tinting colors, available at most paint and art supply stores, to color any of the commercial types of wood putty. The color you want to match is the color the wood will be after it is stained and finished. It may take some experimentation to arrive at this color.

You should practice on some scrap wood. The trick is to judge the colors while they are still damp. At that stage they will give a fairly accurate approximation of the color you will get when the finish is applied. The color of the stain or putty when dry will not be accurate. Keep in mind that ready-made colored putties, usually identified by the names of the woods they are designed to imitate, are not meant to look like the wood after it has been stained. These putties can often be used successfully if you don't intend to stain the wood.

To color a patch, apply your first coat of finish (the sealer coat) to the entire surface in order, see the correct colors you want to imitate. Once this sealer coat is dry, paint in the grain, figure, and the background color, that is, the lightest color visible in the surrounding wood. You may also want to scratch pores into the patch with the point of a knife to imitate deep-porous woods such as oak, mahogany, or walnut.

It's usually best to paint the grain and figure using an artist's brush before painting the background color. Otherwise you will probably make the patch too dark. Once you have the grain and figure close, let it dry, and protect it with a thin coat of finish. Then apply the background color.

For the coloring medium, it's best to use glaze or thinned varnish with some oil-pigment or Japan color added. The advantage of glaze and thinned varnish is that you can remove it if you don't like the result by wiping with paint thinner. The disadvantage is that it takes overnight to cure.

Drawing in grain and figure can be done only on film finishes, such as shellac, lacquer, varnish, polyurethane, and water-based finishes. Oil finishes are too thin to color between coats.

● STAINING WOOD

STAIN is used to decorate wood. You can use or not use a stain depending on how you want the wood to look. Stain changes the color and highlights the grain of wood. But stain also highlights flaws in the wood. You have to prepare the wood extra well if you intend to apply stain to it, and you have to be aware that some woods, especially softwoods like fir and pine, and hardwoods like cherry, poplar, and birch, blotch when you stain them. These woods blotch no matter how well you prepare them. Always test your stain on scrap pieces of the wood you are using for your project to be sure the stain produces the results you want.

There are several factors to consider in choosing a stain. First, the name of the color on the can is a manufacturer's interpretation. The same color name (English Oak, Red Mahogany, Fruitwood) from two manufacturers may be two very different colors. Pay more attention to the real color of the stain than the name on the can.

Second, the wood the stain is applied to plays a big part in how the stain will look. Woods vary in color, density, and grain pattern. The same stain applied to mahogany and maple will look redder on the mahogany because mahogany is redder than maple to start with. The same stain applied to poplar and maple will be darker on the poplar because poplar is more porous than maple. More stain is absorbed into the poplar. The same

THIN, LIGHTLY PIGMENTED STAINS can usually be brushed and left to dry. With thicker, more heavily-pigmented stains, you usually need to wipe off all the excess to avoid leaving streaks.

stain applied to oak and maple will look very different because oak has a very pronounced grain and maple doesn't.

Stains also often look different on solid wood and veneer of the same species. When you make a project using veneered plywood or medium density fiberboard with solid-wood edgings, there may be a color difference between the two parts. Usually, solid wood stains darker than veneer. The difference may be enough that you will want to even it by leaving a little more stain on some parts than on others.

Applying Stain

There are two ways to apply stain:

- Apply it and wipe off all the excess.
- Apply it and leave some or all of the excess.

When you intend to remove all the excess stain, it doesn't make any difference how you apply the stain or in what direction you apply it. You can wipe on the stain, brush it on, spray it on, or you can even pour on the stain and spread it around. Another option is to dip the wood into the stain if possible. The trick is to wipe off all the excess stain before it dries.

Because stains dry at different rates, removing all the excess can sometimes be a problem when you are staining large surfaces. It's usually wise to divide large projects into parts and apply and remove the excess on each part before moving on. Once you get used to a brand of stain, you will get a feel for how large an area you can stain comfortably.

As a general rule, water-based and lacquer-based stains dry very quickly and oil- or varnish-based stains relatively slowly. Of course, the slower a stain dries, the longer you have to wait before applying a finish. Overnight is minimum for oil and varnish-based stains. A few hours is usually enough for water-based and lacquer-based stains.

Just as it doesn't make any difference in what direction you apply stain, it doesn't make any difference in what direction you remove the stain when you are removing all the excess. Since you're removing it all, you shouldn't leave any streaking. But because of the possibility of missing some, it is good practice to make a final pass with your wiping cloth going with the grain. This will line up any remaining streaks of stain so they will be disguised by the grain.

If you want to make the color a little darker, you may need to leave some of the stain on the wood. In this case, you have to apply the stain with the grain of the wood or you will have cross-grain streaks that show badly.

All commonly available stains contain pigment, which is the same colorant used in paint. It's very difficult to wipe or brush pigment onto wood without leaving some streaking. You will find that the thinner the stain—that is, the less pigment contained in the stain—the easier it will be to brush or wipe successfully without leaving streaks. Of course, the less colorant, the lighter the resulting color. But you can always brush or wipe on another coat.

If the stain you are using is too thick to brush or wipe without leaving streaks, thin it with the appropriate thinner.

THE SAME STAIN looks different on different woods. Here the same stain was applied to mahogany (top left), maple (top right), poplar (bottom left), and oak (bottom right). The stain looks very red on mahogany because mahogany is red to begin with. The stain has only a slight effect on maple because maple is a dense, tight-grained wood that absorbs little stain. The stain darkens poplar because poplar is porous. The stain darkens and highlights the grain of oak because oak is porous with a pronounced grain.

STAINING PROBLEMS

MOST STAINING PROBLEMS can be fixed by applying more stain, the solvent or thinner for the stain, or paint stripper. For example, if the stain you are using dries before you get all the excess wiped off, or if brushing or wiping leaves streaks and you can't get rid of them, remove as much of the stain as you can and start again. You may want to work on a smaller area, work faster, or thin your stain the second time.

To remove stain that has begun to dry, you may be able to just apply more stain, which will soften the existing stain. Then wipe off all the excess. If the stain has dried too much, try wiping with the solvent or thinner for the stain. If the stain is totally cured, you will probably need to use a paint stripper to remove it.

Paint stripper won't take all the color out of the wood, only some of it. There is no way to take out all the color short of sanding, scraping, or planing to below the depth the stain has penetrated. But there is no reason to take out all of the color unless you decide that you would rather not stain the wood at all. Because of the work involved, this is not a decision that should be taken lightly.

Blotching. This is one staining problem that is not easy to correct. Woods often have swirly grain or uneven density which cause uneven stain absorption. The wood blotches darker in some places and lighter in others. On some woods, such as walnut and mahogany, blotching is usually attractive. On other woods, though, blotching is often quite ugly.

The problem with blotching is that it is not easy to fix once it has occurred. The remedy is to sand, scrape, or plane to below the depth the stain has penetrated. On veneered plywoods this may not be possible. The only practical way to fix the problem is to paint the wood. It is essential that you anticipate blotching by testing on scrap wood and taking steps to prevent it.

Prevent blotching by keeping all the stain near the surface of the wood. There are two ways to do this.

■ Use a gel stain, which doesn't flow so it doesn't penetrate.

■ Fill the pores first with a stain controller so the stain can't penetrate.

PINE IS AMONG THE WOODS that commonly blotch when you apply a stain. The blotching is caused by uneven density or swirly grain in the wood.

Gel Stains

Gel stains (also called gelled or paste stains) are commonly marketed as easy to use, but this is not their real value in finishing. Their real value is to reduce blotching.

Gel stains are thick. They resemble latex wall paint. When you roll latex wall paint onto a wall, the nap of the roller pulls the paint out into small nibs that remain just as the roller leaves them. The nibs don't flatten out and run down the wall as they would if you were using enamel paint.

In the same manner, a gel stain doesn't flow unless it is moved by your rag or brush. And because it doesn't flow, it doesn't penetrate into the wood. The thicker the gel stain, the less it penetrates and the more effective it is at reducing or eliminating blotching. Keep in mind that the quality that works so well giving pine and cherry an even coloring works to a disadvantage on woods such as mahogany and bird's eye maple, where you usually want deeper stain penetration to bring out the beautiful figure.

Stain Controllers

Stain controllers can be used before applying a liquid stain to keep the stain from penetrating unevenly. Stain controllers (also called wood conditioner, pre-stain, and grain tamer) are composed primarily of slow-evaporating, petroleum-distillate solvents. They work by filling up the pores and less-dense parts of the wood so the stain can't penetrate. The stain just mixes with the solvent near the surface.

To use a stain controller successfully, apply it to the wood with a brush or rag until all parts of the wood stay wet and no more of the liquid is absorbing into the wood. This usually takes successive applications for five to ten minutes, but the number of applications needed will vary depending on the wood and the ingredients used in the stain controller.

When no more dry spots appear on the wood, wipe off all the excess stain controller and apply the stain as quickly as possible—within thirty minutes is best. If you wait too long, enough of the stain controller will have evaporated, or absorbed deeper into the wood, so that the stain will again penetrate and blotch the wood.

PICKLING

IN RECENT YEARS, PICKLING, which means giving the wood a whitish cast, has become very popular. Pickling is very easy to do. There are two methods. One way is to apply a white or slightly off-white stain or paint to the wood and wipe off all or nearly all the excess before it dries. In other words, simply stain the wood white. The other way is to seal the wood first with your first coat of finish, then apply the stain. Again, the stain can be a regular white or off-white stain, or it can be paint. And, again, you can wipe off all the excess, leaving the colorant only in the grain, or you can leave some of the excess. Oil paint is easier to work with, just like oil stains are easier because they give you more working time. However, when you're working on large surfaces in closed rooms, oil-based products can cause breathing problems because of the large amount of solvent that is released into the air. For this reason, painters often use latex paint when they are pickling built-in cabinets or paneling.

PICKLING can be done by wiping a white stain or paint on bare wood (left) or on sealed wood (right). Then wipe off all or most of the excess. More color will be left on the areas between the grain when you apply the colorant to bare wood.

PRIMING & SEALING WOOD

There is a great deal of confusion about primers and sealers. Because primers are necessary when applying paint to bare wood, it is commonly thought that it's necessary to use a special sealer under a clear finish. This is not the case. Primers and sealers perform entirely different functions.

Primers are necessary on bare wood because paint won't bond well by itself. Paint contains a high percentage of pigment (in order to cover better) and only enough binder to glue the pigment particles to each other and to an underlying level surface. Since wood is porous, and thus not level, more binder is required to achieve a good bond. Paint primer contains a higher binder-to-pigment ratio than does paint. Primer provides a level surface to which subsequent coats of paint will bond.

SANDING SEALER contains a lubricant that causes the finish to powder easily when you sand it.

Sealers, on the other hand, do nothing to make finishes bond better. Finishes are 100 percent binder already. Sealers make sanding easier so production can be sped up.

The first coat of any finish locks raised wood fibers in place, causing the surface to feel rough after the finish cures. This roughness telegraphs through each subsequent coat of finish. It's easiest to sand off the roughness after the first coat of finish because the finish is thin and easier to sand at this point. Once the roughness has been removed, each additional coat will cure smooth.

The problem is that most finishes are difficult to sand even when thin. They gum up the sandpaper. So, manufacturers provide special easy-to-sand finishes to be used for the first coat. These finishes are usually the regular finish with zinc stearate, the same soaplike lubricant used in some sandpapers, added. These finishes are properly called "sanding sealers."

Sanding sealers are useful in production situations where a large surface area must be sanded after the first coat. You can achieve almost the same degree of easy sanding by thinning the first coat of finish with the appropriate thinner. Because this makes the resulting film thinner, it will cure faster, making sanding easier.

However, water-based finishes lose their ability to flow smoothly if thinned too much. But most water-based finishes naturally sand easily.

● CHOOSING A CLEAR FINISH

WHEN YOU LOOK at all the finishes on paint-store shelves, it's easy to feel overwhelmed by the number of choices. To aid in choosing a finish, it helps to have an idea of the qualities you are looking for. The qualities that make the biggest difference are the following:

- Protection for the wood
- Durability
- Ease of application

Protection

The primary protective purpose of a finish is to reduce stresses by slowing moisture-vapor exchange in and out of the wood. When the air around wood is humid, moisture is absorbed into the wood and it expands. When the air around wood is dry, moisture is released from the wood and it shrinks. Most materials expand and shrink with humidity changes. But with wood, this expansion and shrinkage occurs only in one direction, across the grain. Wood doesn't expand or shrink significantly along the grain. Thus, when you cross the grain of wood, as when making useful objects, you build in stresses that can destroy the object.

All plywoods have built-in stresses because the plies run in opposite directions. Particleboard and medium-density fiberboard with veneered faces are more stable, but there are still some stresses because the veneer expands and shrinks more than the substrate. All solid-wood boards glued cross grain, rather than edge to edge, also have built-in stresses.

Don't make the finish too thick though. Film thicknesses greater than about .006 inch (about four or five coats of polyurethane) have a tendency to crack, especially if the weather goes through sudden radical changes. Cracks allow more moisture-vapor exchange.

Durability

Durability is the degree to which the finish film itself resists damage. Some finishes are more resistant to scratches, water, and heat than others. For a decorative object that will sit on a fireplace mantle all its life, finish durability is not very important. But for a vanity, table top, or set of kitchen cabinets, finish durability is very important. The finish will probably be subjected to a great deal of abuse. Just as with protection, a thicker finish film is more durable, but thickness is less important for durability than for protection. For durability, the type of finish is more important than the thickness.

Ease of Application

Assuming you have access to all three finish-application tools—rag, brush, and spray gun—the quality that is most important for making finishes easy to apply is fast drying. This may surprise you until you recall the problems you have with dust getting into slow-drying finishes like polyurethane.

The problem with choosing a fast-drying finish is that it is very difficult to apply without a spray gun. If you don't have a spray gun, you will have to choose a slower-drying finish and learn ways to deal with dust.

TYPES OF FINISHES

There are many types of finishes, but only a few are used for wood. It's more helpful to concentrate on types than on brands because brand differences within each type are small. You probably won't even notice differences between brands, but differences between types are significant. There are five common types of finishes used on wood:

- Oil
- Varnish and polyurethane (polyurethane is a type of varnish)
- Shellac
- Lacquer
- Water-based

Oil finishes are easy to differentiate from the other four types because they don't cure hard, and as a result can not be built up into a hard film finish. Varnish, shellac, lacquer, and water-based finishes do cure hard and can build up into a hard film as you add coats. Oil finishes generally are easier to apply than film finishes, while film finishes offer more protection.

Oil

There are two types of oils: those that cure, and those that don't cure. Oils that cure can be used as finishes because they seal the wood and produce a fairly permanent sheen. Oils that don't cure don't perform well as finishes because they continue to soak deeper into the wood leaving the surface unprotected, or they remain sticky on the surface.

Common examples of oils that don't cure are mineral oil, vegetable oil, and motor oil. There are two commonly available oils that cure and thus perform well as finishes: linseed oil and tung oil.

APPLYING OIL FINISHES

ALL THAT IS REQUIRED to apply an oil finish is to wipe or brush the oil onto the wood; let the oil soak in for five to ten minutes, during which time you rewet any places that dry out; and then wipe off all the excess. Allow boiled linseed oil to cure overnight; tung oil about three days. Then sand or use steel wool lightly to make the wood feel smooth, and apply another coat in the same way as the first. Use 220 grit or finer sandpaper and 000 or 0000 steel wool.

Two or three coats of linseed oil will produce an attractive "rubbed" sheen. You don't need to actually rub the oil. It penetrates into the wood perfectly well without rubbing. In contrast to linseed oil, it may take as many as five or six coats of tung oil to produce a nice sheen. Tung oil cures dull and rough to the touch for the first several coats. Continue to sand lightly between coats with very fine sandpaper (220 grit or finer) until the coats begin to cure smooth.

Though oil finishes are not very protective or durable compared to other finishes, they are easy to repair if they become scratched or dull. Simply wipe on another coat of oil (you don't have to use the same oil you used originally), and wipe off the excess. If the surface feels a little rough to the touch, sand it lightly with very fine sandpaper before applying the oil.

Linseed oil is pressed from the seeds of the flax plant. In its raw form, linseed oil takes a week or longer to cure. This slow curing makes raw linseed oil very impractical to use as a finish. To speed the curing, manufacturers add metallic driers which make the oil cure in about a day. With these driers added, the oil is called "boiled linseed oil," but it is not actually boiled.

Tung oil is pressed from the nuts of the tung tree, which is native to China. Pure tung oil sold in the United States as a wood finish does not have driers added. It takes two to three days for pure tung oil to cure when all the excess is wiped off of wood. Pure tung oil thus cures faster than raw linseed oil, but slower than boiled linseed oil.

Neither type of oil is very protective or durable, but tung oil is more so than boiled linseed oil. Both oils are easy to apply, and that is the main reason for their popularity.

Varnish

Varnish is made by cooking an oil, such as linseed oil, tung oil, or modified soybean oil, with a resin. The resins used in varnishes today are synthetic alkyds, phenolics, and polyurethanes. The product called "polyurethane" is simply a varnish that has been made with polyurethane resins.

When more oil and less resin is used in the manufacture, the resulting varnish is softer and more flexible. This type of varnish, called "spar" varnish, is best for outdoor use because it flexes better with the greater wood movement outdoors.

Varnish comes in sheens that range from gloss to flat. Satin is probably the most popular sheen because it imitates a steel-wool rubbed appearance.

Varnish is one of the most protective and durable of all finishes. But varnish cures slowly. Dust has a lot of time to settle and stick to the finish.

APPLYING VARNISH

VARNISH usually is applied with a brush. It is too thick to wipe on easily, and it is not pleasant to spray because small particles settle and stick to everything, including you.

Brushing varnish is just like brushing paint. The only real difference is that cleanliness is more important because dust and dirt show more in a clear varnish finish than they do in paint. Therefore, make an extra effort to make your work room as dust-free as possible. Use a clean brush; transfer the varnish to a separate container if you don't expect to use it all (so you don't contaminate the remaining varnish with dust); and dust the wood surface well before beginning. If the varnish you are using has dust or cured varnish particles in it, strain the varnish through a paint strainer or cheese cloth before beginning.

To remove dust from the wood, begin by vacuuming or wiping with a tack cloth—a sticky cloth you can buy at paint stores. Don't brush or blow the dust off the wood, or it will simply settle back onto your finish while it is wet. Just before you are ready to begin brushing, wipe over the wood with you hand. You will feel if any dust remains. If it does, your hand will pick it up and you can remove it by brushing your hand against your pant leg. When the surface is dust-free, you can begin brushing the varnish.

Begin spreading the varnish onto the wood in any direction. As you move from section to section, or across a large surface, tip off the varnish in the direction of the wood

TO LINE UP YOUR BRUSH STROKES so they are disguised by the grain of the wood, hold your brush almost perpendicular, and drag it lightly across the surface in the direction of the grain.

TO PREVENT RUNS AND SAGS when brushing finish on a vertical surface, you have to view your work in reflected light.

grain. To tip off, hold the brush almost vertical, and use a light touch. The purpose is to line up the brush strokes with the wood grain so they are less noticeable. On horizontal surfaces begin at the far edge and brush from left to right back toward you so that dust

doesn't fall off your arm onto already applied varnish.

Always work with lights set to reflect off the surface of the wood. If you don't have a reflection, you might as well be blindfolded, because you can't see what is happening. A reflection is especially critical on vertical surfaces where the varnish is likely to run and sag. It is very difficult to apply varnish so that it doesn't run and sag on vertical surfaces. The trick is to see the runs and sags when they occur and remove the excess varnish until the running and sagging stop.

To remove runs and sags before they cure, drag your brush over a clean jar edge to remove excess varnish. Then rebrush the varnish while continuing to remove the excess from the brush. Work a section at a time until running and sagging stops.

To lessen brush marking and air bubbles curing in the finish, add 5 to 10 percent paint thinner to the varnish. The added thinner gives the varnish more time to flatten out. It also gives bubbles more time to pop out and the varnish to flow back level. Bubbles are caused by turbulence created by your brush, not by shaking or stirring the can as is often claimed. You can't avoid bubbles. The trick is to get them to pop out before the varnish skins over and traps them.

There is no way to totally eliminate dust settling on your varnish finish. If the dust nibs are worse than you can tolerate, you will need to sand them out. Sand between coats with 220 or finer-grit sandpaper (gray, lubricated sandpaper works best), and after the last coat with 600-grit, wet-or-dry sandpaper. You can use water or mineral oil as a lubricant with this sandpaper. Then rub the surface with 0000 steel wool to produce an even satin sheen.

WIPING VARNISH

VARNISH can be thinned with any amount of paint thinner and still be used as a finish. When varnish is thinned about half with paint thinner, it is easy to wipe on wood, so it is called "wiping varnish." Unfortunately, many manufacturers label their wiping varnish "tung oil," and this causes confusion.

Varnish and tung oil are two entirely different finishes. Varnish, whether thinned or full-strength, cures overnight to a hard, smooth film if left thick on a surface. Tung oil takes months to cure, and then it cures soft and wrinkled. Because of the confused naming, you will need to test your finish in order to learn which you have. To test, pour some of your finish onto a nonporous surface, such as glass or plastic laminate, and leave it overnight in a warm room. If you get a hard and smooth finish, it is varnish. A soft and wrinkled finish is tung oil.

You can apply wiping varnish just like full-strength varnish by brushing it on the wood and leaving it to cure. Or you can apply it like an oil finish, by wiping or brushing it onto the wood and wiping off the excess. But varnish cures much faster than oil. You can leave a little of the varnish on the wood to achieve a build up and, thus, more protection.

Wiping varnish provides good protection and durability, just like full-strength varnish, it just takes more coats to achieve the same thickness.

OIL / VARNISH BLEND

VARNISH can also be mixed with linseed oil or tung oil in any proportion. When this is done, the product is a little more protective and durable than oil alone, but it still cures slowly to a soft, wrinkled film. Wipe off all the excess finish after each coat. When varnish and oil are mixed, they are called "oil/varnish blend."

Oil/varnish blends are very popular finishes because they are so easy to use. Most are sold under names like "Danish oil" and "teak oil" to suggest a supposed relationship with the finish used on imported Scandinavian furniture. (This furniture is actually finished with two-part, catalyzed lacquer, however, not oil.)

You apply oil/varnish-blend finishes just like boiled linseed oil. Let the first coat soak in for five to ten minutes. Sand or buff with steel wool lightly the next day to make the surface smooth. Then apply one or two more coats.

Many formulas circulate for making your own oil/varnish-blend finish. The most common suggest mixing equal parts of varnish, boiled linseed oil, and turpentine or paint thinner. Turpentine differs from paint thinner in its source, not its qualities. Turpentine is distilled sap from pine trees. Mineral spirits is distilled petroleum. Before the twentieth century, mineral spirits was not available.

Shellac

Shellac is the only natural resin still widely used to make a finish. The resin is secreted from the lac bug, which inhabits certain trees native to India and Thailand. Shellac was once the premier wood finish. Almost all furniture and woodwork made between 1830 and 1930 was finished with shellac. During the 1920s, lacquer replaced shellac in factories because lacquer is a little more durable and it is more versatile to apply when sprayed. Shellac continued to be used on woodwork in houses until the 1940s.

Unfortunately, shellac has gotten an undeserved reputation for poor water resistance and imperfect hardening. Neither are legitimate problems once you understand the finish.

Shellac is actually quite water resistant. It is just not as much so as varnish, lacquer, and water-based finishes. Water rings you often see on old furniture that was finished with shellac are due more to the aging of the finish than to the type of finish. All finishes become more porous as they age and, thus, become more susceptible to water damage. So, shellac is still fine for most types of furniture and woodwork. It is not the best choice, however, for surfaces that take a lot of abuse, like dining-table tops and kitchen cabinets.

Imperfect drying is caused by the shellac deteriorating in the can before it was applied. Shellac begins deteriorating as soon as it is dissolved in its alcohol solvent. The deterioration is slow, but over a period of a year or two you can tell that the shellac takes longer to dry and it never gets as hard. Always buy the freshest shellac you can find. Most cans of shellac are stamped with the date of manufacture. Try to find shellac that is not more than six months to a year old. If the container of shellac is not dated, don't buy it.

Shellac varies in color between orange (amber) and clear. Orange shellac adds warmth to woods like walnut, pine, maple, and oak. Pine, maple, and oak woodwork in old buildings was almost always finished with orange shellac. Clear shellac is best if you don't want to add color to the wood.

Shellac's fast drying property is a real advantage for reducing dust problems. Shellac dries as fast as its alcohol solvent evaporates. In most cases, this is fast enough so that dust doesn't have time to settle and become embedded. The disadvantage of fast drying, of course, is that it makes shellac a little difficult to apply with a brush.

APPLYING SHELLAC

SHELLAC is difficult to brush straight out of the can. It is too thick, it doesn't flow out well, and it dries too quickly. Thin the shellac about half-and-half with denatured alcohol (sometimes sold as shellac thinner). The more you thin shellac, the easier it is to brush without leaving brush marks, but the thinner each coat becomes.

Because shellac dries much faster than varnish, you have to follow a different brushing procedure. Begin brushing shellac close to the way you want the brush strokes to line up. You won't have as much time to come back and line them up as you do with varnish. The trick is to move fast enough so that each new brush stroke overlaps a stroke that is still wet. If the previous stroke has begun to set up, your brush will drag it, resulting in ridges curing in the finish. To get ridges out, if they do occur, let the shellac cure. Then sand the surface until it is level, and apply another coat of shellac.

You can apply three or four coats of shellac in a day if the weather is dry and warm. Just like all finishes, shellac dries slower in cool, damp conditions.

SHELLAC DRIES FAST, so you must work quickly and not continue to go over already-brushed parts.

Lacquer

Lacquer is the primary finish used in factories and by professional finishers and refinishers. This is because lacquer dries very fast, reducing dust problems, and lacquer is easy and very versatile to apply using a spray gun. But the solvent fumes left by spraying lacquer are bad for your health, so it's not wise to spray lacquer unless you have a means of exhausting these fumes. As a result, few home woodworkers use lacquer.

There are lacquers, however, that are made to cure slowly enough so they can be brushed. Though the solvent smell in these lacquers is pretty strong, brushing a "brushing lacquer" is no more difficult than brushing shellac. In fact, the procedure for brushing a brushing lacquer is the same as for brushing shellac. If you can tolerate the increased solvent smell and want the added durability of lacquer, a brushing lacquer is a good choice.

Though it is a bit more expensive, you can purchase lacquer in aerosol spray cans.

Water-Based Finishes

Because of stricter air-quality laws in some parts of the country, a market has been created for water-based finishes. These finishes are often marketed as "varnish," "polyurethane," and "lacquer," which confuses them with like-named solvent-based products. However, water-based finishes are always identifiable by some mention of water cleanup on the can. Though water-based finishes still do contain organic solvents, they contain less than most other finishes.

The easiest way to understand water-based finishes is to think of them as latex paint without the pigment—because that is essentially what they are. It makes little difference whether the resin in the finish is polyurethane or acrylic. Just as in comparing oil paint and latex paint, the significant difference is finish type rather than the particular resins used.

Water-based finishes have many of the same good and bad qualities of latex paint. The most important good qualities are reduced solvent smell and easy brush cleanup. The significant limitations are pronounced brush marking and reduced durability. Compared to oil-based varnishes, water-based finishes level poorly and are much less resistant to heat, solvent, acid, and alkali damage.

APPLYING WATER-BASED FINISHES

WEATHER CONDITIONS are critical to achieving good results when brushing water-based finishes. Work in conditions as close as possible to 70° Fahrenheit and 40-percent humidity. Use a synthetic-bristle brush, and don't over-brush the finish. Continuing to brush a water-based finish raises more bubbles. The best procedure is to try to lay down a level coat without having to go back over it. It also helps to keep the coats as thin as possible. Bubbles pop out of thin coats easier than thick coats.

Beyond this, brushing a water-based finish is similar to brushing shellac. Try to brush only in the direction of the wood grain because you won't have much time to line up your brush strokes after they are applied. And apply each brush stroke rapidly enough so that the previous stroke is still wet when you overlap it.

FINISHING THE FINISH

ALL FINISHES can be improved in appearance and feel by rubbing them with an abrasive after they have cured. It is wise to practice this step on a scrap before doing it on a project because you need to experience how much you can rub before cutting through. Rubbing through a finish causes added work repairing the damage, especially when you have stained the wood.

The easiest way to rub a finish is with 0000 steel wool or synthetic steel wool. Using one or both hands and medium to heavy pressure, rub in long straight strokes in the direction of the wood grain. Avoid making arcs with your strokes. Keep the pressure even over the entire surface, and overlap each stroke by 80 to 90 percent. Be very careful not to rub over the edge, or you will cut through the finish and expose bare wood.

To avoid cutting through edges at the ends of your strokes, rub right up to the edge first, using short strokes. Then rub the entire length using long strokes, stopping just short of the edge.

When you've gone over the entire surface once, remove the dust to see what you've done. It's best to blow the dust off using compressed air, or suck the dust off with a vacuum. Then wipe lightly with the grain using your hand to be sure no dust remains. If you don't have compressed air or a vacuum, wipe with a dampened cloth going with the grain. If you wipe across the grain, you may put noticeable cross-scratches in the finish.

Look at the surface in reflected light. If you're not happy with it, determine what is wrong and begin rubbing again to correct the problem.

The Ultimate Fix. Any number of problems can occur applying finishes, including runs and sags, dust and dirt getting into the finish, severe brush marking or streaking, blisters or bubbles, too-slow or too-fast curing, and rubbing through the finish. No matter what goes wrong, you can always fix it by stripping off the finish and starting over.

TYPES OF PAINT

THE FIRST RULE of buying paint is to never buy cheap paint because it is never good. Among top-of-the-line paints, there are variations in quality. Reputable paint suppliers usually sell top-of-the-line paint that is very good and always better than cheaper products. Read the can labels to compare paint ingredients. And remember, the heavier the can, the better the paint.

Latex Versus Oil-Based Paints

Paint is composed of pigment, a vehicle, solvents, and additives, all of which affect the flow and drying characteristics of the paint. With latex paint, the vehicle is a water-based emulsion. With oil-based paint, the vehicle is natural or synthetic (alkyd) oil.

Choosing Latex Paint. Homeowners and professional painters like latex paint because it dries in just a few hours and because cleanup is easy. Quick drying allows the application of two coats in one day. When the job is done, everything can be cleaned with soap and warm water.

Latex paint is environmentally friendlier than its oil-based cousin. Unlike oil-based paint, latex does not emit volatile organic compounds (VOCs), which have been virtually outlawed in some states. Compared to oil-based paint, latex paint is easier on the eyes, nose, lungs, and skin.

In the past, however, many professional painters have resisted using latex paint. They preferred oil-based paint, especially for woodwork and areas where the paint has to hold up to a lot of scrubbing, such as the kitchen and bathroom. The truth was that even the best latex enamel did not dry quite as hard, smooth, or shiny as a good oil-based paint. Some painters complained that latex paint did not flow off the brush as smoothly as oil-based paint.

Recently however, as more states pass laws restricting the use of VOCs, paint manufacturers have put all their research dollars into improving latex paints. Today, many professional painters use oil-based paint only to prime or recoat old oil-based paint.

Choosing Oil-Based Paint. If you do choose to use oil-based paint, mineral spirits or turpentine are necessary to clean brushes, rollers, drips, and yourself. These solvents are relatively costly (especially compared to water); they smell bad (do not be fooled by labels that say "odorless"); and can be irritating to eyes, nose, lungs, and skin. In addition, after you have cleaned tools and skin with mineral spirits, a final cleanup with soap and water is necessary, as well.

Usually you have to wait at least overnight before recoating oil-based paint. This can be inconvenient, especially if you can only work on weekends.

Most municipalities have strict rules regarding the disposal of leftover solvents and oil-based paints, which means you may find yourself stuck with half-empty containers.

Choosing a Sheen

In addition to choosing the color and whether you want latex or oil-based paint, you also need to choose the degree of sheen you want. The range runs from flat to gloss.

The degree of sheen is determined by the proportion of resin in the paint. The resin determines the degree to which the paint is absorbed into the painted surface and how much pigment is left to form a film on the surface. In short, the more resin, the less the absorption, and thus the glossier the paint.

Flat or Matte. A low-gloss finish hides surface flaws and flaws in prepaint preparation. Because the paint is slightly rough, flat paints do not take scrubbing as well as glossier finishes.

Eggshell and Satin. This is glossier than flat paint, with slightly better abrasion resistance. Satin is glossier than eggshell.

Semigloss. Semigloss paints take scrubbing moderately well. They are available in latex or oil-based.

Gloss. This is the highest gloss classification. It is highest in resin and lowest in absorption. Gloss paints take scrubbing well and are easiest to clean. However, gloss paints highlight surface flaws.

Enamel. Years ago, this term was synonymous with oil-based paint. These days, it is a loose term that refers to the glossiness of paint. The term is reliable only in that you can be reasonably sure that a paint labeled "enamel" is a semigloss or gloss paint.

6 living room

WHEN STORAGE OFTEN MEANS PUTTING ITEMS ON DISPLAY

living room storage ideas

Make sure your wall units can multitask to keep books, files, baskets, and DVDs neat and organized.

Clockwise (from top right) Corner cabinets provide space-saving storage solutions. Louver-style drawer fronts add a casual note to this hallway unit. Exposed posts and beams complement the design of this built-in wall unit. The open shelving in this hutch puts collectibles on display.

living room storage ideas

Clockwise (from below) A tall, narrow bookcase fits neatly in the space next to an exposed post; although painted a different color, the bead-board on the inside of the cabinet matches the wainscoting. An entertainment unit is designed around the needs of a large flat-screen TV. Combine two storage units to create one attractive design.

entertainment center

THIS TRADITIONAL-LOOKING entertainment center is a sophisticated solution for housing your entire entertainment system. At 3 feet wide by 7 feet high, it has plenty of room for a TV, DVD player, stereo system, and all of the discs or tapes in your collection.

Depending on your needs and space, you can build the entertainment center alone, or you can create a wall unit by adding the tall bookcase featured on page 81.

Inside the center's traditional exterior is a space designed specifically for storing today's electronic equipment. The shelves are open at the back to vent heat and allow plenty of space for wiring. The doors are mounted with inset hinges, which open a full 180 degrees.

Before the age of plywood, large cases like this were backed with narrow boards. This entertainment center recreates that look simply and inexpensively by using wood-grain paneling for the back. Wood paneling is available in dozens of colors and grain patterns, so pick one that fits with the rest of the room.

The wall unit here is painted with a semigloss enamel latex paint, except for the crown molding and shelf edge strips, which are made of cherry-stained pine.

ENTERTAINMENT CENTER MATERIALS LIST

Difficulty Level: **DIFFICULT**

Qty	Part	Dimensions		Qty	Part	Dimensions
Carcase				**Trim** (crown & baseboard dimensions for stand-alone entertainment center)		
1	Plywood top panel	¾" x 22¾" x 36¼"		1	Front crown molding	¾" x 2" x 41"
2	Plywood fixed shelf & bottom panel	¾" x 22¾" x 36¼"		2	Side crown molding	¾" x 2" x 25¾"
2	Plywood side panels	¾" x 23" x 86"		1	Front base molding	¾" x 4" x 38½"
1	Wood-grain paneling back panel	¼" x 36¼" x 85⅜"		2	Side base molding	¾" x 4" x 24½"
3	Plywood adjustable shelves	¾" x 20" x 35¼"		**(Dimensions for three-piece wall unit)**		
2	Shelf edges	¾" x ¾" x 35¼"		2	Bookcase front crown molding	¾" x 1½" x 32"
2	Stiles	¾" x 2½" x 86"		2	Bookcase side crown molding	¾" x 1½" x 17"
1	Middle rail	¾" x 2½" x 32"		1	Cabinet front crown molding	¾" x 2" x 41"
1	Top rail	¾" x 3" x 32"		2	Cabinet side crown molding	¾" x 2" x 10"
1	Bottom rail	¾" x 5½" x 32"		2	Bookcase front base molding	¾" x 4" x 30¾"
Doors				2	Bookcase side base molding	¾" x 4" x 17"
10	Rails	¾" x 2½" x 13³⁄₁₆"		1	Cabinet front base molding	¾" x 4" x 38½"
4	Top-door stiles	¾" x 2½" x 50¾"		2	Cabinet side base molding	¾" x 4" x 8¾"
4	Bottom-door stiles	¾" x 2½" x 24¾"		**Hardware**		
4	Top-door plywood panels	¼" x 11⅞" x 22⁵⁄₁₆"			4d Finishing nails	
2	Bottom-door plywood panels	¼" x 11⅞" x 20⁷⁄₁₆"			1¼" Screws	
2	Bottom-door plywood panels	¼" x 11⅞" x 20⁷⁄₁₆"			⅞" Brads	
				12	Adjustable shelf pins	
				8	Inset hinges	
				4	Knobs	

BUILDING THE CASE

1. Cut the parts. Cut the top and bottom panels, the fixed shelf, the side panels, and the back panel to the dimensions in the Materials List. Rabbet and dado the side panels as shown in Side Panel Layout. Note that the drawing shows only one side panel. Don't forget to make the other panel in a mirror image. Drill ¼-inch holes into the side panels for the shelf pins. (See "Installing Shelf Pins," page 28.) If you plan to house electronic equipment in your entertainment center, bore a row of 1½-inch holes in the back of the top panel to provide ventilation.

Cut the three adjustable shelves and their solid-wood edges to the dimensions in the Materials List. Attach the edges to the front of the shelves with glue and 4d finishing nails. (If you want to paint the shelves but not the edges, don't add the edges until after the bookcase is assembled and painted.)

2. Assemble the carcase. Attach the fixed shelf and bottom panel to the dadoes in the side with glue and 4d finishing nails. Next, attach the top panel to the case with glue and 1¼-inch screws (the crown molding will conceal the screw heads). Install the back panel flush to the top of the cabinet, and secure it with glue and ⅞-inch brads. (The space at the bottom is to accommodate uneven floors.) If you plan to house electronic equipment in your entertainment center, drill a 1½-inch hole for power-strip cord access.

3. Build and install the face frame. Cut the two stiles, and attach them flush with the outside of the carcase using glue and 4d finishing nails. Cut the three rails to fit, and install them so that their top edges are flush with the fixed shelf and the top and bottom panels.

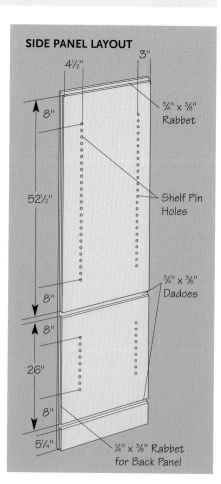

SIDE PANEL LAYOUT

OVERALL VIEW

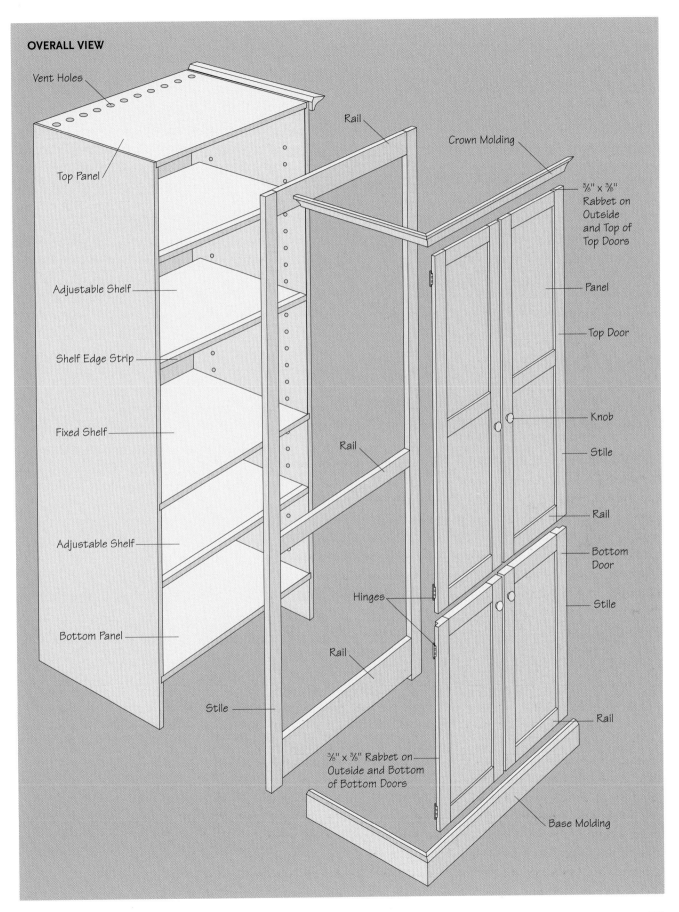

Vent Holes

Top Panel

Adjustable Shelf

Shelf Edge Strip

Fixed Shelf

Adjustable Shelf

Bottom Panel

Stile

⅜" x ⅜" Rabbet on
Outside and Bottom
of Bottom Doors

Rail

Rail

Stile

Rail

Hinges

Rail

Crown Molding

⅜" x ⅜"
Rabbet on
Outside
and Top of
Top Doors

Panel

Top Door

Knob

Stile

Rail

Bottom
Door

Stile

Rail

Base Molding

MAKING AND INSTALLING DOORS

This cabinet uses frame-and-panel doors. The panels are flat and are made of ¼-inch plywood. The top and bottom sets of these doors are virtually identical in construction, except that the top pair has a center rail that serves as a visual break for the larger panel. Don't forget to groove both edges of the center rails to accept the door panels.

Each door has a ⅜-inch x ⅜-inch rabbet on two sides, which allows the doors to be inset in the door opening. (See "Building a Frame-and-Panel Door," page 22 and "Installing Inset Doors," page 27.)

MAKING AND INSTALLING THE TRIM

If you plan to use this cabinet without the matching side bookcases, simply attach the molding with glue and 4d finishing nails when it is still in the shop, and then proceed to finishing. If you'll be adding the bookcases, install the trim after the entertainment center is in place. For information about coping joints and cutting crown moldings, see "Cutting Crown Molding," page 37.

Feel free to select any style of crown or baseboard molding that you wish to trim out the cabinet. However, it is easy enough to make your own baseboard molding with your router and a decorative bit.

ASSEMBLING THE THREE-PIECE WALL UNIT

Assembling the wall unit entertainment center is slightly different from installing the pieces individually. Installing the crown and baseboard moldings on the entire assembly allows the units to fit against each other and creates a more finished look. The trick is to trim the multipiece unit in an order so that any gaps will be concealed by the next piece of molding.

1. Position the cabinets. Position the entertainment center in place, and check the case for level and plumb just as you would do with a base cabinet. (See "Installing Cabinets and Built-ins," page 34.) If your floor is uneven, it is possible at this time to insert small shims (no greater than 3/16 inch). Put the bookcases on either side of the entertainment center so that the back edges are flush and the sides touch.

Use four 1¼-inch screws to fasten the carcases together. Position the screws directly beneath the middle shelf or top panel of the entertainment center.

2. Install the trim. The sequence and joinery for installing the base trim and the crown molding are identical. Start by cutting the trim for the front of the bookcases. These pieces butt against the entertainment center and are mitered on their outside edges. Next, cut the two side pieces for the bookcases. Position the front and side pieces of trim so that they fit tightly at the outside corner, and attach using glue and 4d finishing nails.

Cut the trim for the front. To ensure that the molding is cut exactly to size, you may want to cut it a little longer than you need, tack it in place with double stick tape, and try to fit matching miters to both ends. Don't install this piece just yet.

The short side pieces for the entertainment center are the trickiest because they have a coped end and a mitered end. Cut each piece a little long; cope one end; put the piece in place; and mark the miter cut. Attach using glue and 4d finishing nails.

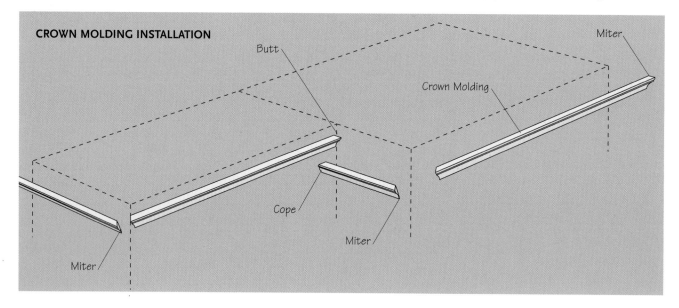

CROWN MOLDING INSTALLATION

Butt

Miter

Crown Molding

Cope

Miter

Miter

tall bookcase

WHILE IT CAN BE QUITE HANDSOME standing alone, this bookcase is designed specifically to flank both sides of the entertainment center on page 77. The dimensions of this case are proportional with those of the entertainment center, and because the construction steps are virtually identical, both units can be built at the same time. Like the entertainment center, the bookcase is made of plywood except for the shelf edge strips, rails, and molding. The back panel is made of a sheet of decorative paneling. It is especially important to purchase or mill all of your crown and baseboard molding at one time for all the units, because the entire assembly will be trimmed as one piece to create a finished look.

TALL BOOKCASE MATERIALS LIST

Difficulty Level: CHALLENGING

Qty	Part	Dimensions
1	Plywood top panel	¾" x 14¾" x 29¼"
1	Plywood bottom	¾" x 14¾" x 29¼"
2	Plywood side panels	¾" x 15" x 86"
1	Wood-grain paneling back panel	¼" x 29¼" x 85⅝"
4	Plywood adjustable shelves	¾" x 13¾" x 28¼"
3	Edge strips	¾" x ¾" x 28¼"
2	Stiles	¾" x 1½" x 86"
1	Top rail	¾" x 2" x 27"
1	Bottom rail	¾" x 5½" x 27"

Qty	Part	Dimensions
Trim (crown & baseboard dimensions for stand-alone bookcase)		
1	Front crown molding	¾" x 1½" x 34"
2	Side crown molding	¾" x 1½" x 17¾"
1	Front base molding	¾" x 4" x 31½"
2	Side base molding	¾" x 4" x 16½"
Hardware		
	4d Finishing nails	
	1¼" Screws	
	⅞" Brads	
16	Adjustable pins	

OVERALL VIEW

Top Panel

Side Crown

Top Rail

Front Crown

Side Panel

Stile

Back Panel

Adjustable Shelves

Edge Strip

Bottom

Bottom Rail

Base Molding

SIDE PANEL LAYOUT

³/₄" x ³/₈" Rabbet

8"

2"

Shelf Pin Holes

¼" x ³/₈" Rabbet

2"

8"

5¼"

³/₄" x ³/₈" Deep Dado

the top and bottom rails to fit; their top edges should be flush with the top panel and bottom shelf, respectively.

4. Install the trim. If you are planning to build the bookcase to stand alone, cut the crown and baseboard moldings to the dimensions in the Materials List and attach with glue and 4d finishing nails. Installing the trim on the wall-unit entertainment center is a little different. (See "Assembling the Three-Piece Wall Unit," page 80.)

1. Cut the parts. Cut the top, bottom, side, and back panels to the dimensions in the Materials List. Rabbet and dado the side panels as shown in *Side Panel Layout*. Note that the drawing shows only one side panel. Don't forget to make the other panel. (See "Dadoes, Grooves, and Rabbets," page 17.) Drill ¼-inch holes into the side panels for the shelf pins. Cut the four adjustable shelves and their solid wood edges. Attach the edging to the shelves using glue and 4d finishing nails.

2. Assemble the carcase. Glue the top and bottom to the side pieces. Attach the top using 1¼-inch screws. (The crown molding conceals the screw heads.) Attach the bottom using 4d nails. Install the back panel flush to the top of the cabinet and secure it with glue and ⅞-inch brads. (The space at the bottom is to accommodate uneven floors.)

3. Build and install the face frame. Cut the two stiles and attach them to the carcase with 4d finishing nails. Cut

window seat with drawers

A WINDOW SEAT is a warm and cozy addition to any room. It's equally suitable in a den as an inviting break in a wall full of floor-to-ceiling bookcases as it is in a bedroom flanked by his-and-her closets. This handsome window seat was designed for double duty with its comfortable cushions and spacious drawers. It is designed to fit a space 48 inches wide, but you can alter its dimensions to fit any available space.

If you have experience upholstering, or if you simply enjoy the challenge, by all means, make your own cushions. Otherwise, you can have them custom made to your specifications at a local upholstery shop.

If you need to remove carpeting and woodwork in the area where you plan to build your window seat, see "Removing Wallboard" and "Removing Carpet," page 34.

WINDOW SEAT WITH DRAWERS MATERIALS LIST

Difficulty Level: CHALLENGING

Qty	Part	Dimensions	Qty	Part	Dimensions
Carcase and face frame			**Hardware**		
2	Solid-wood face frame rails	¾" x 3½" x 48"	12	¼" x 1¼" Wooden dowels	
3	Solid-wood face frame stiles	¾" x 1½" x 9¾"		3" Screws (if attaching side panel to wall)	
2	Plywood side panels	¾" x 16" x 18½"		1½" Screws (if attaching side panels to cabinet)	
1	Plywood back panel	¾" x 16" x 48"		4d Finishing nails	
1	Plywood top panel	¾" x 19½" x 48"	2	Bottom-mount roller-bearing drawer slides	
Drawers			2	Drawer pulls	
4	Sides	¾" x 8¾" x 18"	**Miscellaneous**		
2	Backs	¾" x 8⅛" x 20¾"	2	Upholstered foam cushions	4" x 20" x 24"
2	Fronts	¾" x 8¾" x 20¾"			
2	Bottoms	¼" x 17½" x 20¾"			
2	Solid-wood false fronts	¾" x 10½" x 22½"			

OVERALL VIEW

Top Panel

Rail

¾" x ¼" Rabbet

Back Panel

Dowel

Drawer Slides

Side Panel

Stile

Drawer

Drawer Pull

False Front

1. Cut and rabbet the face frame. Cut the rails from clear 1x4 stock and the stiles from clear 1x2 stock to the dimensions in the Materials List. Rabbet the top rear edge of the top rail.

2. Assemble the face frame. Use a doweling jig to make two holes in each end of each stile. Drill corresponding holes in the center and at both ends of each rail. (See "Reinforcing Joints with Dowels," page 15.)

Attach the rails to the stiles using 12 glued dowels. Draw the rails to the stiles using bar clamps or pipe clamps. Check the frame for square.

3. Cut the carcase panels. Cut the sides, back, and top to the dimensions listed in the Materials List.

4. Attach the back and side panels. Place the back panel against the wall beneath the window, and secure it to the studs using 3-inch screws. Attach the side panels the same way if you are securing them to another wall. If you are securing the side panels to another cabinet, use 1½-inch screws.

5. Install the face frame. Apply glue to the front edges of the side panels; press the face frame against the glued sides; and secure it using four 4d finishing nails.

6. Install the drawer slides. Attach the cabinet portions of the drawer slides to the bottom rail and back panel according to the manufacturer's directions.

7. Attach the top panel. Apply glue to the top edges of the carcase and the rabbet in the top of the face frame. Secure the top panel using 4d finishing nails.

8. Cut and build the drawers. Cut the drawer parts. The solid-wood false fronts are larger than the drawer to allow a ³/₈-inch overhang on all sides. (For reference, see "Building Drawers," page 28.)

Attach the drawer portion of the slides to the drawer bottoms. Attach the drawer pulls using the screws provided by the manufacturer.

decorative shelf

PART OF THE APPEAL OF A FIREPLACE is its mantel-piece—the decorative over-the-hearth shelf meant for displaying special items. With this project, you can have such a mantelpiece, even if you don't have a fireplace to go with it. The shelf shown here is designed with the same built-up thickness and mitered molding that distinguishes many traditional mantelpieces.

As shown in the *Overall View,* the shelf top has a small box, or subassembly, attached to its underside. The subassembly consists of a front, bottom, and two ends. It provides structural support for attaching the project to the ledger strip that is fastened to the wall. It also serves as backing for the crown molding.

The shelf shown here is 48 inches long. You can adjust shelf length to fit available wall space. The installation instructions at the end of this project apply to a wood-frame wall. If you need to install your shelf against a masonry wall, refer to the instructions in "Solid-Wall Fasteners," page 52.

If you plan to paint the shelf, make it from a softwood. For a clear finish, you can choose an attractive hardwood. Unfortunately, you'll find that most lumberyards stock crown molding only in pine or oak. One attractive option is to paint the crown and apply clear finish to the shelf. Even if you build your shelf from hardwood, use softwood for the ledger.

DECORATIVE SHELF MATERIALS LIST

Difficulty Level: EASY

Qty	Part	Dimensions	Part
1	Solid-wood top	¾" x 8½" x 48"	**Hardware**
1	Solid-wood bottom	¾" x 4⅜" x 39¾"	6d Finishing nails
1	Solid-wood front	¾" x 2½" x 41¼"	4d Finishing nails
2	Solid-wood sides	¾" x 2½" x 5⅛"	#8 x 2½" Drywall screws
1	Front crown molding	1¹⁄₁₆" x 3½" x 50"	8d Finishing nails
2	Side crown molding	1¹⁄₁₆" x 3½" x 10"	
1	Solid-wood ledger	¾" x 1¾" x 39⅝"	

OVERALL VIEW

Top

Ledger Attached to Wall

Side Crown Molding

Side

Front

Front Crown Molding

Bottom

BUILDING THE SHELF

1. Cut the shelf parts. Cut the top and bottom to the dimensions in the Materials List. Cut the front and side pieces to the dimensions in the Materials List with 45-degree miters on both ends of the front piece and one end of each side piece.

2. Rout the top. Use a router and $3/8$-inch cove bit to mill a cove along the front and side edges of the shelf top, as shown in the Overall View. Sand the shelf top using 120- and 220-grit sandpaper.

3. Assemble the bottom, front, and sides. Apply glue to the front and side edges of the bottom and to the mitered ends of the front and side pieces. Attach the front and sides to the bottom using 6d finishing nails to form the subassembly. Use four nails into the front and two nails into each side.

4. Attach the top. Glue and nail the subassembly to the top using 6d finishing nails. Use two nails for each side piece and four nails for the front. Predrill for the nails if the top is made of hardwood.

CUTTING AND INSTALLING THE CROWN

1. Cut and attach the front crown. Miter-cut one end of the molding. Position the molding against the front of the shelf assembly, as shown in the *Overall View,* and mark the second cut in place. Glue and nail the front crown to the top and to the subassembly front piece using 4d finishing nails. (See "Cutting Crown Molding," page 37.)

2. Cut and install the side molding. Miter-cut each crown molding side piece a little longer than the dimensions in the Materials List. Position

each against the mitered end of the front crown molding piece, and mark where it meets the rear edge of the shelf assembly. Square-cut that end for a flush fit. Apply glue to the mitered ends and contact surfaces of the side molding pieces. Install the pieces using 4d finishing nails into the top and into the subassembly side pieces.

INSTALLING THE SHELF

1. Install the ledger. Use a stud finder to locate the wall framing. (See "Finding Studs," page 34.) Scribe a level line that crosses at least two studs at the height of your choice. Attach the ledger using $2\frac{1}{2}$-inch screws driven in at each stud.

2. Attach the shelf to the ledger. Fit the shelf over the ledger, and secure the shelf using four 8d finishing nails driven into the ledger.

cd/dvd storage unit

AS VIDEO AND AUDIO TECHNOLOGY has become more sophisticated, we can now enjoy first-quality entertainment in our own homes. More and more people are investing in home theater systems, and with them, the need arises for more storage space for CDs and DVDs. Of course, you can find some disc storage systems at furniture and electronic stores, but with a modest investment in materials and a weekend or two in your home shop, you can build a handsome storage case yourself. This gives you the opportunity to pick the materials and finish to match your decor and the satisfaction of knowing you built it yourself.

For an eye-catching piece, select an attractive hardwood such as, oak, cherry, walnut, or maple with a clear finish; if you want something that's a bit less formal, use pine or poplar, and finish it with paint. You can also create a more eclectic look by mixing a painted finish on the body of the piece with a clear finish on a hardwood top and base cap.

CD/DVD STORAGE UNIT MATERIALS LIST

Difficulty Level: EASY

Qty	Part	Dimensions	Qty	Part	Dimensions
Carcase			1	Solid-wood base back	¾" x 3¼" x 7½"
2	Solid-wood sides	¾" x 6¼" x 62½"	1	Solid-wood base top	¾" x 7¾" x 10½"
2	Solid-wood facing strips	¾" x ⅞" x 62½"			
10	Solid-wood shelves	¾" x 6" x 8"	**Hardware**		
1	Plywood back	¼" x 8½" x 63"		4d finishing nails	
1	Solid-wood top	¾" x 7⅝" x 10¼"		1" brads	
				#8 x 1¼" flathead wood screws	
Base					
1	Solid-wood base front	¾" x 3¼" x 9"	**Miscellaneous**		
2	Solid-wood base sides	¾" x 3¼" x 7"		#20 joining plates (optional)	

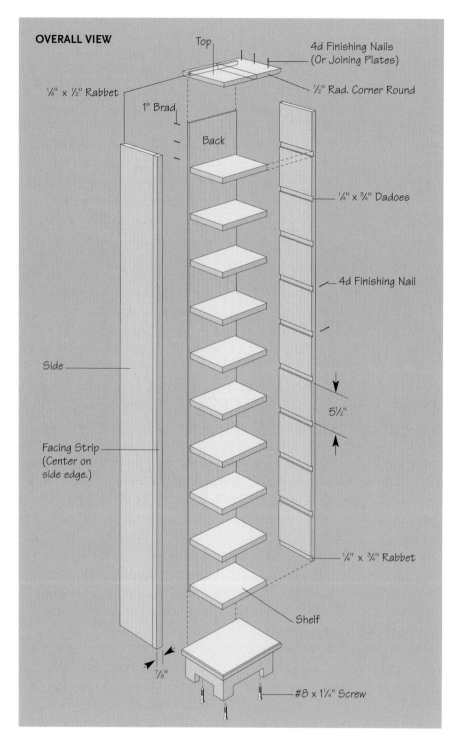

OVERALL VIEW

Top

4d Finishing Nails
(Or Joining Plates)

¼" x ½" Rabbet

½" Rad. Corner Round

1" Brad

Back

¼" x ¾" Dadoes

4d Finishing Nail

Side

5½"

Facing Strip
(Center on
side edge.)

¼" x ¾" Rabbet

Shelf

⅞"

#8 x 1¼" Screw

BUILDING THE BASE

1. Cut the parts. Rip stock for the base front, sides, and back to width. Use a miter saw to cut the parts to length with appropriate miter cuts for the front base joints and square cuts for the back. Next, cut the base top to size.

2. Make the decorative cutouts. Use a saber saw or a band saw to make the decorative cutouts in the base front and side pieces.

3. Assemble the base. Apply glue to the miter and butt joints of the base; then assemble the parts using clamps

to hold them in proper position. Use 4d finishing nails to pin the joints together. If you are using hardwood for the base, you will need to first drill ¹⁄₁₆-inch-diameter pilot holes for the nails.

4. Chamfer the top. Use a 45-degree chamfer bit in the router to cut the small chamfer along the front and side edges of the base top on both the bottom and top surfaces. You can also use a sharp block plane to make these cuts.

5. Attach the base top. Place the top on the base, and fasten it to the front, sides and back using 4d finishing nails. Drill pilot holes through the base top for fastening it to the shelving unit. Wiggle the drill bit perpendicular to the grain of the wood as you drill to slightly elongate the holes. This will allow the base and case to move independently of one another without causing any cracks. Countersink the holes from the bottom side as shown in the *Overall View*.

BUILDING THE CASE

1. Cut the sides, shelves, facing strips, top, and back panel to size as shown in the Material List. Use the drawings as a guide to lay out the position of the rabbets and dadoes in the sides. Use a router with a straight bit, or dado blades in the table saw, to cut the rabbets in the sides for the back panels; then cut the shelf dadoes. (See "Dadoes, Rabbets, and Grooves," page 17). Note that the shelf dadoes are cut across the sides, from the front to the back rabbet. These exposed joints are covered by the facing strips.

2. Apply facing strips. Apply glue to the front edge of one of the sides and apply the facing strip, allowing it to

BASE CONSTRUCTION

⅛" Chamfer on Both Faces

4d Finishing Nails

4d Finishing Nail

1¼"

¾" Overhang on Sides and Front

3½"

1¾"

5½"

1¾"

overhang both the inside and outside surfaces by ¹⁄₁₆-inch. Use clamps to hold the strips in place while the glue sets. If you do not have access to a sufficient number of clamps, you can use 4d finishing nails to pin the joint. Remember to drill pilot holes for the nails if you are using hardwood stock. Allow the glue to set for about 30 minutes; then use an old chisel to remove any glue that has squeezed out of the joint, especially into the shelf dadoes, as this would prevent the parts from fitting properly.

3. Cut joining plate slots. A nice option for fastening the case top to the sides is to use joining plates. These provide a way to positively join the parts without any visible fasteners. However, if you do not have access to a plate joiner, you can also use dowels or simply nail the top to the sides using 4d finishing nails. If you plan to use joining plates, cut matching slots in the top ends of the sides and bottom surface of the case top.

3. Rout top edges and back. Use a ½-inch-diameter roundover bit in the router to shape the front and side bottom edges of the top panel. Then install a straight bit in the router to cut the stopped rabbet in the back edge of the top to house the case back. Because the router leaves a round-end cut, stop the router about ¼-inch shy of the layout marks on both ends, and use a sharp chisel to square the ends of the cut.

4. Assemble sides and shelves. Lay both sides on a worktable or saw horses with the inside surface facing up. Spread a small amount of glue in the dadoes in both case sides. Place the shelves into the dadoes of one side; then place the opposite side over the shelf ends. Adjust the parts so that the back ends of the shelves are flush with the edges of the rabbets in the sides; then apply clamps to hold the joints tight while the glue sets. If you do not have sufficient clamps, you can use 4d finish nails to pin the joints together. Turn the assembly on its back

and compare opposite diagonal measurements to check that the case is square. (See "Squaring a Carcase," page 21.) After the glue has cured, remove the clamps.

5. Attach the top. If you are using joining plates, spread glue in the slots, and place the top into position, clamping it lightly until the glue sets—otherwise, nail the top to the sides using 4d finish nails.

6. Install the back. Turn the case back-side up on the table, and place the back in position. Use 1-inch brads to fasten the panel to the sides, top, and shelves.

7. Attach the base. With the case lying on its back on the table, position the base so that there is the proper overhang on the front and sides. Use a clamp to temporarily hold the parts in proper position while you bore pilot holes; then fasten them together using #8 x 1¼-inch flathead screws.

FINISH THE PROJECT
1. Fill all nailholes. Use matching wood filler to fill all nailholes. Allow the filler to dry thoroughly before sanding.

2. Sand all exposed parts. Use 120-, 150-, 180-, and 220-grit sandpaper to sand all exposed cabinet parts. Remember to thoroughly remove the sanding dust whenever you change to a finer-grit paper.

3. Apply the finish. Apply the finish of your choice following the techniques outlined in Chapter 5, "Wood Finishing." If you stain the piece, allow the stain to dry completely before applying the initial top coat of finish.

coffee table

WITH STRAIGHT, SIMPLE LINES that are consistent with either Shaker or Arts and Crafts motifs, this coffee table will provide an attractive and useful addition to your living or family room. Its classic details and proportion will fit with most design schemes. It provides an ample top for display and serving, and a handy drawer that can hold remote controls, coasters, and napkins—or other small items—in a convenient but unobtrusive spot.

Construction details of this table are quite simple, using dowels to join the aprons and legs. For the most impressive results, you should choose an attractive hardwood lumber, such as oak, cherry, maple, ash, or walnut, for the exposed parts of the table. To save a bit on materials, the interior drawer guides, corner and fastener blocks, and cleats can all be made of a less expensive secondary wood, such as poplar.

COFFEE TABLE MATERIALS LIST

Difficulty Level: CHALLENGING

Qty	Part	Dimensions	Qty	Part	Dimensions
Table base			4	Corner blocks	¾" x 4" x 4¾"
1	Solid-wood top	¾" x 24" x 48"	8	Table top fastener blocks	¾" x 2" x 2"
	glue up from narrow boards		**Drawer**		
4	Solid-wood legs	2¼" x 17¼"	1	Solid-wood drawer false front	¾" x 2⅜" x 17⅞"
	glue up from ¾" thick boards		1	Solid-wood drawer front	¾" x 2⅜" x 16⅞"
2	Solid-wood end aprons	¾" x 4" x 18"	1	Solid-wood drawer back	¾" x 1⅞" x 16⅞"
1	Solid-wood back apron	¾" x 4" x 42"	2	Solid-wood drawer sides	¾" x 2⅜" x 20"
1	Solid-wood front apron	¾" x 4" x 42"	1	Plywood drawer bottom	¾" x 16⅞" x 19½"
	glue up from 4 pieces listed below		**Hardware and Miscellaneous Supplies**		
2		¾" x ¾" x 42"	8	¼" x 1" wood dowels (front apron, optional)	
2		¾" x 2½" x 12"	16	⅜" x 1½" wood dowels	
2	Solid-wood drawer guides	¾" x 4" x 20"	1	knob	
4	Solid-wood guide cleats	¾" x 4" x 2½"		#8 x 1¼" screws	
2	Solid-wood drawer runners	¾" x ¼" x 20"		#6 x 1" screws	

BUILDING THE TABLE BASE

1. Cut the parts. Rip and crosscut ³⁄₄-inch-thick material for the legs, leaving the pieces slightly oversized. Next, cut the stock to finished dimension for the aprons, drawer guides, runners, guide cleats, and corner and fastener blocks. Note that the front apron is assembled from 4 separate parts to create the opening for the drawer.

2. Assemble leg blanks. Use a foam roller or brush to spread glue on the mating surface of the individual pieces for each leg. Assemble the parts using clamps to hold the joints tight while the glue sets. After the glue has cured, rip and crosscut the legs to finished dimension.

3. Assemble the front apron. You will find that it simplifies assembly if you use dowels as an aid in locating the individual apron parts in relation to one another. Use a doweling jig to drill ¼-inch-diameter holes for dowels in the mating edges; then apply glue to the edges and holes; insert the dowels; and join the parts. Use clamps to pull the joints tight, and allow the apron to sit for at least one hour to allow the glue to set.

4. Drill dowel holes for leg/apron joints. Use a doweling jig to bore ³⁄₈-inch-diameter holes for dowels in the ends of the aprons and also in the leg faces as shown in the plans. Note: when laying out the leg holes, you should orient the parts so that the faces with exposed glue joints are all facing the same direction.

5. Assemble the base. Begin assembly by joining the front and back rails to the legs. Spread a small amount of glue in the dowel holes and also on

OVERALL VIEW

#8 x 1¼" Screw

#8 x 1¼" Screw

Back Apron

Tabletop Fasteners

Guide Cleat

Drawer Guide

#6 x 1" Screw

Corner Blocks

Drawer Runner

End Apron

Front Apron Pieces

³⁄₈" x 1½" Dowel

Leg (Glue up from ³⁄₄"stock.)

each dowel before joining the parts. Use bar clamps to pull the joints tight, and allow the glue to set.

Next, join the front and back sub-assemblies to the end rails. Clamp the parts to pull the joints together; then set the base on a flat table or on the floor to check that all legs rest evenly on the surface. If the base rocks, adjust the position of the clamps to eliminate the problem.

6. Install the drawer guides. Bore and countersink pilot holes for screws in the drawer guides, runners, and guide cleats. Install the cleats to the inside of the aprons; then screw the drawer guides to the cleats. Note that the faces of the drawer guides must be flush with the drawer opening in the front apron. Finally, screw the runners to the drawer guides.

7. Install the table top fastener blocks. Drill and countersink pilot holes in each fastener block. Create

an elongated hole by either wiggling the drill bit as you bore the hole, or by drilling two holes side-by-side and removing the waste between them with a small chisel. This will allow the top to expand and contract with seasonal humidity changes without causing any cracks. Apply glue to one edge of each block, and then clamp them to the inside of the apron as shown in the *Overall View*.

MAKING THE SOLID-WOOD TABLE TOP

1. Edge-glue the boards. Build the top by joining several boards to form a slightly oversize blank. (See "Edge-Gluing Stock," page 14.) After the glue has cured, rip and crosscut the top to final dimensions.

2. Sand the top. Use 120-grit sandpaper to smooth the top, taking care to ease all sharp edges with a sanding block.

DRAWER CONSTRUCTION

¼" x ¼" Groove (Sides and Front)

2⅜"

#8 x 1¼" Screws

4d Finishing Nails

³⁄₁₆" x ¾" Groove

DRAWER AND GUIDE SECTIONS

1⅝"

¾"

1⅝"

¹³⁄₁₆"

¾"

¹³⁄₁₆"

¼"

¼"

INSTALLING THE TOP TO THE BASE

1. Place the top upside down on a padded worktable, and invert the base over it. Adjust the position of the base so that the top extends an equal amount beyond the aprons on all sides.

2. Drill pilot holes in the top. Bore directly through the pilot holes in the fastener blocks.

3. Attach the top to the base with screws. Use #8 x 1¼-inch screws to fasten the top to the base.

BUILDING THE DRAWER

1. Cut the parts to size. Rip and crosscut the drawer face, front, back, sides, and the bottom panel to the dimensions shown in the Materials List. When selecting the material for the drawer face, try to pick stock that matches the color and grain of the front apron.

2. Cut drawer joints. Cut the rabbets and grooves in drawer front and sides as shown in *Drawer Construction*.

3. Cut guide grooves. Use dado blades in the table saw or a straight bit in the router to cut grooves for drawer guides in the outside faces of the drawer sides.

4. Assemble the drawers. Spread glue in the rabbets in the drawer sides; then attach the front and rear panels to the sides using 4d finish nails. Take care to keep the top edges flush. Slide the bottom panel into position, and fasten it by driving 1-inch brads into the bottom edge of the drawer back.

5. Sand and fit the drawer. Sand the drawer box, and test its fit in the table. If you find that it does not slide easily, you can either sand the drawer guides or the grooves in the drawer sides.

6. Mount the drawer face. Drill and countersink pilot holes in the drawer front, and then mount the face to the drawer box using #6 x 1-inch screws. When installed in the table, there should be a space of ¹⁄₁₆-inch between the drawer face and apron on all edges. Bore a pilot hole for the knob through the drawer face and the

drawer box front. Mount the knob to the drawer. Depending on the length of the mounting screw, you might need to counter bore the pilot hole on the inside of the drawer—or you can get a longer screw.

FINISHING THE TABLE

1. Disassemble the table. For ease of sanding and finishing the table, remove the drawer and the top from the base.

2. Finish sand all parts. Sand all parts to 220 grit, following the instructions in "Sanding Wood," page 57.

3. Apply the finish. Apply a stained or clear finish using the techniques outlined in "Staining Wood," page 62 or "Choosing a Clear Finish," page 66.

4. Reassemble the table parts. Once the final coat of finish is completely dry, reattach the top to the table base. Apply a light coat of wax to both the drawer runners and drawer sides to guarantee smooth operation; then reinstall the drawer.

end table with shelf

THIS OCCASIONAL TABLE packs a lot of appeal into a small and relatively approachable project. Whether you use it as an end table beside a sofa or armchair to support a lamp or as a stand-alone piece to show-case photos, sculpture, or souvenirs, its simple and straightforward design is sure to draw attention. You could even use this table in the bedroom as a night-stand—if necessary, you can adjust the length of the legs to suit the height of your mattress.

The table features a drawer on full-extension slides so that you won't have to struggle to access items in the back; you'll find it a handy spot for books, maga-zines, coasters, or remote controls. The open shelf pro-vides a spot for either display or storage, making this an extremely versatile and functional piece of furniture.

For this table, select a hardwood species that com-plements your design scheme. Remember that you can create an interesting and eclectic atmosphere by combining a variety of materials and styles in a room—so the wood you select doesn't necessarily need to match your existing furniture.

END TABLE WITH SHELF MATERIALS LIST

Difficulty Level: CHALLENGING

Qty	Part	Dimensions
Base		
4	Solid-wood legs	1¾" x 1¾" x 26"
3	Solid-wood aprons	¾" x 4" x 15"
2	Solid-wood rails	¾" x 2½" x 15"
2	Solid-wood slide blocking	¾" x 3½" x 15"
2	Shelf cleats	¾" x ¾" x 15"
Top and Shelf		
1	Solid-wood top glue up from narrow stock	¾" x 20" x 20"
1	Solid-wood shelf glue up from narrow stock	¾" x 15" x 16½"

Qty	Part	Dimensions
Drawer		
1	Solid-wood drawer face	¾" x 3¹⁵⁄₁₆" x 14⅞"
2	Solid-wood drawer sides	¾" x 3½" x 16"
1	Solid-wood drawer front	¾" x 3½" x 13"
1	Solid-wood drawer back	¾" x 3" x 13"
1	Plywood drawer bottom	¼" x 13" x 15½"
Hardware and Miscellaneous Supplies		
20	⅜" x 1½" wood dowels	
	1" brads	
	#6 x 1¼" flathead screws	
1 set	16" full-extension, side-mount drawer slides with ½" side clearance	
1	knob or pull	
	#20 joining plates	

BUILDING THE TABLE BASE

1. Cut the parts. Cut the table legs from planed ⁸/₄ stock to the size shown in the plans. If you cannot find thick lumber, you can always glue up 3 ³/₄-inch-thick boards to form blanks, then rip the legs from them. Rip and crosscut the aprons, rails, shelf cleats, and side blocking to the dimensions shown in the Materials List.

2. Drill dowel holes. Use a doweling jig to bore the ³/₈-inch-diameter x ¹³/₁₆-inch-deep dowel holes in legs, rails, and aprons.

3. Cut joining plate slots. Use a plate joiner to cut the joining plate slots in the top edges of the aprons. The joining plates will provide a simple and strong joint between the aprons and top panel. Because the slots are located only on the sides and back, the top will be able to expand and contract slightly with changes in humidity without breaking the joints or cracking the top.

4. Join aprons and rails to legs. Apply glue to the dowel holes and dowels, and assemble the side rails and aprons to the legs. Use clamps to pull the joints tight, and check that the assemblies are square before setting them aside to allow the glue to cure. (See "Squaring a Carcase," page 20.) After the glue has set, remove the clamps and join the two side assemblies to the back rail. Again, use clamps to pull the joints tight. Set the base upright on a flat table top or floor to check that all legs rest evenly on the surface. If the base rocks, adjust the clamps to remedy the problem—then let the glue set for at least one hour before removing the clamps.

OVERALL VIEW

Top

³/₈" Rad. Quarter Round

#20 Joining Plate

Apron

Drawer Slide

Slide Blocking

Shelf Cleat

Apron

#6 x 1¼" Screw

Shelf

Rail

³/₈" x 1½" Dowel

5. Install the shelf cleats and side blocking. Bore and countersink pilot holes in the shelf cleats and drawer blocking; then install them to the rails and aprons as shown in the plans using #6 x 1¼-inch flathead screws.

BUILDING THE TOP AND SHELF

1. Rip and crosscut ¾-inch-thick stock to be edge-glued for the top and shelf panels. These pieces should be cut so that the panels will be slightly larger than the finished dimensions— you can trim the panels after glue-up.

2. Assemble the panels. Glue and clamp the two panels. (See "Edge-Gluing Stock," page 14.) Allow the glue to set for at least one hour before removing the clamps. Trim the panels to the dimensions specified.

3. Shape the top edges. Use a ³/₈-inch-radius roundover/beading bit to cut the edge profile on the table top.

4. Cut joining plate slots. Use the plate joiner to cut slots in the bottom face of the top panel to create the joints with the table aprons.

DRAWER CONSTRUCTION

Back

Side

Bottom

#6 x 1¼" Screw

¼" x ⅜" Rabbet

Front

4d Finishing Nail

Pull

Face

¼" x ¼" Groove (Front and Sides)

FRONT VIEW SECTION

1/16" Reveal

Top

½"

¾"

2½"

Blocking

Apron

¼"

Cleat

Shelf

⅝"

1¼"

½"

Rail

Leg

4¾"

INSTALLING THE TOP AND SHELF

1. Install the shelf. Place the shelf in position, with its ends resting on the shelf cleats. Place a clamp on either end to temporarily hold it in position; then invert the table so that you can drill pilot holes into the bottom of the shelf. Guide the drill bit through the holes already drilled in the cleats. Fasten the shelf in place with #6 x 1¼-inch screws.

2. Install the top. Spread a small amount of glue in the joining plate slots in both the aprons and table top. Insert joining plates in the slots; then place the top over the aprons. Use clamps, or place heavy weights on the top, to draw the joints together, leaving them in place until the glue sets—at least one hour.

BUILDING THE DRAWER

1. Cut the drawer parts. Cut the drawer face, sides, back, and front to size as specified in the Materials List. Also cut a piece of ¼-inch-thick plywood to size for the drawer bottom.

2. Cut drawer joints. Cut the rabbets for corner joints in drawer sides and grooves for drawer bottoms in the

sides and front panel. (See "Drawer Construction," page 28.) You can use either a router or the table saw with dado blades to make these cuts.

3. Assemble the drawer. Apply glue to the rabbets in the drawer sides, and assemble the drawer box. Use 4d finishing nails to pin the joints together. Slide the drawer bottom into the groove in sides and front, and fasten it by nailing it to the back.

4. Attach the drawer face. Drill and countersink pilot holes in the drawer front; then use #6 x 1¼-inch flathead screws to mount the face to the drawer. Drill a pilot hole for the knob, and attach it to the drawer. If the mounting screw is not long enough, you can counter bore the hole on the inside of the drawer.

5. Attach drawer slides. Mount the drawer slides to both the table and drawers as indicated in the slide instructions. Install the drawer in the table, and check for proper operation. Most slides have slotted mounting holes that allow you to adjust the drawer position as required.

FINISHING THE PIECE

1. Remove hardware. Temporarily remove the drawer slides and knob. It's very difficult to do a thorough job of sanding and finishing when you must work around obstacles. The small time and effort required to remove and reinstall these parts will be made up by the superior finish that you will achieve.

2. Sand and finish. Sand all exposed parts, finishing up with 220-grit sandpaper. Remember to remove all sanding dust whenever you switch to finer grit paper. Apply the stain (if desired) and clear top coat following the guidelines in "Wood Finishing," on page 55.

3. Reinstall the hardware. Using the pilot holes already established, reinstall the drawer slides and drawer knob. Then check the operation of the drawer in the table. Most slides have extra holes that allow you to make adjustments.

wall unit

BUILT-IN CABINET AND SHELVING UNITS are always near the top of "dream" lists of home improvements. These multipurpose projects fulfill a variety of roles in the home, combining storage, display, and decorative functions. The piece shown on our cover photo is a great example of this type of project, designed to be adaptable for a living room, family room, or even a bedroom. It features open, adjustable shelves that can be used to display books, photos, and collectible items, as well as provide generous cabinet storage. You will also find six ample drawers that can store anything from CDs and DVDs to clothing and table linens. This project is designed to be painted, so you can use cost-effective paint-grade materials like pine, poplar, or birch plywood.

Of course, a project of this size and complexity cannot be approached casually. You will need to plan carefully and study the construction details so that you fully understand the steps before starting to cut any materials. The design of the piece lends itself to being approached as two distinct parts, so you can build the lower and upper units separately and then simply fasten them together with screws before attaching the entire unit to the wall. This modular technique makes it easier to manage the details of construction, and it also means that you will require less space to assemble the individual components.

WALL UNIT MATERIALS LIST

Difficulty Level: **DIFFICULT**

Qty	Part	Dimensions
	Lower Cabinet Carcase	
2	Plywood sides	¾" x 17¼" x 29¼"
3	Plywood partitions	¾" x 17" x 23"
1	Plywood bottom	¾" x 17" x 91"
2	Plywood back panels	¼" x 29⅛" x 23½"
1	Plywood back panel	¼" x 33¼" x 23½"
1	Solid-wood nailer	¾" x 3½" x 91½"
6	Blocking for slides	1¼" x 4" x 16"
	Lower Cabinet Face Frame	
2	Solid-wood stiles	¾" x 2" x 29¼"
1	Solid-wood top rail	¾" x 1½" x 88"
1	Solid-wood bottom rail	¾" x 3" x 88"
4	Solid-wood drawer rails	¾" x 1½" x 27"
3	Solid-wood mullions	¾" x 2" x 21¼"
	Lower Cabinet Top Frame	
1	Solid-wood front rail	¾" x 5½" x 93½"
1	Solid-wood back rail	¾" x 5½" x 82½"
2	Solid-wood end rails	¾" x 5½" x 18¾"
3	Solid-wood center blocking	¾" x 5½" x 7¾"
	Upper Cabinet Carcase	
2	Plywood sides	¾" x 15¼" x 52¾"
3	Plywood partitions	¾" x 15" x 51½"
1	Plywood bottom	¾" x 15" x 91"
1	Plywood top with edging	¾" x 18" x 96"
	1 Plywood top panel	¾" x 17¼" x 94½"
	1 Solid-wood edging strip	¾" x ¾" x 96"
	2 Solid-wood edging strips	¾" x ¾" x 18"
1	Solid-wood nailer	¾" x 3½" x 91½"
2	Plywood back panels	¾" x 29¾" x 52"
1	Plywood back panel	¼" x 32" x 52"
	Upper Cabinet Face Frame	
2	Solid-wood stiles	¾" x 2" x 52¾"
1	Solid-wood top rail	¾" x 3¼" x 88"
1	Solid-wood bottom rail	¾" x 1½" x 88"
3	Solid-wood mullions	¾" x 2" x 48"
	Miscellaneous Cabinet Parts	
1	Solid-wood baseboard	¾" x 5" x 93½"
2	Solid-wood baseboards	¾" x 5" x 18¾"
1	Shoe molding	¾" x ½" x 94½"
2	Shoe molding	¾" x ½" x 19¼"
1	Crown molding	⁹⁄₁₆" x 2¾" x 95¼"
2	Crown molding	⁹⁄₁₆" x 2¾" x 17⅝"
3	Blocking	¾" x 5½" x 15"
6	Plywood shelves with edging	¾" x 15⅛" x 14⅛"
	6 Plywood shelf panels	¾" x 15⅛" x 14⅛"
	6 Solid-wood edging strips	¾" x ¾" x 15⅛"

Qty	Part	Dimensions
6	Plywood shelves with edging	¾" x 28¾" x 14⅛"
	6 Plywood shelf panels	¾" x 28¾" x 14⅛"
	6 Solid-wood edging strips	¾" x ¾" x 28¾"
2	Plywood shelves with edging	¾" x 15¾" x 16⅛"
	6 Plywood shelf panels	¾" x 15¾" x 16⅛"
	6 Solid-wood edging strips	¾" x ¾" x 15¾"
	Lower Cabinet Doors (2 – ¾" x 13⅞" x 21⅛")	
4	Solid-wood stiles	¾" x 2" x 21⅛"
4	Solid-wood rails	¾" x 2" x 11⅛"
2	Plywood panels	¼" x 10⁹⁄₁₆" x 17¹³⁄₁₆"
	Upper Cabinet Doors (4 – ¾" x 13⁷⁄₁₆" x 47⅞")	
8	Solid-wood stiles	¾" x 2" x 47⅞"
12	Solid-wood rails	¾" x 2" x 11⁷⁄₁₆"
8	Plywood panels	¾" x 10⅛" x 20⅝"
	Drawer Faces	
2	Solid-wood faces	¾" x 4⅛" x 26⅞"
4	Solid-wood/plywood faces	¾" x 6⅞" x 26⅞"
	8 Solid-wood frame	¾" x 2" x 26⅞"
	8 Solid-wood frame	¾" x 2" x 6⅞"
	4 Plywood panels	½" x 3⅝" x 23⅝"
	Drawer Boxes (2 – 3½" x 16" x 26" and 4 – 6¼" x 16" x 26")	
4	Solid-wood sides	¾" x 3½" x 16"
2	Solid-wood fronts	¾" x 3½" x 25"
2	Solid-wood backs	¾" x 3" x 25"
8	Solid-wood sides	¾" x 6¼" x 16"
4	Solid-wood fronts	¾" x 6¼" x 25"
4	Solid-wood backs	¾" x 5¾" x 25"
6	Plywood bottoms	¼" x 25" x 15½"
	Hardware and Miscellaneous Supplies	
	#20 joining plates	
	#0 joining plates	
	¼" x 1½" wood dowels	
6	door knobs	
12	drawer pulls	
6	door catches	
56	¼" shelf pins	
16	2½" x 1½" butt hinges	
6	16" full-extension drawer slides with ½" side space	
	1" brads	
	4d finishing nails	
	6d finishing nails	
	#8 x 1¼" flathead wood screws	
	#8 x 1¾" flathead wood screws	
	#10 x 3" flathead wood screws	

OVERALL VIEW, LOWER CASE

Miter Front Frame Corners

21⁷⁄₈"

11¹⁄₈"

6d Finishing Nail

Top Frame

#20 Joining Plate

½" Rad. Quarter Round

½" x 1" Recess for Nailer

Drawer Slide Blocking

2" (2½" on Other Face)

Plywood Shelf

4½"

4½"

5¾"

Bottom

Solid Wood Edging

2"

6¼"

Nailer Notch

Partition

Back Panel

Nailer

Side

1" Brads

4d Finishing Nail

Joining Plates for Locating Top (Optional)

¼" Dado

¼" x ⅜" Shelf Pin Hole

15⁷⁄₈"

15⁷⁄₈"

¼" Dado

28½"

¼" x ½" Rabbet along Inside Edge for Back

#8 x 1¾" Screw

6d Finishing Nail

BUILDING THE CARCASES

1. Cut the parts. Cut the plywood sides, bottom, back, and upper case top panel to size as specified in the Materials List. Next, cut the solid wood edging strips for the upper case top and parts for the lower case top frame, as well as the nailer strips that are used to fasten the case to the wall. Cut the dadoes and rabbets, as specified in the *Overall Views,* using either the table saw and dado blades or router with a straight bit. (See "Dadoes, Grooves, and Rabbets," page 17.) When cutting the wide rabbets in the side panels for the solid-wood nailers, you can remove most of the waste with a router and finish the cuts with a sharp chisel, creating sharp inside corners. Use a saber saw or handsaw to cut notches

for the nailers in the back edges of the partitions.

Cut #20 joining plate slots in the lower top frame parts. (See "Reinforcing Joints with Biscuits," page 16.) If you do not have access to a plate joiner, you could instead use a doweling jig to bore holes, and then use dowels to form these joints.

2. Assemble the lower case top frame. Apply glue to the joining plate slots and also to the faces of the joining plates; then assemble the lower case top frame. Use clamps to pull the joints tight, leaving them in place until the glue sets for at least one hour. Install a ½-inch-radius beading bit in the router, and use it to shape the front and two ends of the frame as shown

in the drawings. Drill and countersink pilot holes in the top frame for attaching the upper cabinet. Elongate the pilot holes slightly to allow the case parts to move independently with changes in humidity.

3. Assemble the upper case top. Apply glue to the edges of the top panel, and apply the solid-wood edging strips. (See "Finishing Edges," page 12.) Use masking tape or clamps to hold the strips in place while the glue sets. Install a ⅜-inch-radius roundover bit in the router to shape the top and bottom edges of the top on the front and two ends. You will need to use an accessory edge guide with the router to make these cuts.

OVERALL VIEW, UPPER CASE

Top Panel

6d Finishing Nail

⅜" Rad. Half-Round Edging

½" x 1" Recess for Nailer

1" Brads

Side

Nailer Notch

4d Finishing Nail

Plywood Shelf

2" (2½" on Other Face)

Solid-Wood Edging

Nailer

Joining Plates for Locating Top (Optional)

¼" x ⅜" Shelf-Pin Hole

Back Panel

¼" Dado

¼" x ½" Rabbet along Inside Edge for Back

¼" Dado

2"

Partition

6¼"

6d Finishing Nail

Blocking

15¼"

29⅞"

¾"

4. Cut joining-plate slots. You will find it much easier to assemble the carcases if you provide a means to accurately locate the partitions and sides in relation to the top panels. One simple method of achieving this is to cut two or three joining plate slots in the tops of each part, and then a matching set of slots in the tops. You can then install joining plates in the slots to locate the parts, and use nails to provide fastening power—glue is optional. Of course, if you do not have a plate joiner to use, you can substitute dowels.

5. Drill shelf-pin holes. Use a drilling jig to bore ¼-inch-diameter x ⅜-inch-deep holes for shelf pins in the carcase sides and partitions where appropriate. (See "Installing Shelf Pins," page 28.)

Note that where these holes are located on both sides of a single partition, vary the setback distance on opposite sides so that the holes do not intersect.

6. Assemble the carcases. Begin assembly with the lower case because it is smaller and will be simpler to handle. Spread glue in the dadoes in the case bottom, and place the partitions into the grooves. Drive 6d finishing nails through the bottom into the partition ends to fasten the joints. Next, apply glue to the dadoes in the side panels, and fit them over the ends of the case bottom. Again, fasten the joints using 6d finishing nails. Place joining plates in the slots in the partitions and side panels (if used); then place the top frame into position.

Drive nails through the frame into the plywood parts to fasten the joints. Lay the assembly on its face, and compare opposite diagonal measurements to check that it is square. (See "Squaring a Carcase," page 21.) Make any necessary adjustments; then apply glue, and fasten the nailer strip to the notches in partitions and side panels using 4d finishing nails. You can also drive nails through the top panel into the edge of the nailer. Install the back panels, and fasten them using 1-inch brads.

Next, begin assembly of the upper case. Use the same techniques employed for the lower unit. Join the bottom to the partitions; then add the side panels. Fasten the top and nailer strip and finally the back panels. Set the carcase units aside.

BUILDING THE FACE FRAMES

1. Cut the parts. Cut the parts for both upper and lower face frames according to the dimensions in the Materials List. Use a doweling jig to bore holes in the stiles, rails, and mullions for face frame joints. (See "Reinforcing Joints with Dowels," page 15.)

2. Assemble the face frames. Begin with the smaller, lower-case face frame. Because there are so many parts, and glue has a limited "open time" (the amount of time before it begins to set), it is best to work in stages. This technique will allow you to focus on achieving tight, square joints and eliminate errors due to rushing the assembly. First, apply glue to the dowel holes, and join the mullions to the top and bottom rails. Use bar clamps to pull the joints tight; then check that the assembly is square before setting it aside for the glue to cure. Next, join the drawer rails to the mullions. And finally, join the stiles to the ends of the rails. When it comes to clamping the stiles to the long rails, you can fashion a make-shift clamp from rope. Simply tie a loop of rope around the assembly, and use a short stick to twist it, applying pressure to the joints. Use a small clamp to hold the wooden "tightening stick" in place to maintain pressure.

Use the same steps to assemble the upper face frame. Begin by joining the mullions to the top and bottom rails; then, when the glue cures on those joints, add the stiles.

3. Install the face frames. Place the lower case on its back, and apply glue to the front edges of the sides and partitions. Arrange the face frame over the carcase, and fasten it in place with 4d finishing nails. Repeat the process to install the upper-case face frame.

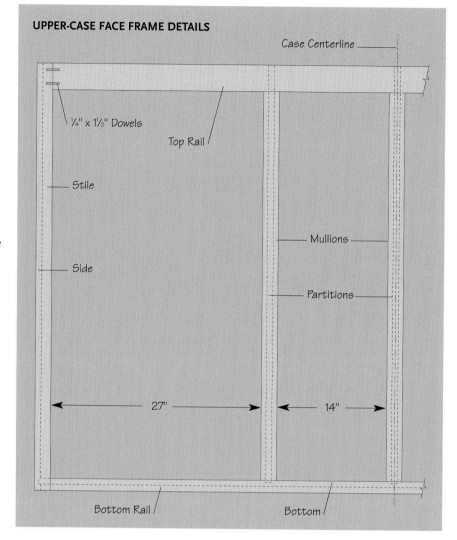

UPPER-CASE FACE FRAME DETAILS

Case Centerline

¼" x 1½" Dowels

Top Rail

Stile

Mullions

Side

Partitions

27"

14"

Bottom Rail

Bottom

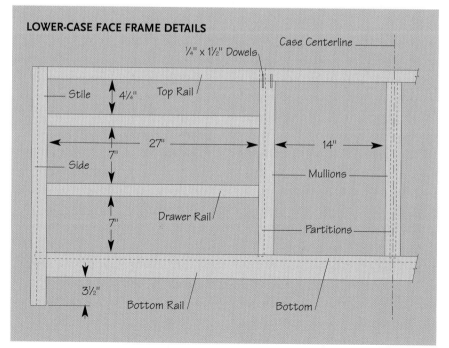

LOWER-CASE FACE FRAME DETAILS

¼" x 1½" Dowels

Case Centerline

Stile

4¼"

Top Rail

27"

14"

7"

Side

Mullions

7"

Drawer Rail

Partitions

3½"

Bottom Rail

Bottom

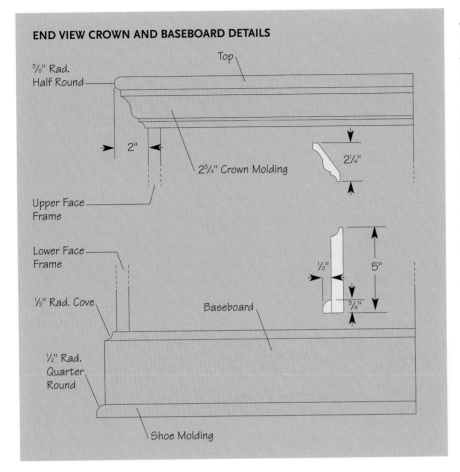

END VIEW CROWN AND BASEBOARD DETAILS

3/8" Rad. Half Round

Top

2"

2¾" Crown Molding

2¼"

Upper Face Frame

Lower Face Frame

½" Rad. Cove

Baseboard

½"

5"

¾"

½" Rad. Quarter Round

Shoe Molding

INSTALLING ACCESSORY PARTS

1. Add blocking to upper case.
Because the bottom of the upper case sits ¾-inch above the bottom edge of the face frame and sides, you need to install blocking to keep the bottom from sagging and also to provide a means of attaching the upper and lower cases. Cut blocks to the dimensions shown in the Materials List; drill and countersink pilot holes; and screw them to the bottom of the case under each partition—use #8 x 1¼-inch flat-head screws.

2. Install crown molding. Use a miter saw to cut crown molding strips to the dimensions in the Materials List, and nail it using 4d finishing nails between the upper-case face frame and sides and the case top. Remem-

ber to apply glue to the mating faces of the miter joints at the molding corners before tacking the joint with 1-inch brads.

3. Install baseboard molding. Rip solid stock to width for baseboard molding. Install a ½-inch-radius cove bit in the router, and use it to shape the top edge of the molding strips. Cut the molding to length with appropriate bevel joints at the front corners; then nail it to the lower case using 4d finishing nails. Again, remember to apply glue to the faces of the bevel joints at the outside corners.

4. Cut and edge-band the shelves. Cut plywood and solid-wood edging to size for the adjustable shelves—see the Materials List. Spread glue on the front edge of the plywood pieces, and

clamp the edging in place. (See "Finishing Edges," page 12.) Check that the shelves fit in their respective openings; then set them aside.

5. Install blocking for drawer slides. Cut blocking for drawer slides from solid wood or plywood. If you do not have material thick enough to provide the full 1¼-inch thickness, you can build up thinner material—for example, ½-inch plus ¾-inch plywood strips. Drill and countersink pilot holes in the blocking material, and then install them to the lower-case sides.

BUILDING THE DOORS

1. Cut the parts. The doors for this project are built with traditional mortise-and-tenon joints and use ¼-inch-thick plywood door panels. Cut the door stiles and rails to the dimensions specified in the Materials List. Follow the instructions in "Building a Frame and Panel Door," pages 22–23 for door construction details and techniques. Note that the doors are sized to provide a 1/16-inch gap between the doors and face frame on all edges.

2. Assemble the doors. Assemble one door at a time, beginning with the bottom-case doors. First apply glue to the mortises in the door stiles; then spread a light coating of glue on the rail mortises. Insert the top and bottom rails into the mortises in one of the stiles; then slide the panel into position. Finally, place the second stile over the exposed tenons on the rails, and apply clamps to pull the joints tight. Compare opposite diagonal measurements to check that the door is square—if necessary, you can easily readjust the position of the clamps to square up the assembly.

FRAME-AND-PANEL DOOR DETAILS

¼" x 1¼" x 1¹⁄₁₆" Mortise

⅜" Tenon Haunch

2"

Top/Bottom Rail

Butt Hinge

¼" Panel

Middle Hinge
(Upper Doors
Only)

¼" x ⅜" Groove

Middle Rail (Upper
Doors Only)

¼" x1" Tenon

Stile

and install them; install the door catches.

It will be much easier to install the cabinet if you temporarily re-move the doors from the case. Set them aside in a safe place until after the final installation.

BUILDING THE DRAWERS

1. Cut the parts. Cut the drawer sides and front and back panels from solid wood as specified in the Materials List. Cut the bottom panels from ¼-inch-thick plywood. Use the table saw with dado blades or the router with a straight bit to cut the rabbets and grooves for drawer joints. (See "Building Drawers," page 28.)

2. Assemble the drawer boxes. Apply glue to the rabbets in drawer sides and also the ends of the drawer front and back panels. Use 4d finish-ing nails to fasten the joints; then check that the box is square before sliding the bottom panel into place. Fasten the bottom to the drawer back using 1-inch brads. Repeat the process for each of the case drawers.

Follow the same procedure for the rest of the doors. The doors for the upper case are different only in that they include a center rail and two pan-els—otherwise the techniques are the same.

3. Check the fit of the doors. Place each door in its opening in the face frame. If the door fits properly, you should be able to fit a ¹⁄₁₆-inch-thick shim between the door and frame on each edge. If the door is too tight, you can adjust the fit by cutting, planing, or sanding the door edges.

4. Install the doors. Mark the loca-tion of hinges on the door edges; then cut the appropriate mortises, and in-stall the hinges. (See Installing "Flush-Fit Doors," pages 25–26.) Place each door in its opening to transfer the hinge locations to the face frame. Once again, support the door by plac-ing ¹⁄₁₆-inch-thick shims between the door and face frame on all edges. Use a sharp knife to mark the face frame to indicate the top and bottom edges of each hinge. Cut the hinge mortises in the frame stiles and mullions; then drill pilot holes and install the doors. Bore pilot holes for the door knobs,

3. Build the drawer faces. Cut the drawer faces for the top drawers from solid wood. The faces for the middle and bottom drawers have a flat-panel configuration. These faces are formed by constructing a solid-wood frame around a panel of ½-inch-thick plywood. (See *Drawer Front Sections*, opposite, and *Large Drawer Face Details*, page 104.) Rip solid wood to a width of 2 inches for the frame material—leave the strips several inches longer than finished dimension to allow you to safely machine their edges. Use dado blades in the table saw to cut a ¼-inch-wide by ⅜-inch-deep groove on the inside edge of the frame stock;

DRAWER DETAILS

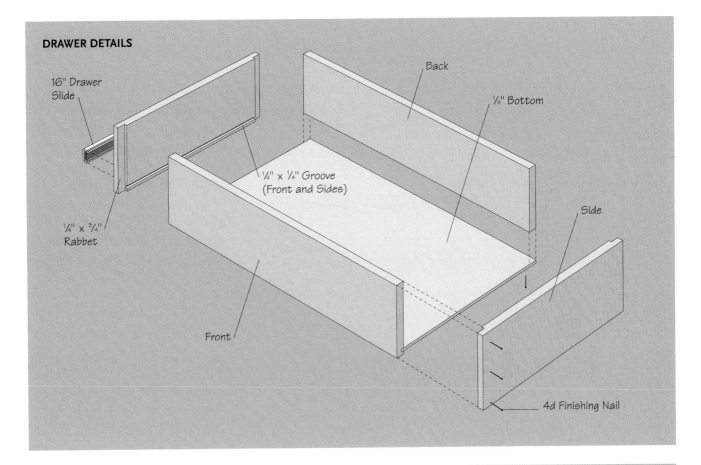

16" Drawer Slide

Back

¼" Bottom

¼" × ¼" Groove (Front and Sides)

¼" × ¾" Rabbet

Side

Front

4d Finishing Nail

then use a miter saw to cut the 45-degree joints for the corners. Use the plate joiner to cut slots for #0 joining plates for the corner joints.

Cut the plywood panels to size; then cut rabbets around the edges with the table saw or router.

To assemble the frames, apply glue to the joining plate slots and also the mating faces of the corner joints. Install the joining plates, and then fit the frame parts together around one of the plywood panels. Apply clamps to pull the joints tight. If the corner angles are cut accurately, you will be able to tell if the assembly is square when the joints are tight. Allow the glue to set for at least one hour before removing the clamps.

4. Mount the drawer faces. Drill and countersink pilot holes in the drawer faces, and then mount the faces to drawers using #8 x 1¼-inch flat-head screws. Note that when mounting the paneled faces, the screws should be driven into the solid-wood frame, not the plywood panel. Drill pilot holes for the drawer pulls, and mount them to the drawers.

5. Install the drawers. Drawer slides have two components—the slide unit mounts to the cabinet, and the drawer rails mount directly to the drawer sides. Study the instructions that are provided with your slides; then install them to the case and drawers; and slide the drawers into position. You should calculate the position of the slides to allow the drawer faces to sit flush with the face frame when the drawers are closed. In most cases, the slides will be provided with slotted holes for initial mounting. These allow you to adjust the position of the

DRAWER FRONT SECTIONS

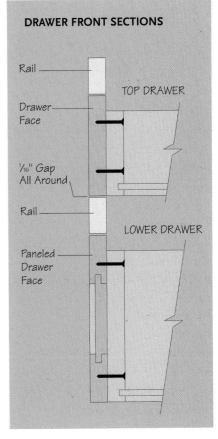

Rail

TOP DRAWER

Drawer Face

¹⁄₁₆" Gap All Around

Rail

LOWER DRAWER

Paneled Drawer Face

LARGE DRAWER FACE DETAILS

No. 0 Joining Plate

¼" x ⅜" Rabbet Around Panel

45° Miter Joint

½" Panel

¼" x ⅜" Groove

end. Fasten the cabinets together by driving screws through the top frame of the lower case into the blocking strips on the bottom of the top cabinet. Fasten the top case to the wall by driving screws through the nailer into wall studs.

3. Reinstall doors and drawers. Slide the drawers into their respective openings, and re-hang the doors. Check the operation of all moving parts. It sometimes happens that a cabinet can be pulled out of alignment during installation—especially if the wall is not perfectly plumb. If you notice that the doors are slightly misaligned, you can loosen some of the screws that hold the cases to the wall, and use small shims to fill those spaces behind the cabinet. If there are any gaps between the cabinet sides and wall surface, you can caulk these joints.

4. Finish the project. Temporarily remove all doors, drawers and hardware from the case to make finishing easier. Set all exposed nailheads below the wood surface, and use a drying wood putty to fill the resulting holes. Slightly mound the filler over each hole to allow for shrinkage during drying. When completely dry, sand the filler smooth. Sand, prime, and paint the cabinet and accessory parts following the guidelines in "Wood Finishing," pages 55 to 72. Finally, reinstall the doors, drawers, and shelves.

drawer in the opening. When you are satisfied with the position and operation of all drawers, install the remaining screws to keep the slides from shifting.

Temporarily remove the drawers from the unit while you install the cabinet against the wall.

INSTALLING THE CABINET

1. Install the lower cabinet. Remove any existing baseboard on the wall where the cabinet is to be located. Use an electronic stud finder to locate the wall studs behind the cabinet; then place a mark to indicate each stud center on the wall, just above the height of the cabinet. Slide the cabinet into position, and check that it is level from side to side and front to back. If necessary, slide tapered shim shingles

under the cabinet to adjust its position. Drill and countersink pilot holes through the nailer, and drive screws (#10 x 3-inch flathead wood screws) into the wall studs to fasten the cabinet in place. Use a sharp utility knife to score the shingles, and then break off the exposed portion of each shim. Cut shoe molding to length with mitered ends at the front corners, and install it using 4d finishing nails, driving the nails into the baseboard, not the flooring material. The shoe molding will cover any gaps between the baseboard and the floor.

2. Install the upper cabinet. Have a helper assist you in lifting the upper cabinet unit and positioning it on top of the lower case. Adjust the cabinet so that the top frame of the lower case extends ¾-inch past the sides on each

7 bedroom

MAXIMIZING STORAGE SPACE WITH SHELVES AND ACCESSORIES

bedroom storage ideas

Clockwise (from right) What could be better than a fireplace and built-in storage in the bedroom? This headboard features open shelves and a hidden storage compartment. Here's an idea taken from kitchen cabinets—a pullout that holds shoes and purses.

Count the storage possibilities in this room: armoire, window-seat drawers, reach-in closet, open shelving, and desk.

When not in use, this Murphy-style unit provides storage and floor space; open it to reveal a pull-down bed.

bedroom storage ideas

The more you look, the more storage you discover. Note the bank of cabinets near the ceiling.

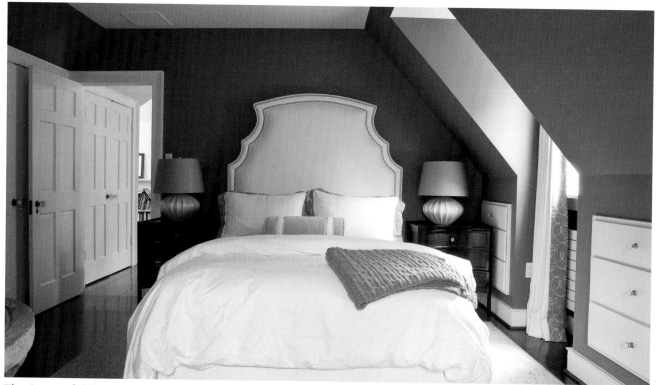

The owner of this attic bedroom installed groups of drawers in the space behind the knee walls.

chest of drawers

THIS CHEST OF DRAWERS is a great example of how you can use modern methods and materials to create a traditional heirloom-quality piece that will serve your family for generations to come. Old-time cabinetmakers used hand tools, great skill, and patience to plane boards by hand and cut complex joints. You'll still need the patience, but plywood, power tools, modern fasteners, and glue simplify joinery and eliminate the need for great skill.

In this project, the plywood is used for the big, flat expanses—the sides and back. Select a hardwood plywood, such as cherry, walnut, or oak; then make the rest of the project from solid hardwood to match.

CHEST OF DRAWERS MATERIALS LIST

Difficulty Level: DIFFICULT

Qty	Part	Dimensions
Base		
1	Solid-wood base front	¾" x 3½" x 31"
1	Solid-wood base back	¾" x 3½" x 29½"
2	Solid-wood base sides	¾" x 3½" x 17½"
4	Solid-wood base cleats	1¼" x 1¼" x 3½"
1	Solid-wood apron front	¾" x 2½" x 31½"
2	Solid-wood apron sides	¾" x 2½" x 18½"
1	Solid-wood apron back	¾" x 2½" x 26½"
Carcase		
2	Plywood side panels	¾" x 17" x 40½"
1	Plywood back panel	¼" x 29¼" x 40½"
12	Drawer supports front & back	¾" x 3½" x 29¼"
12	Drawer supports sides	¾" x 3½" x 9¾"
6	Runners	¼" x ¾" x 16¾"
1	Apron cleat front	¾" x 3½" x 28½"
1	Apron cleat back	¾" x 3½" x 22½"
2	Apron cleat sides	¾" x 3⅛" x 13¼"
2	Face frame stiles	¾" x 1½" x 40½"
7	Face frame rails	¾" x 1½" x 27"

Qty	Part	Dimensions
4	Corner blocks	¾" x 3½" x 3½"
1	Top panel	¾" x 18½" x 31½"
Drawers		
6	Drawer false fronts	¾" x 5¾" x 28"
12	Drawer sides	¾" x 4½" x 16½"
6	Drawer fronts	¾" x 4½" x 25¾"
6	Drawer backs	¾" x 4" x 25¾"
6	Plywood drawer bottoms	¼" x 16¾" x 25¾"
12	Runner tracks	¼" x ¾" x 16½"
Hardware		
	#6 x 1¾" Flathead wood screws	
48	¼" x 1¼" Wood dowel pins	
	#6 x ¾" Flathead wood screws	
	⅞" Brads	
	2½" Wood screws	
	6d Finishing nails	
	#6 x 1¼" Flathead wood screws	
12	Drawer pulls	

OVERALL VIEW

BASE AND APRON CONSTRUCTION

Apron Side   18½"   Apron Back

Base Cleats

Base Side

4"

Apron Front   23"

1¾" Radius Curve

11"

3¼"   1¾" Radius Curve

Base Front

SIDE PANEL DETAILS

¼" x ⅜" Rabbet   6½"

6½"

¾" x ⅜" Dadoes   6½"

40½"   6½"

6½"

6½"

1½"

17"

DRAWER SUPPORT CONSTRUCTION

Drawer Support

14¼"

Apron Cleats

#6 x ¾" Flathead Wood Screws

Runner

⅜"

Apron Cleat

Countersunk #8 x 2½" Flathead Wood Screw

BUILDING THE BASE

1. Cut the parts. Cut the base front, back, sides, and base cleats to the dimensions in the Materials List. Use a band saw or saber saw to make the decorative cuts shown in *Base and Apron Construction.*

2. Assemble the base. Using 1¾-inch flathead wood screws, glue and screw two base cleats to the back of the base and one cleat flush with the front end of each side piece. Apply glue to the mating sides of the rear cleats; then assemble the sides to the back. Next, apply glue to the mating sides of the front cleats, and assemble the front to the sides. Clamp the base together; then measure across diagonals to make sure the base is square. Secure the joints using screws through the cleats into the base.

3. Make and attach the apron. Cut the apron front to the dimensions in the Materials List with a 45-degree miter on each end. Clamp the apron front in place so that it creates a ¼-inch overhang along the front. Next, cut the two mitered side pieces a bit

longer than the given dimensions. Position them in place, and mark the square back cuts in place. Clamp the side pieces in place. Cut the back piece to fit.

Glue and clamp the entire apron assembly onto the base. When the glue dries, use a router equipped with a ¾-inch half-round bit to rout the front and side edges of the apron. (See "Router, Bits, and Accessories," page 43, for details on routing options.)

BUILDING THE CARCASE

1. Cut the side and back panels. Cut the sides and back panels to the dimensions in the Materials List. Rabbet and dado the side panels as shown in *Side Panel Details.* Note that the drawing shows one side panel. Don't forget to make the other panel as a mirror image. (See "Dadoes, Grooves, and Rabbets," page 17.)

2. Build the drawer supports. Cut the pieces for the drawer supports, drawer runners, and apron cleats to the dimensions in the Materials List. Note that only the bottom drawer support will be attached to the apron cleats. Assemble the supports with glue and dowels as shown in *Drawer Support Construction* on page 111. Clamp the supports together, measuring the diagonals to ensure that the assembly is square. Using ¾-inch flathead wood screws, attach the runner centered across the front and rear pieces.

3. Assemble the carcase. Apply glue to the dadoes in the side panels, and slide the drawer supports in place so that they are flush with the front edges of the side panels. Attach the back panel to the assembly using glue and ⅞-inch brads. Glue and clamp the apron cleats in place beneath the bottom drawer support.

4. Attach the carcase to the apron. Place the carcase on the apron, making sure they are flush at the back. Make sure the apron extends past the carcase by ¾-inch all around the front and sides. Predrill countersunk holes for 2½-inch flathead wood screws through the bottom drawer supports and apron cleats into the apron. Remove the carcase. Apply glue to the top of the apron; then screw the carcase to the apron.

5. Build and install the face frame. Cut the stiles and rails. Join the rails to the stiles using dowels. (See "Reinforcing Joints With Dowels," page 15.) Be sure that the top of each rail is 6½ inches from the top of the rail below so that the rail tops will be flush to the top of the drawer supports. Attach the face frame to the carcase using glue and 6d finishing nails.

DRAWER CONSTRUCTION

Space runner tracks ⅞" apart.

Center runner tracks on underside of bottom.

Back

Bottom

Side

¾" x ¼" Rabbets

False Front

Front

¼" x ¼" Dado Located ¼" from Bottom

1"

4½"

½"

6. Build the top. Cut boards to be edge-glued to form the top panel. Cut the boards so the top will be slightly larger than the dimensions given in the Materials List. Glue and clamp the boards together. Cut the glued panel to its finished dimensions. Use a ¾-inch half-round bit to rout the front and side edges of the top trim to match the apron.

7. Install the corner blocks. Predrill and countersink each corner block for two 1¼-inch wood screws. Position so as not to penetrate the exterior of the carcase. Glue and screw the blocks into the top corners of the carcase, flush with the top of the carcase. As you predrill the screw holes in the corner blocks for the chest top, wiggle the bit to elongate the hole from front to back. This allows room for wood movement.

8. Attach the top. Lay the top in place, flush with the back edge of the carcase and with an equal overhang at front and sides. Secure the top using 1¼-inch screws driven up through the center of each corner block.

BUILDING THE DRAWERS

1. Cut the drawer parts. Cut the drawer sides, fronts, and backs. Dado the sides and groove the front and sides as shown in *Drawer Construction.*

2. Build the drawers. Follow directions in "Building Drawers," page 28, to build the six drawers in this project using the dimensions in the Materials List.

3. Make the false drawer fronts. Cut the false drawer fronts. Round over the outside edges of the false fronts with your router and a ⅜-inch roundover bit set to round the edges slightly. Attach the drawer front using four 1¼-inch screws. Attach the drawer pulls using screws provided.

4. Attach the runner tracks. Apply glue to the runner tracks, and attach them to the plywood drawer bottoms, clamping them in place. After the glue has dried, test the drawers in the carcase. If the drawers don't slide smoothly, use a block plane or sandpaper on the runners or runner tracks until the drawers slide easily.

three-drawer dresser

IT'S A COMMON DILEMMA to feel that you don't have adequate storage space for your clothes, especially if you're one of those who find it easy to buy new things and hard to toss old ones. One way to address the storage shortage might be to build our three-drawer dresser. This piece offers many advantages for efficient bedroom use. Its drawers are wide and deep, providing ample room for items small and delicate, or large and bulky; and unlike many commercial dressers, the drawers are mounted on full-extension slides so that you can easily find items hidden in the back corners. The overall height of the piece is just 30¾ inches, giving you the option of using the top to display pictures or to hold toiletries—or you could mount a mirror, painting, or TV over the dresser, using the wall space to maximum advantage.

From a construction viewpoint, this dresser is not a difficult piece to build. The side panels, back and base cap are all made of hardwood plywood—only the case top requires glue-up from solid wood. The face frame joinery utilizes dowels, and other glue joints can be reinforced with finishing nails, so you can get by with a minimum of clamps for assembly.

For a classic look, select hardwood lumber and matching plywood that complements your bedroom decor or, for a lower cost project, you could follow a less-formal direction and build the dresser entirely from paint-grade materials. Regardless of the material you choose for the exposed parts, you can always use a less expensive secondary wood, such as poplar, for the interior parts of the dresser.

THREE-DRAWER DRESSER MATERIALS LIST

Difficulty Level: CHALLENGING

Qty	Part	Dimensions	Qty	Part	Dimensions
Carcase			1	Solid-wood base front	¾" x 4" x 40"
2	Hardwood plywood sides	¾" x 19¼" x 25¼"	2	Solid-wood base sides	¾" x 4" x 20"
1	Top, glued-up solid-wood panel	¾" x 20¾" x 41½"	1	Solid-wood base back	¾" x 4" x 38½"
1	Hardwood plywood back	¼" x 39½" x 25¼"	***Drawer***		
6	Blocking for slides	¾" x 4" x 19"	1	Solid-wood drawer face	¾" x 5¾" x 37¾"
	solid wood or plywood		2	Solid-wood drawer faces	¾" x 7¾" x 37¾"
2	Solid-wood frames	¾" x 39" x 19"	2	Solid-wood drawer sides	¾" x 4½" x 18"
4	Front and back	¾" x 3½" x 39"	4	Solid-wood drawer sides	¾" x 6½" x 18"
6	Frame rails	¾" x 3½" x 12"	1	Solid-wood drawer front	¾" x 4½" x 35"
Face Frame			2	Solid-wood drawer fronts	¾" x 6½" x 35"
2	Solid-wood stiles	¾" x 1½" x 25¼"	1	Solid-wood drawer back	¾" x 4" x 35"
2	Solid-wood rails	¾" x 1¾" x 37"	2	Solid-wood drawer backs	¾" x 6" x 35"
2	Solid-wood rails	¾" x 1⅜" x 37"	3	Plywood drawer bottoms	¼" x 17½" x 35"
Base			***Hardware and Miscellaneous Supplies***		
1	Base cap panel, plywood with	¾" x 41¼" x 20⅝"	3 pair 18" full-extension side-mount drawer slides, ½" width		
	solid wood edging		16 ¼" dia. x 1½" wood dowels		
1	Plywood panel before edging	¾" x 39¾" x 19⅞"	6 Drawer knobs		
1	Solid-wood edging strip	¾" x ¾" x 41¼"	4d finishing nails		
2	Solid-wood edging strips	¾" x ¾" x 20⅝"	1" brads		
			#8 x 1¼" flathead wood screws		

BUILDING THE BASE

1. Cut base parts. Rip stock to width for the base front, sides, and back; then use a miter saw to cut the parts to length with 45-degree bevel cuts for the front joints and square cuts for the back joints as shown in *Base Assembly*. Use a saber saw or band saw to make the decorative cuts in the front and sides. Remember to keep the saw kerf on the waste side of the layout lines when cutting. Smooth the cut surfaces with a plane or sandpaper to remove the saw marks.

2. Assemble the base. Apply glue to the joint surfaces, and assemble the base. Drill ¹⁄₁₆-inch-diameter pilot holes; then use 4d finishing nails to pin the joints together. Compare opposite diagonal measurements to check that the assembly is square; then set it aside to allow the glue to cure.

OVERALL VIEW

Screw top panel to upper frame.

¼" x 1½" Dowel

Back

Elongated Screw Holes

¼" x ½" Rabbet for Back

¼" Rabbet for Frame

#8 x 1¼" Screws

Drawer Blocking

Drawer Slide

5"

7"

7"

4¾"

4¾"

1⅜"

1" Brad

Side

Face Frame Rail

Lower Frame

Face Frame Stile

BASE ASSEMBLY

Base Top

Base Top Trim

Base Back

3¼"

Base Front

Miter Front Corners

1⅜"

Base Side

TOP AND BASE TRIM DETAIL

⅟₁₆" Reveal

¾" Solid Wood

TOP DETAIL (Assemble panel from narrow boards.)

¾" Overhang (Front and Sides)

¾"

4d Finishing Nail

¾" Plywood

⅝"

Wooden Trim with ½" Ogee

BASE TRIM DETAIL

3. Build the base cap. Cut the plywood panel and edging strips for the base cap to the sizes specified in the Materials List. Use a miter saw to cut the 45-degree miter cuts for the joints at the front corners of the edging. Spread glue on the panel edges, and apply the edging strips using masking tape as clamps. (See "Finishing Edges," page 12.)

Use a ½-inch ogee bit in the router to shape the solid edge of the base cap panel. Drill and countersink pilot holes for screws; then fasten the base cap panel to the base, allowing it to overhang ⅝ inch on the two sides and front.

BUILDING THE CARCASE
1. Cut the side and back panels.
Cut the back and side panels to the sizes shown in the Materials List. Use a router and straight bit or dado blades in the table saw to cut the rabbets in the side panels.

2. Build the top and bottom frames. Cut frame parts to size; then use a doweling jig to bore the dowel holes as shown in the *Overall View*. Apply glue to the dowel holes; insert the dowels; and assemble the frames. Use clamps to pull the joints tight, and then compare opposite diagonal measurements to make sure that the frames are square before setting them aside. After you remove the clamps, drill and countersink pilot holes in the frames for attaching the case top and base. Elongate the holes as shown in the drawings by either wiggling the drill bit or boring two holes side-by-side and removing the waste between them with a chisel. This will allow the parts to expand and contract with seasonal variations in humidity without causing cracks.

3. Assemble the carcase. Apply glue to the rabbets in the side panels, and join the sides to the top and bottom frames. Use clamps to pull the joints

tight. If you do not have adequate clamps, you can use 4d finishing nails to pin the joints together—first drill a ⅟₁₆-inch-diameter pilot hole for each nail. Install the back panel to the case, fastening it by nailing with 1-inch brads.

4. Build and install the face frame. Cut face frame parts to finished dimension; then use a doweling jig to bore dowel holes in the stiles and rails. (See "Reinforcing Joints with Dowels," page 15.) Apply glue to the holes and dowels, and assemble the face frame, pulling the joints tight with bar clamps. Check that the assembly is square before setting it aside for the glue to cure.

Apply glue to the front edges of the carcase, and install the face frame. If you do not have enough clamps to pull the joints tight while the glue sets, you can drill pilot holes and use 4d finishing nails to fasten the face frame to the sides and top and bottom frames.

SECTION THROUGH DRAWER AND FACE FRAME

Top Rail

Side

Drawer Front

Drawer Face

Bottom

Middle Rail

Back

#8 x 1¼" Screw

30° Bevel around Drawer Faces

¼" x ¼" Groove (Sides and Front)

Middle Rail

4d Finishing Nail

¼" x ¾" Rabbet

DRAWER TOP VIEW

5. Install drawer slide blocking. Cut blocking to size; then drill and countersink pilot holes; and fasten the blocking to the case sides as shown in the *Overall View*. Use #8 x 1¼-inch flathead screws.

6. Assemble the base to the carcase. Place the carcase on the base, adjusting its position so that the base cap extends beyond the sides and face by ⅝-inch. Use #8 x 1¼-inch flathead screws to fasten the parts, using the pilot holes previously drilled in the bottom frame.

7. Build and install the top panel. Cut boards to be edge-glued for the top panel. Select lumber for similar color and grain pattern to create a uniform appearance. Cut the boards so

that the panel will be slightly larger than finished dimension. Apply glue to the edge joints, and clamp the boards together. (See "Edge-Gluing Stock," page 14.) Trim the assembled panel to finished dimension, and then use a ½-inch-radius roundover/beading bit to shape the top edge.

Place the top on the case, adjusting its position so that it overhangs the sides and front by ¾-inch. Fasten the top to the case using #8 x 1¼-inch flathead screws, driven through the pilot holes in the top frame. Do not use any glue on these joints.

BUILDING THE DRAWERS

1. Cut the drawer parts. Cut the drawer faces, front, back, side, and bottom panels to finished size as shown in the Materials List. Cut rabbets in the sides, and groove the sides and front panels as shown in the plans. (See "Building Drawers," page 28.) Install a 30-degree chamfer bit in the router to shape the edge profile on the drawer faces.

2. Assemble the drawers. Apply glue to the rabbets in drawer sides; then assemble the drawer boxes using 4d finishing nails to pin the joints. Slide the bottom panels into the grooves in sides and fronts, and fasten them to the bottom edge of the backs using 1-inch brads. Drill and countersink pilot holes in the drawer fronts; then use clamps to temporarily hold the faces on the drawer boxes. Check that the drawer faces overhang the drawer boxes as shown in the plans; then drive #8 x 1¼-inch flathead screws to fasten them in place.

Bore pilot holes for the knobs through the faces and drawer fronts, and mount the knobs. If the mounting

screws are too short, you can counterbore the pilot holes on the inside of the drawer box.

3. Attach the drawer slides. Follow the manufacturer's instructions to mount the drawer slides on the drawer boxes and also on the case sides. Use the slotted holes for initial mounting so that you can adjust the height of the slides as required. Install the drawers to the case, and check that they operate properly. Make any necessary adjustments, and then install the remaining screws.

FINISHING THE DRESSER

1. Fill all nailholes. Carefully set all nailheads below the wood surface; then fill the holes with wood filler that matches the case. Slightly mound the filler over each hole because fillers have a tendency to shrink slightly as they dry. Allow the filler to dry completely before proceeding.

2. Sand all parts. Remove the drawers from the case, and temporarily remove the knobs and drawer slides. Carefully sand all exposed parts, starting with 120-grit sandpaper, moving through finer abrasives to end at 220 grit. Remember to carefully remove all sanding dust when switching to a finer grit paper. (See "Preparing Wood," page 57.)

3. Apply a stain (if desired) and clear finish of your choice. (See "Wood Finishing," pages 55 to 72.) When the final coat is completely dry, replace the hardware, and reinstall the drawers in the dresser.

bunk beds

KIDS LOVE BUNK BEDS, and so should you, especially if your children share a small bedroom. This project really maximizes floor space; not only do the bunk beds take up less room than a pair of conventional twin beds, they also provide two dressers' worth of built-in drawers! You can install the bottom bunk as shown here, or you can turn it so that the length of both beds are along the same wall in conventional bunk bed fashion.

These beds will be permanently installed in a corner of the room, so you must prepare the room prior to installation. First, you'll need to remove any trim or molding so that the headboards and sideboards can be fastened onto the walls. (See "Removing Trim," page 37.) Once you've located and marked the studs, scribe a level line on the walls 16 inches above the floor for the sideboard and headboard of the lower bed, and 56¼ inches above the floor for the upper bed.

These beds are designed to work with 4 x 39 x 75-inch foam mattresses. If you intend to use the beds with thicker mattresses, make the upper bunk rail supports longer so that the top of the rails is at least 5 inches above the mattress.

BUNK BEDS MATERIALS LIST

Difficulty Level: DIFFICULT

Qty	Part	Dimensions	Qty	Part	Dimensions
Cabinet			**Ladder and guardrails**		
2	Plywood side panels	¾" x 17¾" x 49"	2	Solid-wood sides	1½" x 3½" x 56"
2	Plywood top & bottom panel	¾" x 17½" x 39¾"	8	Solid-wood steps/nailers	1½" x 2½" x 16"
1	Plywood back panel	¼" x 39¾" x 49"	1	Solid-wood foot guardrail	¾" x 3½" x 30"
2	Solid-wood stiles	¾" x 2" x 49"	1	Solid-wood side guardrail	¾" x 3½" x 77¾"
4	Solid-wood rails	¾" x 2" x 36½"	9	Solid-wood supports	1½" x 1½" x 8"
1	Solid-wood bottom rail	¾" x 3½" x 36½"			
8	Solid-wood guide hangers	1¼" x 1½" x 17½"	**Cabinet drawers** (overall dimensions:		
			1 at 18¼" x 16½" x 35½"; 3 at 5¾" x 16½" x 35½")		
Lower bunk			1	Solid-wood false front	¾" x 19½" x 37¼"
2	Plywood headboard/footboard	¾" x 15¾" x 39¾"	1	Plywood front panel	¾" x 18¼" x 35"
1	Plywood sideboard	¾" x 15¾" x 75"	1	Plywood rear panel	¾" x 17½" x 35"
1	Plywood long support	¾" x 12" x 75"	2	Plywood side panels	¾" x 18¼" x 16½"
6	Plywood platform supports	¾" x 12" x 38⅝"	3	Solid-wood false fronts	¾" x 7" x 37¼"
2	Screen molding	¼" x ¾" x 39¾"	3	Plywood front panels	½" x 5¾" x 35"
1	Screen molding	¼" x ¾" x 75"	3	Plywood rear panels	½" x 5" x 35"
2	Solid-wood long stiles	¾" x 1½" x 16"	6	Plywood side panels	½" x 5¾" x 16½"
2	Solid-wood short stiles	¾" x 1½" x 7"	4	Plywood bottom panels	⅜" x 16¼" x 35"
1	Solid-wood rail	¾" x 3½" x 73½"			
1	Solid-wood rail	¾" x 5½" x 73½"	**Hardware**		
6	Plywood cleats	¾" x 1½" x 23½"		4d Finishing nails	
1	Plywood mattress platform	½" x 39" x 75"		⅞" Brads	
				¼" x 1¼" Dowels	
Upper bunk				1¾" Drywall screws	
1	Solid-wood headboard	¾" x 7¼" x 39¾"	4 sets	16" Side-mounted metal drawer slides	
1	Solid-wood inner sideboard	¾" x 7¼" x 93½"		#10 x 1¼" Flathead wood screws	
2	Solid-wood headers	1½" x 3½" x 93½"		#10 x 3½" Flathead wood screws	
5	Solid-wood joists	1½" x 3½" x 36"		1¼" Drywall screws	
1	Plywood backerboard	¼" x 39" x 93½"	3 sets	28" Side-mounted metal drawer slides	
1	Solid-wood outer sideboard	¾" x 7¼" x 95"		1½" Wood screws	
1	Solid-wood footboard	¾" x 7¼" x 40½"		3" Galvanized deck screws	
1	Plywood mattress platform	½" x 39" x 93½"		#6 x 2½" Flathead wood screws	
			64	⅜" Wood plugs	
Lower-bunk drawers (overall dimensions: 6½" x 22½" x 30")				#8 x 2" Flathead wood screws	
3	Solid-wood false fronts	¾" x 7¾" x 24¼"	11	Drawer pulls	
3	Plywood front panels	½" x 6½" x 22"			
3	Plywood rear panels	½" x 5¾" x 22"			
6	Plywood side panels	½" x 6½" x 30"			
3	Plywood bottom panels	⅜" x 22" x 29¾"			

BUILDING THE CABINET

1. Cut the parts. Cut the sides, top, bottom, and back panel to the dimensions in the Materials List. Dado and rabbet the side panels as shown in *Cabinet Construction*. Also, make a ¼-inch-wide by ⅜-inch-deep rabbet along the inside back edge of each side panel. These rabbets will house the back panel. (See "Dadoes, Rabbets, and Grooves," page 17.)

2. Assemble the cabinet. Apply glue to the rabbets and dadoes and the ends of the top and bottom. Then secure the panels using 4d finishing nails. Apply glue to the side-panel rabbets and to the rear edges of the horizontal panels, and nail the back panel in place using ⅞-inch brads.

3. Build the face frame. Cut the stiles and rails to the dimensions in the Materials List. Use a doweling jig to drill ¼-inch dowel holes. (See "Reinforcing Joints with Dowels," page 15.) Apply glue to dowels, and insert them into the holes in the stiles and the rails. Pull the frame together using bar or pipe clamps. Square up the frame, and let it stand until the glue sets.

4. Attach the face frame. Apply glue to the front edges of the cabinet. Then nail the face frame in place using 4d finishing nails every 12 inches.

CABINET CONSTRUCTION

- Stile
- ¼" Dowels
- Top Panel
- ¾" x ⅜" Rabbet
- ⅜" x ¼" Rabbet Along Back Edge of Sides
- 36½"
- 6¼"
- 6¼"
- 6¼"
- 18¾"
- Rail
- Bottom Rail
- Drawer Guides
- Guide Hangers
- Bottom Panel
- Back Panel
- Side Panel

5. Attach the guide hangers and drawer guides. Draw layout lines on the inside of the cabinet. Make the lines flush to the tops of the rails, and square to the front of the cabinet.

From ¾ dimension lumber, cut the guide hangers to the dimensions in the Materials List. Align the tops of the hangers to the lines, and fasten them using glue and 1¾-inch drywall screws. Follow the manufacturer's directions and use the screws furnished to attach the guide portion of the 16-inch-long drawer slide hardware.

119

BUILDING THE LOWER BUNK FRAME

1. Cut and assemble the parts. Cut the lower bunk headboard, footboard, sideboard, supports, and screen molding to the dimensions in the Materials List. Rabbet and dado the long support as shown in *Lower Bunk Construction*.

Attach screen molding to the top edges of the headboard, footboard, and sideboard using glue and ⁷⁄₈-inch brads.

Apply glue to one broad side of four of the platform supports, and sandwich them together to make two double-thick supports. Reinforce this joint using eight 1¼-inch flathead wood screws as shown in *Lower Bunk Construction*.

2. Install the headboard and sideboard. Set the headboard snugly into the corner. Level the panel with shims as necessary before attaching it to the wall using two 3½-inch flathead wood screws into each stud. Butt the sideboard against the headboard, and check for level. Make any necessary adjustments before attaching it using 3½-inch screws.

3. Install the footboard. Apply glue to the foot end of the sideboard, and attach the footboard to it using four 4d finishing nails. Use a framing square to keep the footboard perpendicular to the wall as you nail; then let it stand until the glue sets.

4. Install the supports. Apply glue to the two dadoes and the two rabbets in the long support, and insert the doubled platform supports in the dadoes and the single platform supports in the rabbets, securing each to the long support using 1¼-inch drywall screws.

LOWER BUNK CONSTRUCTION

Mattress Platform

Headboard

Screen Molding

Long Support

Sideboard

Drawer Guides

1½" × ⅜" Dado

¾" × ⅜" Rabbet

Rail

Platform Supports

#10 × 1¼" Screws

Platform Supports

23½"

23½"

Short Stiles

Footboard

Cleat

Long Stile

¼" Dowels

Apply glue to the wall side of the long support; press the subassembly in place against the sideboard; and secure it using nine 1¼-inch drywall screws. Glue and screw the two single supports to the inside of the headboard and footboard. Attach the guide portion of the 28-inch-long drawer-slide hardware.

INSTALLING THE LOWER BUNK FACE FRAME & PLATFORM

1. Cut the parts. Cut the stiles, rails, plywood cleats, and platform to the dimensions in the Materials List.

2. Assemble the face frame. Using a doweling jig, drill dowel holes in the stiles and rails. Insert dowels into the holes; apply glue; and draw the pieces together with bar or pipe clamps. Check that the face frame is square, and let the frame stand until the glue sets. (See "Reinforcing Joints with Dowels," page 15.)

3. Attach the face frame and platform. Apply glue to the ends of the headboard, footboard, and the platform supports, and attach the face frame using four 4d finishing nails,

tacking them in at first in case you need to make an adjustment. Position each plywood cleat between the platform supports and flush with their top or bottom edges. Then glue and screw the cleats to the inside of the rails, using four 1¼-inch screws for each connection.

Apply glue to the top edges of all platform supports and top cleats, and lay the platform atop the supports. Weigh down the platform with some books or tools until the glue dries.

UPPER BUNK CONSTRUCTION (See following page for instructions.)

Mattress Platform

Header

Headboard

Inner Sideboard

Joist

21½"

21½"

21½"

21½"

Footboard

Backerboard

Outer Sideboard

BUILDING THE UPPER BUNK

1. Cut the parts. Cut the headboard and inner sideboard to the lengths in the Materials List. Cut two headers and five joists from common 2x4s to their listed lengths. Cut the backerboard from ¼-inch plywood.

2. Attach the headboard and sideboard. Align the top edge of the headboard with the 56¼-inch level line, and attach it to the wall using one 3½-inch flathead wood screw into each stud. Align the sideboard along the adjacent wall, and secure it using screws.

3. Assemble the frame. Attach the joists to the header using two 3-inch deck screws or 16d nails at each joint, spacing the joists as shown in *Upper Bunk Construction,* page 121. Attach the other header the same way. Measure diagonals to ensure the frame is square.

Attach the backerboard onto one face of the frame using glue and 4d finishing nails every 12 inches.

4. Install the frame. Place the cabinet in position. With the aid of a couple of helpers, position one end of the frame atop the cabinet. Level the frame, and then attach it to the walls using two 3½-inch wood screws driven into each wall stud.

5. Attach the cabinet. Secure the cabinet to the frame using two 1½-inch wood screws driven up through the top panel of the cabinet into the bed frame. Secure the cabinet to the wall using three 3½-inch wood screws driven into a stud.

6. Install the sideboard and footboard. Cut the outer sideboard square at the wall ends and mitered at the outside corner. Apply glue to the end of the headboard and outside header, and attach the sideboard using 4d finishing nails.

Miter-cut one end of the footboard; then double-check the distance from the mitered end of the outer sideboard to the wall. Cut the other end of the footboard to that finished length. Apply glue to the end of the inner sideboard, the outer face of the joist, and the mitered ends of the footboard and outer sideboard; then attach the footboard using 4d finishing nails.

7. Cut and install the platform. Cut the mattress platform from ½-inch plywood. Apply glue to the top surfaces of the frame; lay the platform on top of the frame; and secure it using 4d finishing nails every 12 inches.

BUILDING & INSTALLING THE LADDER

1. Cut the parts. Cut the ladder sides, steps, and nailers to the dimensions in the Materials List.

2. Mark the step notches. Hold the ladder sides together, face to face, align their ends, and clamp them together using a C-clamp at each end. Starting 8 inches from the bottom ends, use a framing square to lay out seven lines 8 inches apart. Scribe a second guideline 2½ inches beneath the other guidelines.

3. Cut the step notches. Set the circular saw for a 1½-inch cutting depth. Using an angle square as a saw guide, make cuts across the 2x4s just inside each guideline. Then cut away the material between the guidelines by making several more cuts at each location and chiseling out the material.

LADDER CONSTRUCTION

Notch for Nailer

Nailer

2½"

Side

Notches for Steps

Steps

2½" Flathead Wood Screw

8"

8"

Nailer

2½" Drywall Screw

4. Mark and cut the nailer notches. Turn the ladder sides over, and scribe lines across the rear surfaces 2½ inches from each end. Then cut away the material from the lines to the ends the way you did for the step notches.

5. Counterbore and drill the steps and nailers. Use a ⅜-inch bit to counterbore a pair of holes ¾ inch from each end and ¾ inch from the

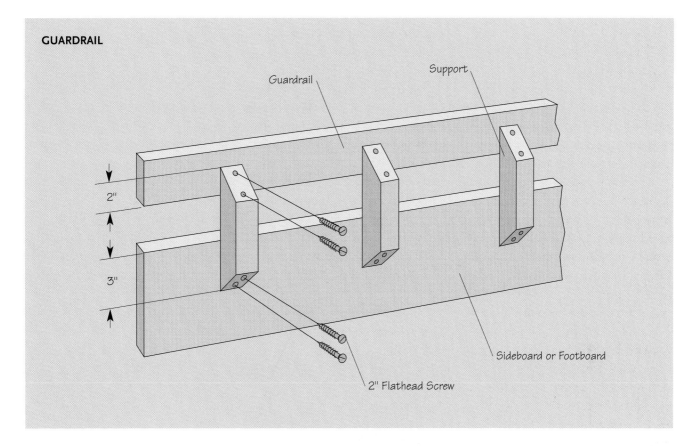

GUARDRAIL

Guardrail

Support

2"

3"

Sideboard or Footboard

2" Flathead Screw

top and bottom of each step and nailer. Counterbore two centered holes into the front of each nailer, 3 inches from each end. Then drill through the center of each hole using an $^{11}/_{64}$-inch bit. (See "Countersink and Counterbore Bits," page 42.)

6. Attach the steps and nailers. Apply glue to the nailer notches. Lay the nailers in place, and secure each using two 2$^1/_2$-inch flathead wood screws. Attach each step to the step notches using two 2$^1/_2$-inch screws, and glue in each notch.

7. Install the ladder. Center the ladder against the side of the cabinet, and attach it with four 2$^1/_2$-inch screws. Plug all the counterbored screw holes with glued wood plugs. When the glue sets, cut the plugs off flush, and sand as required.

BUILDING & INSTALLING THE GUARDRAILS

1. Cut the parts. Cut the foot guardrail, side guardrail, and their nine supports to the dimensions in the Materials List. Cut a 45-degree bevel at each end of the 2x2 supports. Counterbore and drill for the two screws that will be installed at each end of each support.

2. Attach the supports. Attach two supports 6 inches from the ends of the foot guardrail and 1$^1/_2$ inches from the top edge of the rail using two 2-inch screws in each support. Then attach a support to the center of the side rail and two more located on 12-inch centers on each side of the center support.

3. Install the guardrails. Using glue and two 2-inch screws in each support, attach the side guardrail to the sideboard and foot guardrail to the

footboard, keeping a 3-inch space between the guardrails and the sideboard or footboard.

4. Plug the screw holes. Plug the screw holes with $^3/_8$-inch wood plugs and glue. When the glue sets, cut off the plugs, and sand them smooth.

BUILDING THE DRAWERS

Make the cabinet drawers and bed drawers. Make the false drawer fronts from solid wood and the rest of the parts from plywood. (See "Drawer Construction," page 28, for instructions on making $^3/_8$-inch overlay drawers, and see "Edge-Gluing Stock," page 14, for instructions on making a wide, solid-wood false drawer front from narrow boards.)

Apply finish to the project before attaching the drawer pulls and the drawer sections of the side-mounted metal drawer slides. Attach hardware using the screws provided.

toy box

IF YOU HAVE CHILDREN in your household or on your gift list, here's a dandy project you can put together in a few evenings or over a weekend.

In a child's room, this box will hold all sorts of toys and games in its roomy interior. But thanks to its functional and sturdy design, this handsome chest is sure to remain in service long after its owner outgrows the need to store toys. In a teenager's room, it becomes a catchall or a gear locker for sports equipment. In a young adult's first apartment, it's a handy storage unit that doubles as an accent table or coffee table. Line it with aromatic cedar and it becomes a cedar chest worthy of a spot in any adult's home.

You can build this toy box from softwood and softwood plywood and paint it, or make it with hardwood and hard-wood plywood and finish it naturally. Just make sure to use nontoxic finishing materials and special spring-loaded toy-box lid supports that prevent the lid from slamming on little fingers.

You can decorate the front and side plywood panels with wooden numbers or alphabet letters you can make yourself or buy at any home center. You could use a scroll saw to cut out geometric designs or other shapes to attach to the exterior with glue and brads. Or simply paint or stencil decorations onto the finished surface.

To make the unit mobile, install the optional swivel casters, available at any hardware store or home center. Match the casters to the flooring in the room, and follow the manufacturer's directions for installation.

TOY BOX MATERIALS LIST

Difficulty Level: CHALLENGING

Qty	Part	Dimensions	Qty	Part
2	Plywood front and rear panels	¾" x 17¼" x 38½"		*Hardware*
2	Plywood side panels	¾" x 17¼" x 18"		4d Finishing Nails
2	Solid-wood top trim strips	¾" x 1½" x 20"		1 ¼" Brads
2	Solid-wood top trim strips	¾" x 1½" x 40"		1" Brads
2	Solid-wood base trim strips	¾" x 2½" x 20"	1	36" Piano hinge
2	Solid-wood base trim strips	¾" x 2½" x 40"	2	Toy-box lid supports
4	1" Corner guard	¼" x 1" x 1" x 13¼"	2	Chest or trunk handles
2	Cleats	¾" x ¾" x 37"		
2	Cleats	¾" x ¾" x 15½"		
1	Plywood bottom panel	¾" x 16⅞" x 36⅞"		
1	Solid-wood lid	¾" x 21" x 42"		

ASSEMBLING THE FRONT, REAR, AND SIDE PANELS

1. Cut the parts. Cut the front, rear, and side panels to the dimensions in the Materials List.

2. Rabbet the front and rear panels. Rabbet the ends of the front and rear panels as shown in the *Overall View*. (See "Making Rabbets with a Router," page 20.)

3. Assemble the parts. Assemble the side panels to the rabbets in the front and back panels using glue and 4d finishing nails. Square up the box using corner clamps at two diagonal top corners and the two opposite diagonal bottom corners, and let stand until the glue sets. (See "Squaring a Carcase," page 21.)

ATTACHING THE TRIM AND CORNER GUARD

1. Chamfer the trim stock. Use a router with a chamfering bit or a table saw to cut a ½-inch chamfer along one edge of the 1x2 and 1x3 trim stock.

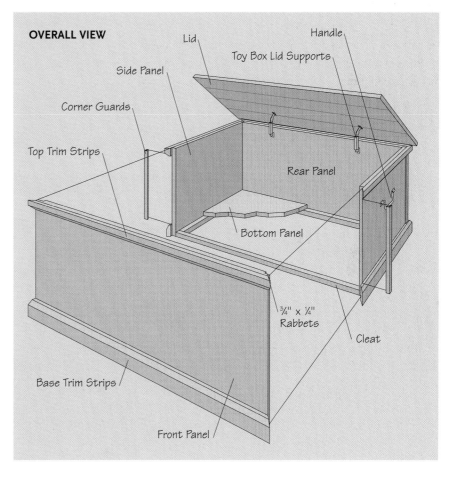

OVERALL VIEW

2. Cut and attach the top trim. Cut the top trim strips from the chamfered 1x2 stock with 45-degree miters at the ends. Then attach the trim, chamfered edge down, using glue and 1¼-inch brads flush with the top edges of the plywood panels.

3. Cut and attach the base trim. Cut the base trim strips from the chamfered 1x3 stock the same as you did the top trim, and install it the same way, but with the chamfered edge up.

4. Cut and attach the corner guard. Cut four strips of corner guard to fit the corners of the box between the top and base trim. Attach the strips using glue and 1-inch brads.

INSTALLING THE PIANO HINGE

Piano Hinge

INSTALLING THE TOY-BOX BOTTOM

1. Cut the parts. Cut the bottom panel and the four cleats to the dimensions in the Materials List.

2. Attach the cleats. Turn the box upside down, and attach the front and rear cleats using glue and 1¼-inch brads flush with the bottom edges of the front and rear panels. Then attach the side cleats flush with the bottom edges of the side panels.

3. Install the bottom panel. Turn the box upright, and run a bead of glue along the top edges of the cleats. Lay the bottom panel atop the cleats, and let it stand until the glue sets. If necessary, put several heavy objects atop the bottom panel so it maintains full contact with the cleats while the glue dries.

BUILDING THE LID; FINISHING AND INSTALLING HARDWARE

1. Glue up the lid. For the lid, you'll need a slab made from nominal 1-inch stock to fit the dimensions in the Materials List. (See "Edge-Gluing Stock," page 14, for instructions on building up large pieces from narrow boards.)

2. Apply finish. Fill any remaining nailholes or flaws with wood filler; let it dry; and sand the lid and box as required. Then apply the finish of your choice, and let dry.

3. Attach the hinge to the box. Center the piano hinge along the top edge of the back of the box as shown in *Installing the Piano Hinge,* and use it as a template to mark for pilot holes.

Drill pilot holes, and mount the hinge to the box using the screws provided.

4. Attach the lid. Position the lid atop the box so it overhangs the front and sides by 1 inch and is flush with the rear edge. Use the hinge to mark for pilot holes in the rear edge of the lid; make the holes; and attach the hinge to the lid.

5. Attach the lid supports. With the lid propped open, attach the supports to the inside of the rear panel and underside of the lid according to the manufacturer's directions and using the screws provided.

6. Attach the handles. Center a chest or trunk handle on each end of the box about 6 inches from the top edge, and mount it using the screws provided.

under-bed drawer

IN THE SEARCH FOR STORAGE around the house, most of us overlook an area with excellent potential: the space under the bed. This project provides under-bed storage that's out of sight but readily accessible. This pullout drawer is designed to fit under your bed, and it's just the place for storing off-season clothing or children's toys. It has an easy-open top that keeps stored items free from dust. And you'll never have to struggle to pull the unit in and out because installed near the drawer's bottom cor-

ners are four wooden wheels (available at most hobby and craft shops or through mail-order suppliers).

Before you begin cutting parts to size, measure the clearance under your bed. The dimensions in the Materials List will yield a drawer that measures 6¼ inches high—a size that will fit under most beds—but you can adjust the width of the drawer's sides and ends if your under-bed clearance demands a shallower drawer, or a deeper one, if space allows.

UNDER-BED DRAWER MATERIALS LIST

Difficulty Level: EASY

Qty	Part	Dimensions	Qty	Part
2	Plywood sides	¾" x 5¼" x 24"		*Hardware*
2	Plywood front & back	¾" x 5¼" x 23¼"		6d Finishing nails
1	Plywood bottom	⅜" x 23¼" x 23¼"		1" Brads
1	Plywood top	¼" x 22¾" x 22¾"		4d Finishing nails
1	Solid-wood edging blank	¾" x 2⅛" x 50"	1	Wood knob
			4	2" to 4" Wooden wheels with axles

OVERALL VIEW

Top

Rabbet

Edging

Back

Miter

Side

2"

¾" x ⅜" Rabbet

Wheel

2"

⅜" x ⅜" Rabbet

Front

FINISHING THE DRAWER

1. Apply the finish. After sanding, stain and varnish or paint the drawer and top. Paint or stain the wheels before installation.

2. Install the knob. Center the screw hole for the knob, and install the knob.

3. Install the wheels. Drill two axle holes in each side panel 2 inches inside each front and rear corner and at a distance from the bottom edge to provide ¼-inch clearance when wheels are attached. Then insert an axle through each wheel hub, and glue each axle in a hole. Keep glue off the axle where it contacts the wheel.

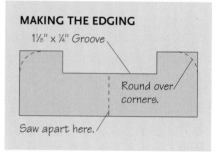

MAKING THE EDGING

1⅛" x ¼" Groove

Round over corners.

Saw apart here.

SECTION THROUGH SIDE

½" x ¼" Rabbet

Edging

Top

Finishing Nail

Side

Wheel

Axle

⅜" x ⅜" Rabbet

Bottom

MAKING THE PARTS

1. Cut the parts. Cut the parts to the dimensions in the Materials List using clear pine for the solid-wood edging.

2. Cut the rabbets. Rabbet the ends of the side panels and the bottoms of the front and back as shown in the *Overall View*. Rabbet the bottoms of the side panels as shown in *Section Through Side*. (See "Dadoes, Grooves, and Rabbets," page 17.)

3. Make the top edging. Groove the edging as shown in *Making the Edging*. Using a router and ⅜-inch or ½-inch roundover bit, round-over two corners of the blank as shown. Then rip the blank in half to form two strips of top edging.

ASSEMBLING THE DRAWER

1. Assemble the box. Fasten the front and back to the end rabbets in the sides using glue and 6d finishing nails. Fasten the bottom to the bottom rabbets in the box using glue and 1-inch brads.

2. Install the top edging. Miter-cut four strips of edging to fit the top edges of the drawer, with the rabbet in each strip facing the inside of the drawer. Attach the strips using glue and 4d finishing nails so that the outside surfaces of the edging and drawer panels are flush.

3. Drill the top. Use a 1-inch spade or Forstner bit to drill a finger hole centered about 2 inches from one edge of the plywood top.

platform bed

A PLATFORM BED makes sense in several ways. The platform provides excellent support of the mattress for comfortable sleeping and is particularly advantageous for those who suffer from back problems. Bedding expenses are cut in half because there's no need for box springs. Moreover, platform beds appeal especially to do-it-yourselfers because they can be built in the home workshop. This bed offers the added advantage of convenient storage.

The bed shown here is sized to accommodate a queen-size mattress. The platform itself folds in half with a piano hinge to make it easier to maneuver in and out of the bedroom.

While the platform bed is a great project in its own right, it's designed to be combined with the bedroom wall unit, making it one of the most functional and attractive bed ensembles you can build.

PLATFORM BED MATERIALS LIST

Difficulty Level: DIFFICULT

Qty	Part	Dimensions
Pedestal		
4	Solid-wood side-frame rails	¾" x 1½" x 74½"
4	Solid-wood side-frame stiles	¾" x 3½" x 9½"
2	Plywood side-frame panels	¾" x 9½" x 20"
4	Solid-wood cleats	¾" x 1½" x 1½"
4	Solid-wood cleats	¾" x 1½" x 3½"
2	Solid-wood supports	1½" x 3½" x 48½"
2	Solid-wood supports	1½" x 1½" x 48½"
2	Plywood headboards/footboards	¾" x 12½" x 50"
4	1" corner guard	¼" x 1" x 1" x 12½"
Platform		
2	Plywood bed slabs	¾" x 40¼" x 61"
2	Solid-wood headboards/ footboards	¾" x 2½" x 62½"
4	Solid-wood sideboards	¾" x 2½" x 40¼"
4	Solid-wood platform stops	¾" x ¾" x 8"

Qty	Part	Dimensions
Drawers (with ⅜" overlay)		
8	Plywood sides	½" x 9" x 24"
4	Plywood fronts	½" x 9" x 22¼"
4	Plywood backs	½" x 8½" x 22¼"
4	Plywood bottoms	⅜" x 22¼" x 23¾"
4	Solid-wood false fronts	¾" x 10¼" x 24½"
Hardware		
28	⁵⁄₁₆" x 1½" Wood dowels	
	1¼" x #6 Flathead wood screws	
	4d Finishing nails	
8	3" Metal corner braces with screws	
	6d Finishing nails	
4	Side-mounted drawer slides	
	1" Brads	
1	48" Piano hinge with screws	
8	Drawer pulls	

OVERALL VIEW

Sideboards

Bed Slabs

Platform Footboard

2x4 Drawer-Guide Support

Drawer Guides

Platform Headboard

Pedestal Footboard

2x2 Drawer-Guide Support

2x4 Platform Support

Cleats

Pedestal Headboard

Metal Corner Braces

Side-Frame Stile

Side-Frame Rail

Side-Frame Panels

Corner Guards

SIDE-FRAME CONSTRUCTION

Rail

Panel

Dowels

Stile

Stile

#6 x 1¼" Flathead Wood Screws

BUILDING THE PEDESTAL

1. Cut the side-frame parts, and drill the cleats. Cut the side-frame rails, stiles, panels, and cleats to the dimensions in the Materials List. Use a #6 countersink bit to drill and countersink two pilot holes in each cleat as shown in *Side-Frame Construction*.

2. Assemble the side frames. Assemble the rails to the stiles and side-frame panels using glue and two dowels at each joint, locating the parts as shown in *Side-Frame Construction*. (See "Reinforcing Joints with Dowels," page 15.)

PEDESTAL CORNER DETAIL

¾" x ½" Rabbet

Headboard or Footboard

Corner Brace

Corner Guard

Rail

Stile

3. Attach the cleats. Apply glue to the back of each cleat, and install each using two #6 x 1¼-inch screws on the inside surface of each side frame, locating them as shown in *Side-Frame Construction*.

4. Cut the remaining pedestal parts. Cut the drawer-guide supports, platform supports, and pedestal headboard and footboard to the dimensions in the Materials List. (Wait until the pedestal is assembled to cut and install the corner guard.)

5. Rabbet the headboard and footboard. Rabbet each end of the inside surface of the headboard and footboard as shown in *Pedestal Corner Detail*. (See "Making Rabbets with a Router," page 20.)

6. Assemble the pedestal. Attach the headboard and footboard to the side frames using glue and 4d finishing nails as shown in *Overall View*. Then install two corner braces at each corner using screws provided as shown in *Pedestal Corner Detail*.

7. Install the supports. Apply glue to the ends of the 2x2 and 2x4 supports and to the tops of the cleats. Lay the supports atop the cleats, and attach them using 6d finishing nails as shown in *Overall View*.

8. Install the drawer slides. Attach the cabinet portions of the drawer slides to the drawer-guide supports according to the manufacturer's directions. (See "Installing Drawer Slide Hardware," page 31.)

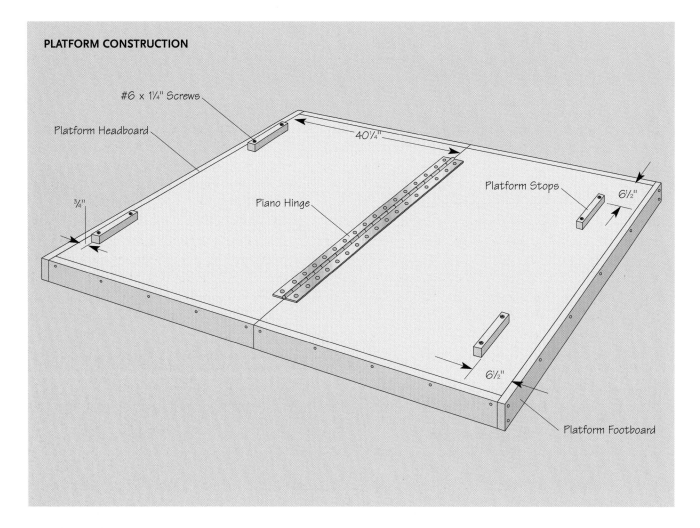

PLATFORM CONSTRUCTION

#6 x 1¼" Screws

Platform Headboard

40¼"

Piano Hinge

Platform Stops

6½"

¾"

6½"

Platform Footboard

9. Attach the corner guard. Measure each corner of the pedestal, and cut a piece of corner guard to fit. Apply glue to the inside surfaces of the corner guard, and attach it using 1-inch brads.

BUILDING THE PLATFORM

1. Cut the parts. Cut the platform bed slabs, headboard, footboard, sideboards, and stops to the dimensions in the Materials List.

2. Build the platform. Apply glue to the side edges of each slab, and attach the sideboards using 4d finishing nails as shown in *Platform Construction*. Apply glue to one end of each slab, and attach the footboard to one and headboard to the other using 4d finishing nails.

3. Attach the stops. Use a #6 countersink bit to drill and countersink pilot holes in each stop. Turn the slabs upside down, and attach each stop with glue and two #6 x 1¼-inch screws, positioning them as shown in *Platform Construction.*

4. Attach the piano hinge. With the slabs positioned together, attach the piano hinge to them with the screws provided.

BUILDING THE DRAWERS AND FINISHING THE BED

The pedestal drawers are designed to overlay the pedestal openings by ⅜ inch on all sides. Make the false fronts from solid wood and the rest of the parts from plywood according to the

dimensions in the Materials List. (See "Drawer Construction," page 29, for instructions on making ⅜-inch overlay drawers, and see "Edge-Gluing Stock," page 14, for instructions on making solid-wood false drawer fronts from narrow boards.)

Fill any remaining nailholes or flaws with wood filler; let dry; and sand all components. Then apply the finish of your choice, and let it dry.

Attach a drawer pull to the false front of each drawer. Then attach the drawer portions of the drawer slides to the drawers according to the manufacturer's directions.

bedroom wall unit

HERE'S AN IDEAL PROJECT for the master bedroom—a modular unit that stands 6 feet tall and spans nearly 11 feet of wall space. Combine this project with the platform bed on page 129, and you'll have the perfect bedroom ensemble. In each bedside cabinet are three roomy drawers and three spacious shelves.

Two large bridge shelves span the head of the bed and join the two cabinets. The lower shelf also features built-in fluorescent lighting.

You can build the project from softwood or hardwood, and then paint it or finish it naturally. Plans call for trimming the cabinets with 1-inch corner guard. This finishing touch conceals plywood edges and provides a pleasing contemporary visual appeal. The softwood version of the corner guard has 1-inch outside and $\frac{3}{4}$-inch inside dimensions. Hardwood corner guard might be as much as $\frac{1}{8}$ inch wider, but will work just as well. Although dimensions are provided in the Materials List, be sure to carefully measure and miter-cut each strip individually.

Holes drilled in cabinet panels and fitted with brass hardware help keep electrical cords out of sight. Because of the narrow diameters of the holes and hardware, it's necessary to remove plugs from lights and other electrical appliances before threading the cords through. You can then replace the plugs with new snap-on or other standard two-prong plugs.

BEDROOM WALL UNIT MATERIALS LIST

Difficulty Level: **DIFFICULT**

Qty	Part	Dimensions	Qty	Part	Dimensions
Face frames			**Top Drawers** (with ⅜" overlay)		
12	Solid-wood rails	¾" x 1½" x 25½"	4	Solid-wood false fronts	¾" x 7¼" x 12¾"
2	Solid-wood bottom rails	¾" x 3½" x 25½"	4	Plywood fronts	½" x 5½" x 11"
2	Solid-wood stiles	¾" x 1½" x 6½"	4	Plywood backs	½" x 4⅞" x 11"
4	Solid-wood stiles	¾" x 1½" x 22½"	8	Plywood sides	½" x 5½" x 16"
4	Solid-wood stiles	¾" x 1½" x 48"	4	Plywood bottom panels	⅜" x 11" x 15¾"
Carcases			**Bottom Drawers** (with ⅜" overlay)		
2	Plywood cabinet tops	¾" x 11½" x 29½"	2	Solid-wood false fronts	¾" x 10¼" x 26¼"
2	Plywood nightstand tops	¾" x 17¼" x 28½"	2	Plywood fronts	½" x 8½" x 24½"
6	Plywood cabinet shelves	¾" x 10⅛" x 28⅜"	2	Plywood backs	½" x 7⅞" x 24½"
2	Solid-wood nightstand edging	½" x ¾" x 28½"	4	Plywood sides	½" x 8½" x 16"
2	Solid-wood top panel edging	½" x ¾" x 29½"	2	Plywood bottom panels	⅜" x 24½" x 15¾"
4	Plywood side panels	¾" x 18" x 72"	**Hardware and Electrical Items**		
2	Plywood back panels	¼" x 29½" x 71¾"		2½" Drywall screws	
12	Solid-wood shelf cleats	½" x ¾" x 10¼"		1" Brads	
4	Solid-wood face frame stops	½" x ¾" x 22½"		1" x #6 Flathead wood screws	
4	Solid-wood back cleats	¾" x 1½" x 28½"		⅞" Brads	
2	Solid-wood bottom back cleats	¾" x 3½" x 28½" "		4d Finishing nails	
4	Rear corner guard	¼" x 1" x 1" x 72½"		1" Brads	
4	Top horizontal corner guard	¼" x 1" x 1" x 12½"	6	Drawer pulls	
4	Top vertical corner guard	¼" x 1" x 1" x 49¾"	6	17" Bottom-mount drawer slides	
4	Nightstand corner guard	¼" x 1" x 1" x 7"		18", 15-watt Under-cabinet fluorescent lamps	
4	Bottom vertical corner guard	¼" x 1" x 1" x 23¾"		¼" x 1½" Brass roundhead machine screws	
4	Bottom horizontal corner guard	¼" x 1" x 1" x 18½"		¼" Brass flat washers	
Bridge Shelves				¼" Brass hex nuts	
2	Plywood bridge shelves	¾" x 9¾" x 65"		2" ⅜ IP Brass nipples	
2	Solid-wood bridge shelf faces	¾" x 2½" x 66½"		⅜ IP Brass knurled locknuts	
4	Solid-wood bridge shelf ends	¾" x 2½" x 9¾"		⅜ IP Brass hex nuts	
				Snap-on, two-prong electrical plugs	

MAKING THE FACE FRAMES

1. Cut the parts. Cut all the face frame rails and stiles to the dimensions in the Materials List.

2. Build the upper face frames. Clamp the four upper face frame stiles together face up, making sure they are flush at top and bottom. Draw lines across all the stiles laying out the positions of the bottom of each rail as shown in *Upper Face Frame Construction*, page 136. Use an ⁱ¹⁄₆₄-inch bit to drill pilot holes through the sides of the stiles. Drill one hole ³⁄₄ inch above

each layout line. Then assemble the two upper face frames using glue and 2¹⁄₂-inch drywall screws.

3. Build the lower face frame. Clamp the four lower face frame stiles together as you did for the upper face frames, and lay out the position of one side of the center rails as shown in *Lower Face Frame Construction*, page 136. Then do the same with the 1x2 upper rails to lay out the positions of the center stiles. Predrill, glue, and screw the lower face frames together as you did the upper face frames, using two screws for each bottom rail connection as shown.

MAKING THE CABINET TOPS AND SHELVES

1. Cut the parts. Cut the cabinet and night stand tops, cabinet shelves, and the nightstand and top panel edging to the dimensions in the Materials List.

2. Rabbet the cabinet tops. Rabbet the back edge of each cabinet top as shown in the *Overall View*. (See "Dadoes, Grooves, and Rabbets," page 17.)

3. Attach the shelf edging. Use glue and 1-inch brads to attach the edging to the front of the top panels and nightstands.

OVERALL VIEW

¼" x ½" Rabbet

Top

Top Panel Edging

¾" x ½" Rabbet

Back Panel

Bridge Shelf End

Side Panel

Bridge Shelf

Bridge Shelf Face

Stile

Cabinet Shelf

Rail

Night-stand Top

Nightstand Edging

Center Stile

Stile

Corner Guard

Bottom Rail

4. Predrill the shelves. To make the wall units lighter and easier to maneuver, don't install the shelves until you assemble the unit in the bedroom. For now, just drill pilot holes for the 1-inch brads that will secure the shelves to the cleats. Use a ¹⁄₁₆-inch-diameter bit to drill two holes through the top of each shelf about 1 inch from the front and rear edges and ¼ inch from the ends.

SEE INSTRUCTIONS "MAKING THE FACE FRAMES," ON PAGE 134.

UPPER FACE FRAME CONSTRUCTION

Stile

2½" Drywall Screw

Layout Line

Rail

34¼"

22¼"

11¾"

LOWER FACE FRAME CONSTRUCTION

Rail

Stile

Center Stile

Layout Line

12"

13"

Bottom Rail

2½" Drywall Screw

MAKING THE SIDE AND BACK PANELS

1. Cut the parts. Cut the cabinet sides, back panels, shelf cleats, face-frame stops, and back cleats to the dimensions in the Materials List. If you don't want to rip your own stock for the cleats and stops, you can buy ½ x ¾-inch stock called parting bead.

2. Make the nightstand cutaways. As shown in *Side and Back Panel Construction,* lay out the cuts that will reduce the cabinet sides to 12 inches wide above the nightstand. Make the cuts with a saber saw and saw guide.

3. Rabbet the cabinet sides. Rabbet the top and back edges of the cabinet sides as shown in *Side and Back Panel Construction.* (See "Making Rabbets with the Router," page 20.) Remember to rout the right sides on faces that will oppose the left sides.

4. Attach the side cleats. Use a pencil to lay out the positions of the shelf cleats and face frame stops as shown in *Side and Back Panel Construction.* Drill and countersink two holes for #6 x 1-inch screws in a wide edge of each cleat and four holes in each face-frame stop as shown. The cleats and stops are attached with glue and screws. Align the top of each cleat and the front of the stops to the layout lines, and attach them using #6 x 1-inch wood screws.

5. Attach the back cleats. Lay out the position of the back cleats on the back panels. Then flip the panels over, and lay out nailing lines on the outside face of the back panel. Apply glue to the back of each bottom back cleat, and clamp each cleat in place flush with the bottom of each back panel.

SIDE AND BACK PANEL CONSTRUCTION

12"

12¼"

24¼"

36¼"

½" x ¼" Rabbet Along Back of Side Panel

Shelf Cleat

Back

Back Cleat

1½"

6"

Side

#6 x 1" Screw

23¼"

Face Frame Stops

1½"

Bottom Back Cleat

22½"

14½"

Glue and clamp the remaining cleats the same way. Turn the panels over, and drive $\frac{7}{8}$-inch brads, about 6 inches apart, through the back panels and along the nailing lines.

ASSEMBLING THE CARCASES

1. Install the lower face frames. In these cabinets, the face frames fit between the side panels, against the face frame stops and recessed $\frac{3}{4}$ inch from the front edges of the side panels. Apply glue to the front edges of the face frame stops and the side edges of the lower face frames, and attach the side panels to the face frames using 4d finishing nails spaced about 6 inches apart.

2. Attach the back panels. Apply glue to the rabbets in the rear edges of the side panels and to the side edges

CORNER GUARD DETAILS

Top Horizontal Corner Guard

Top Vertical Corner Guard

Rear Corner Guard

Nightstand Corner Guard

Bottom Vertical Corner Guard

Bottom Horizontal Corner Guard

of the back panels. Lay each back panel in place; check it for square; and secure it using 4d finishing nails spaced about 8 inches apart.

3. Install the nightstand tops. Apply glue to the side and rear edges of each nightstand top, the top of each face frame stop, and the top edge of the upper cleat on each back panel. Lay the tops in place, and secure them using 4d finishing nails driven through the side and rear panels.

4. Install the upper face frames. Apply glue to the front edges of the shelf cleats and side edges of each upper face frame. Set each face frame in place, snug against the nightstand top, and secure using 4d finishing nails.

5. Install the cabinet tops. Apply glue to the upper rabbets in the side panels, the rabbets in the rear of the top panels, the top edges of the back panels, and the top edges of the upper face frames. Then secure the tops using 4d finishing nails.

ATTACHING THE CORNER GUARD

Note: When attaching the corner guard, put glue on both inside surfaces of the guard and on all the miter joints.

1. Attach the rear corner guard. Measure and miter-cut corner guard to fit the rear of the cabinet side panels as shown in *Corner Guard Details*. Attach the guard using glue and bar clamps placed across the side panels.

2. Attach the top corner guard. Miter-cut strips of corner guard to fit the top horizontal edges of the side panels. Attach the guard using glue and 1-inch brads.

3. Attach the remaining corner guard. Cut corner guard pieces to fit the top vertical edges at the front of the side panels, and attach them using glue and bar clamps or glue and brads. Cut guard pieces to fit the nightstand cutaway, and attach them using glue and brads. Cut guard pieces to fit the bottom vertical front edge, and attach them using glue and bar clamps or glue and brads. Finally, cut guard pieces to fit the bottom horizontal edges, and attach them using glue and brads.

BUILDING THE BRIDGE SHELVES AND DRAWERS

1. Cut and assemble the shelves. Cut the bridge shelves, shelf faces, and shelf ends. Attach each shelf end and then both shelf faces using glue and 4d finishing nails as shown in *Bridge Shelves Details*, page 134.

2. Drill the shelf ends. Lay each shelf upside down, and counterbore two $\frac{1}{2}$-inch diameter attachment holes $\frac{3}{8}$ inch deep into the inside surface of each shelf end, 1 inch inside the front and rear edges of each shelf end. Then drill through each hole using a $\frac{1}{4}$-inch bit. In the bottom shelf only, drill a centered $\frac{13}{32}$-inch wiring hole through each shelf end.

3. Build the Drawers. The drawers are designed to overlay the face frames by $\frac{3}{8}$ inch on all sides. Make the false drawer fronts from solid wood and the rest of the parts from plywood according to the dimensions in the Materials List. (See "Drawer Construction," page 28, for instructions on making $\frac{3}{8}$-inch overlay drawers, and see "Edge-Gluing Stock," page 14, for instructions on making solid-wood false drawer fronts from narrow boards.)

BRIDGE SHELVES DETAILS

Attachment Holes

Bridge Shelf

3"

18"

Wiring Hole

Shelf End

4d Finishing Nail

Attachment Holes

Shelf Face

BORING HOLES AND APPLYING FINISH

1. Drill the cabinet sides. Lay the left cabinet on its left side and the right cabinet on its right side. Lay out the positions of the bridge shelves. Stand the top bridge shelf on end on the left side panel, aligned with the guide marks, and drill ¼-inch holes through the holes in the shelf ends. Align the bottom shelf with the lower marks, and drill through using ¼-inch and ¹³/₃₂-inch bits. Do likewise on the right side panel.

2. Drill the cabinet backs. Drill a ¹³/₃₂-inch hole through the back of each cabinet, near the same-size hole in the side panel. If you will need access to an electrical outlet from the nightstand top (for clock, radio, etc.), drill a ¹³/₃₂-inch hole in the cabinet back near a bottom corner of the open area.

3. Fill, sand, and finish the unit. Fill any remaining nailholes or flaws with wood filler; let dry; and sand all components. Then apply the finish of your choice, and let it dry.

ASSEMBLING THE UNIT

1. Attach the pulls. Attach one drawer pull to each small drawer and two pulls to each large drawer using the screws provided by the manufacturer.

2. Attach the drawer slides. Follow the manufacturer's directions and use the screws provided to attach a drawer section of a slide to the bottom center of each drawer. Attach the cabinet sec-

tions to the lower face frames and rear supports as shown in the *Overall View*.

3. Install the lamps. Lay the lower bridge shelf upside down, and mount a light fixture 3½ inches inside each end, snug against the back of the shelf face, according to the manufacturer's directions. Cut the plug off the cord end using wire cutting pliers.

4. Assemble the unit. In the bedroom, lay the cabinets on their backs, and attach the bridge shelves using brass machine screws, washers, and nuts. Insert a brass nipple into each ¹³/₃₂-inch hole, and secure with a knurled locknut on the outside and hex nut on the inside. With a helper, stand the assembly upright, and move it back against the wall. Thread the lamp cords through the brass nipples, and attach the snap-on plugs. See to other wiring chores, and plug the lamps into extension cords, if necessary, and then into wall outlets. Lay the cabinet shelves atop the cleats, snug against the upper face frame rails, and secure them using 1-inch brads driven through the pilot holes.

INSTALLING THE FLUORESCENT LAMPS

3½"

Fluorescent Lamps

dressing table and mirror

IF YOUR BATHROOM must serve as a storage area for cosmetics and other personal products, it is likely that you have noticed a shortage of space. As the number and variety of these items have grown, and as their use has become a much more integral part of our culture, they can easily overtake the available space in a medicine cabinet or vanity, sometimes leading to conflict over the use of shared real estate. Fortunately, a simple solution can be found by rediscovering a piece of furniture that was once a common feature in the bedroom—the dressing table.

Our design offers six drawers that can provide plenty of space for all sorts of personal items, not only cosmetics. Its modest proportions make it a reasonable addition to most bedroom layouts and you can select materials that match or complement your existing furniture. The plans include details for a matching mirror that can be mounted to the table. Your efforts in building this project will be amply rewarded by yielding an attractive and useful piece of furniture, offering the promise of a more peaceful and less cluttered home.

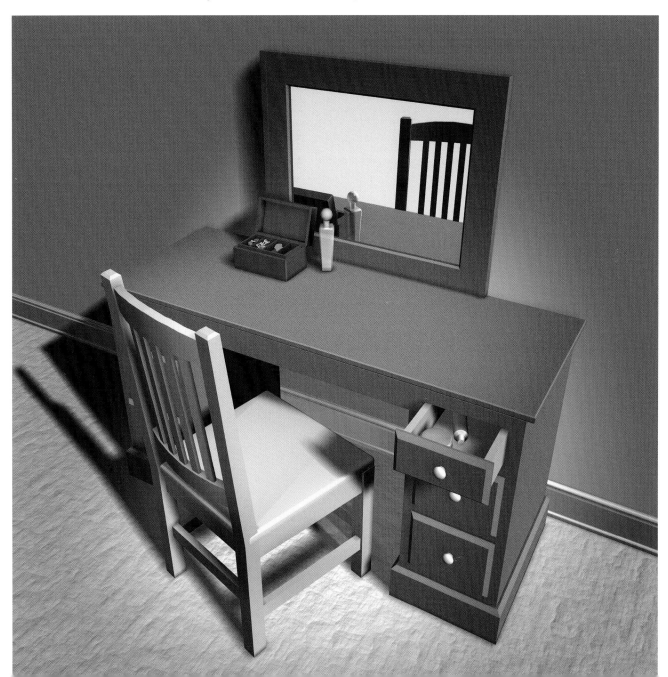

DRESSING TABLE AND MIRROR MATERIALS LIST

Difficulty Level: CHALLENGING

Qty	Part	Dimensions	Qty	Part	Dimensions
Pedestals			2	Solid-wood fronts,	¾" x 3¾" x 7⅞"
4	Plywood sides	¾" x 19¼" x 29¼"	4	Solid-wood fronts	¾" x 6¾" x 7⅞"
8	Plywood drawer dividers & tops	¾" x 11" x 19"	2	Solid-wood backs	¾" x 3¼" x 7⅞"
2	Plywood backs	¼" x 11½" x 23¾"	4	Solid-wood backs	¾" x 6¼" x 7⅞"
1	Solid-wood baseboards	¾" x 4¾" x 13½"	6	Plywood bottoms	¼" x 7⅞" x 17½"
2	Solid-wood baseboards	¾" x 4¾" x 20¾"	12	Solid-wood drawer guides	¼" x ¾" x 17¼"
6	Solid-wood drawer runners	¼" x ¾" x 19"	2	Solid-wood faces	¾" x 4¾" x 9¾"
Face Frames			4	Solid-wood faces	¾" x 7¾" x 9¾"
4	Solid-wood stiles	¾" x 1½" x 29¼"	**Mirror Frame**		
2	Solid-wood top rails	¾" x 1½" x 9"	2	Solid-wood frame	¾" x 3" x 24"
4	Solid-wood middle rails	¾" x 1¾" x 9"	2	Solid-wood frame	¾" x 3" x 30"
2	Solid-wood bottom rails	¾" x 3" x 9"	1	Solid-wood edging	¾" x 1¼" x 31½"
Apron Assemblies			2	Solid-wood edging	¾" x 1¼" x 24¾"
2	Solid-wood aprons	¾" x 3" x 30"	1	Plywood backer panel	¼" x 24" x 30"
1	Solid-wood center stretcher	¾" x 3½" x 18½"	**Hardware and Miscellaneous Supplies**		
2	Solid-wood side stretchers	¾" x 3" x 18½"	1	Mirror	¼" x 18⅞" x 24⅞"
4	Corner blocks	¾" x 3" x 4"		¼" x 1½" wood dowels	
Top				¼" x 1¼" wood dowels	
1	Plywood top panel	¾" x 19¼" x 54"	6	Drawer knobs	
1	Solid-wood edging	¾" x ¾" x 54"		#8 x 1½" flathead wood screws	
2	Solid-wood edging	¾" x ¾" x 20¾"		#8 x 1¼" flathead wood screws	
1	Solid-wood edging	¾" x ¾" x 55½"		#8 x ¾" flathead wood screws	
Drawers				#6 x ¾" flathead wood screws	
4	Solid-wood sides	¾" x 3¾" x 18"		4d finishing nails	
8	Solid-wood sides	¾" x 6¾" x 18"		1" brads	
			2	1½" x 6" Steel mending plates	

BUILDING THE PEDESTALS

1. Cut the plywood parts. Cut the pedestal side, top, divider, and back panels to the sizes listed in the Materials List. Lay out and cut the dadoes and rabbets in the side panels as shown in the *Pededal Assembly*. (See "Dadoes, Grooves, and Rabbets," pages 17 to 20.) Cut drawer runners to size; then drill and countersink pilot holes in the runners and fasten them to the drawer divider panels. Drill and countersink pilot holes in the pedestal top panels for attaching the dressing table top.

2. Assemble the pedestal carcases. Apply glue to the rabbets and dadoes in the plywood side panels; then join

PEDESTAL ASSEMBLY

OVERALL VIEW

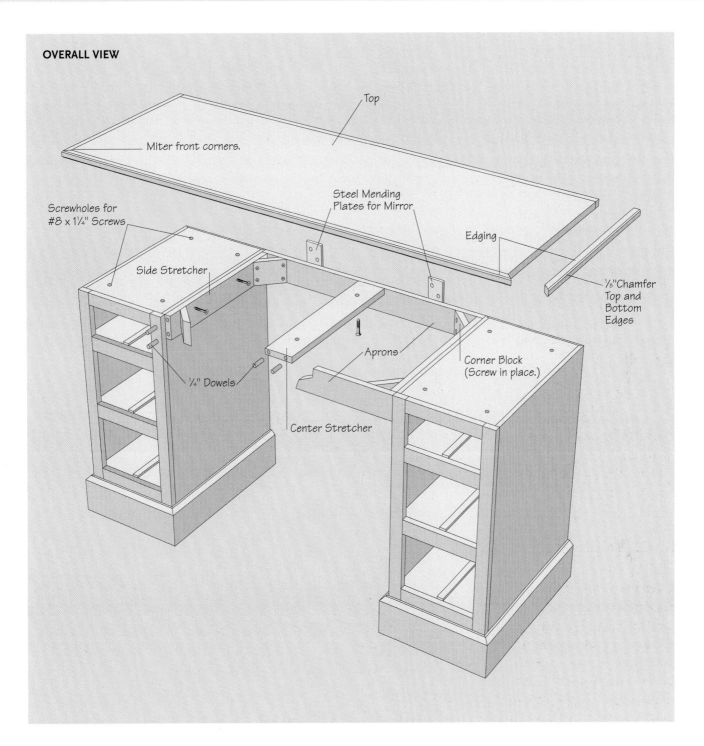

Top

Miter front corners.

Steel Mending
Plates for Mirror

Edging

Screwholes for
#8 x 1¼" Screws

Side Stretcher

⅛"Chamfer
Top and
Bottom
Edges

¼" Dowels

Aprons

Corner Block
(Screw in place.)

Center Stretcher

them to the drawer dividers and top. You can either clamp the assembly to pull the joints tight or, if you do not have adequate clamps, you can use 4d finishing nails to fasten the joints. Check that the pedestals are square by comparing opposite diagonal measurements; then install the back panels with 1-inch brads.

3. Build and install the face frames.
Cut the face frame parts. Lay out the position of the dowels for face frame joints; then use a doweling jig to bore the dowel holes. (See "Reinforcing Joints with Dowels," page 15.) Apply glue to the dowel holes and to the individual dowels; then assemble the face frames. Use clamps to pull the joints tight; then

check that the frames are square, and if not, adjust the position of the clamps to correct the situation. Allow the glue to set for at least 30 minutes before removing the clamps.

Apply glue to the front edges of each carcase, and install the face frames. Use clamps or 4d finishing nails to fasten them.

141

4. Cut and install baseboards.
Rip stock to width for the baseboard molding, leaving the stock a few inches longer than finished length at this time. Install a 45-degree chamfer bit in the router, and use it to shape the molded top edge of the baseboard material as shown in the *Pedestal Assembly*. Use a miter saw to cut the stock to finished dimension, and install it using 4d finishing nails. To ensure tight joints, apply glue to the faces of the miter joints before nailing them.

BUILDING AND INSTALLING THE APRON ASSEMBLY

1. Cut the parts. Cut the aprons, stretchers, and corner blocks to finished dimension. Use a miter saw to make the 45-degree bevel cuts on the ends of the corner blocks. Use a doweling jig to bore the dowel holes in the aprons and stretchers; then apply glue and assemble the parts. Clamp the assembly to pull the joints together; then check that it is square before setting it aside for the glue to cure. Bore and countersink pilot holes in the corner blocks; then install them using #8 x 1½-inch flathead screws.

2. Install the aprons to the pedestals. Bore and countersink pilot holes in the side stretchers and also in the center stretcher (for attaching the dressing table top). Position the apron assembly between the two pedestals—align the face of the front apron with the face frames of the pedestals to form a continuous plane. In addition, the top edges of the aprons should be perfectly flush with the top edges of the pedestals. You can use clamps to hold the apron assembly in position while you fasten it to the pedestal sides using #8 x 1¼-inch flathead screws.

DRAWER CONSTRUCTION

¼" x ¼" Groove (Sides and Front)

Side

Back

¼" x ¾" Rabbet

Nail back edge of bottom to back.

Bottom

Front

Guides

¹³⁄₁₆"-Wide Space between Guides

4d Finishing Nails

BUILDING AND INSTALLING THE TOP

1. Cut the parts. Cut the top panel and edging strips to size. Use a miter saw to cut the 45-degree joints on the edging strips for the front corners.

2. Apply the edging strips. Apply glue to the back edge of the top panel, and place the back edging strip in position. Use clamps or masking tape to hold the strip tight to the panel while the glue sets. Apply the side and front edging strips using the same techniques, remembering to apply some glue to the mating surfaces of the front corner miter joints.

3. Shape the top edges. Use a 45-degree chamfer bit in the router to shape the chamfered profile on the front and sides of the top. Place the top upside down on a worktable to shape the bottom edges; then flip it over to repeat the procedure for the top edges.

4. Install the top. Place the top on the base assembly, and arrange it so that there is a ¾-inch overhang on the two sides and front—the back edge of the top should be flush with the back of the pedestals. Fasten the top by driving screws through the pedestal top panels and also through the center stretcher of the apron assembly—use #8 x 1¼-inch flathead screws. Note: Because you will need to work inside the top drawer compartments, a stubby or right-angle screwdriver will be necessary.

BUILDING THE DRAWERS

1. Cut the parts. Cut the fronts, sides, backs, bottom panels, and drawer guides to the dimensions in the Materials List. Cut rabbets and grooves in the sides and fronts as shown in the plans. (See "Building Drawers," page 28.)

2. Assemble the drawers. Apply glue to the rabbet joints in the drawer sides, and assemble the drawer boxes using 4d finishing nails to fasten the joints. Slide the bottom panels into position, and use 1-inch brads to fasten them to the bottom edges of the drawer backs. Apply glue to the drawer guide strips, and clamp them to the drawer bottoms.

DRAWER DETAILS

DRAWER SIDE DETAIL

#8 x 1¼" Screws

⅝"

⅜"

¼"

DRAWER FRONT DETAIL

Drawer Face with ½" Chamfer

½"

Side

Drawer
Guides

Drawer
Runner

Bottom

MIRROR DETAILS

No. 20 Joining
Plate

4d Finishing
Nail

Edging

#6 x ¾"
Screws

Frame

¼" Chamfer

Mirror

¼" x ½"
Rabbet

Back

¼"

¼"

Secure mirror to rear apron with
2¼" steel mending plates.

3. Make the drawer faces. Cut the drawer faces to the proper sizes. Use the router with 45-degree chamfer bit to shape the outside edges. Bore and countersink pilot holes in the drawer fronts, and attach the faces using #8 x 1¼-inch flathead screws. Drill pilot holes for knobs, and install them. If the mounting screws are not long enough, you can either counterbore the pilot holes on the inside of the drawer front or purchase longer screws.

4. Install the drawers. Test the operation of each drawer in the pedestal openings. If you find that a drawer does not slide easily, you can sand the drawer guides or runners.

BUILDING THE MIRROR

1. Cut the parts. Rip stock for the mirror frame and edging strips. Use a router with 45-degree chamfer bit to shape the top inside edge; then rabbet using inside back edge of the frame stock with either the router or table saw. (See "Making Rabbets with a Table Saw," page 18, and "Making Rabbets with a Router," page 20.) Use a miter saw to trim the frame pieces and edging strips to finished length with 45-degree angled ends where appropriate. Trim the back panel to finished dimensions.

Use the plate joiner to cut slots in the ends of the frame parts. (See "Making Biscuit Joints," page 16.)

2. Assemble the mirror frame. Apply glue to the slots in the ends of the frame parts; insert the joining plates; and assemble the frame. Use clamps across both the width and length of the frame to tighten the joints. By manipulating the clamp pressure, you can adjust the position of the joints until they fit perfectly. Check that the assembly is square.

3. Install the mirror. Place the frame face down on the worktable, and gently lower the mirror into the rabbet in the frame. Lay the ¼-inch-thick plywood backer over the mirror, and screw it to the frame using #6 x ¾-inch flathead screws.

4. Attach the edging strips. Edging strips are required only on the top and sides of the frame. Nail the strips to the frame using 4d finishing nails. The face of the edging should protrude ¼-inch beyond the face of the frame.

5. Mount the mirror. Screw the steel mending plates to the back side of the mirror, allowing half of each plate to overhang the bottom edge. Stand the mirror on the tabletop, and drive screws through the mounting plates to fasten it to the back apron. Slide the back of the table against the wall to reduce stress on the attachments.

nightstand

A NIGHTSTAND can take many forms, ranging from a simple table to an enclosed cabinet. Offering some of the best features of a table and a cabinet, this nightstand provides an attractive combination of form and function. The tabletop is slightly larger than a standard-size nightstand, allowing you room for a lamp, phone, and radio or clock without crowding. The drawer is deep enough to hold a variety of items and is mounted on full-extension slides to provide easy access, even to the back corners. And one fixed and one adjustable shelf provide room for books, magazines, or display of decorative objects.

The materials list and the techniques that follow describe a table made primarily of solid hardwood lumber, requiring that you edge glue narrow stock to form the top, sides, back, and shelves. But if you are not enthused by the prospect of so much stock preparation, you can substitute hardwood plywood for these parts instead and still have an attractive table. This substitution would require you to apply solid-wood edging on all edges of the tabletop and also on the front edges of the bottom panel and adjustable shelf. You can also save some money by using a less-expensive lumber for the drawer blocking and drawer box. It is common practice to use a secondary wood for these less visible parts—it can also provide a nice visual contrast with the primary wood of the piece.

NIGHTSTAND MATERIALS LIST

Difficulty Level: CHALLENGING

Qty	Part	Dimensions
Table Base		
4	Solid-wood legs	1¾" x 1¾" x 25¼"
2	Solid-wood sides glue up from narrow stock	¾" x 15½" x 19¾"
1	Solid-wood back glue up from narrow stock	¾" x 17" x 19¾"
1	Solid-wood bottom glue up from narrow stock	¾" x 16½" x 18"
2	Blocking for slides plywood or solid wood	½" x 15½" x 4½"
Top and Shelf		
1	Solid-wood top glue up from narrow stock	¾" x 20½" x 22"
1	Solid-wood shelf glue up from narrow stock	¾" x 17⅞" x 17⅞"

Qty	Part	Dimensions
Drawer		
1	Solid-wood drawer face	¾" x 4¹⁵⁄₁₆" x 16⅞"
2	Solid-wood drawer sides	¾" x 4½" x 16"
1	Solid-wood drawer front	¾" x 4½" x 15"
1	Solid-wood drawer back	¾" x 4" x 15"
1	Plywood drawer bottom	¼" x 15" x 15½"
Hardware and Miscellaneous Supplies		
	#8 x 1¼" flathead screws	
	4d finishing nails	
	1" brads	
1	pr. 16" full-extension side-mount drawer slides, ½" side space	
	#20 joining plates	
4	¼" shelf pins	

OVERALL VIEW

Top

½" Leg Offset

Back

Blocking

Shelf

½" Rad. Quarter Round

¾" Overhang at Leg

Drawer Slide

¼" Shelf Pin

Bottom

No. 20 Joining Plate (3 per Joint)

Curve leg inside surfaces.

5"

1"

¼" Shelf Pin Hole, 1½" Apart

SHELF AND BOTTOM DETAILS

½" x ½" Notch (Typical)

16½"

BOTTOM PANEL

18"

½" x ½" Notches

17⅛"

SHELF

½" x 1¼" Notches

17⅞"

BUILDING PANELS

1. Cut the stock. Rip and crosscut material for the side, back, top, bottom, and shelf panels. Plan these cuts so that the panels will be slightly larger than the finished dimensions shown in the materials list.

2. Assemble the panels. Apply glue to the mating edges of the panel stock, and clamp them together. (See "Edge-Gluing Stock," page 14.) After the glue sets, remove the clamps, and trim the panels to finished dimension.

3. Notch panels. Use a saber saw to cut the notches in the bottom and shelf panels as shown in the *Shelf and*

Bottom Details. These allow the panels to fit around the table legs.

BUILDING THE TABLE BASE

1. Cut the legs. Rip and crosscut the legs from 1¾-inch-thick stock. If you cannot find thick lumber, you can glue up ¾-inch-thick stock and then cut the legs from these blanks. Mark the legs to indicate the eventual orientation of each in the table. If you are using glued-up stock for the legs, arrange them so that the exposed glue joints face the sides of the table, rather than the face.

Draw the curved taper profile on the legs, and use a saber saw or band saw to cut the legs to this shape. Note

that the curved profile should be cut only on the inside surfaces; the outside faces remain straight. When making these cuts, keep the saw kerf on the waste side of the layout line—then use a sharp block plane to remove the saw marks and refine the shape.

2. Cut joints. Use the plate joiner to cut joining plate slots in the legs, side, back, and bottom panels as shown in the plans. (See "Reinforcing Joints with Biscuits," page 16.) If you do not have access to a plate joiner, you could substitute dowels. (See "Reinforcing Joints with Dowels," page 15.) Cut matching slots in the top ends of the sides and back and bottom face of the table top.

3. Drill shelf-pin holes. Use a drilling jig to bore holes for the adjustable shelf pins in the side panels. (See "Installing Shelf Pins," page 28.)

DRAWER DETAILS

¼" x ¼" Groove (Sides and Front)

Side

¼" x ¾" Dado

Back

Bottom

1" Brad

Front

Face

⁷⁄₁₆"

#8 x 1¼" Screw

Face

⁷⁄₁₆" Overhang at Sides

4d Finishing Nail

¼"

4. Assemble the base. Begin assembly by joining the legs to the side panels. Apply glue to the joining plate slots, and also spread a thin coating on the plates. Insert the plates in their respective slots, and join the parts. Apply clamps to pull the joints tight—allow the glue to set for at least 30 minutes before removing the clamps.

Next, join the back to the bottom panel. Again, apply glue to the plate slots and plates, and clamp the parts together. Finally, join the two sides to the back/bottom subassembly using the same techniques.

5. Install drawer slide blocking. Cut material for the drawer slide blocking to size. Drill and countersink pilot holes in the blocks; then screw them to the drawer sides.

INSTALL THE TOP

1. Shape the edges. Install a ½-inch-diameter roundover bit in the router to shape the edges of the table top.

2. Apply glue to the joining plate slots and also on the joining plates; then assemble the top to the table base. Use clamps to pull the joints tight—if you do not have adequate clamps for the job, you can place heavy weights on the top instead.

BUILDING THE DRAWER

1. Cut the parts. Cut the drawer front, sides, back, bottom, and face panel to finished dimensions as shown in the Materials List.

2. Cut drawer joints. Use dado blades in the table saw or a router with straight bit to cut rabbets and grooves in the drawer sides and front. (See "Building Drawers," page 28.)

3. Assemble the drawer. Apply glue to the rabbets in drawer sides; assemble the box; and use 4d finishing nails to pin the joints together. Slide the drawer bottom into the groove in sides and front, and nail it to the

bottom using 1-inch brads. Drill and countersink pilot holes in the drawer front; then attach the drawer face using #8 x 1¼-inch flathead screws. Drill a pilot hole for the knob, and install it to the drawer. If the mounting screw is too short to reach through the face and front panels, counterbore the pilot hole on the inside of the drawer or use a longer screw.

INSTALL THE DRAWER

1. Mount slides. Install the cabinet portion of the drawer slides to the table base, and then mount the drawer portion to the drawer sides—use the slotted holes for mounting, if available, leaving the other holes unused at this point. Follow the manufacturer's instructions for installing the slides.

2. Install drawer. Slide the drawer into position in the table, and check that it operates properly. Check that there is a uniform space of ¹⁄₁₆ inch on each side and on the top edge of the drawer face. Adjust the drawer position using the slotted mounting holes. When you are satisfied, install the remaining screws.

FINISHING THE PIECE

1. Remove hardware. You will find it much easier to sand and finish the table if you temporarily remove the drawer slides and knob.

2. Sand the table. Start sanding with 120-grit paper; then move to 150 grit, then 180 grit, and 220 grit. Remove all sanding dust when switching to a finer grit.

3. Apply the finish. Apply a stain and clear finish of your choice, or paint the nightstand.

8 kitchen

MAKING THE HEART OF THE HOME AS EFFICIENT AS POSSIBLE

kitchen storage ideas

This cabinet glows, thanks to small lights hidden behind frosted leaded-glass panels on the doors.

Clockwise (from above) Most cabinet manufacturers offer pullout units, turning every available inch of dead space into valuable storage. Attached to the bottom of a wall-hung cabinet, this handy shelf keeps spices close at hand. Plate racks eliminate stacking, which keeps chipping and scratching to a minimum. Here's an unusual arrangement: a hard-working counter that doubles as a display cabinet.

kitchen storage ideas

Clockwise (from top right) Open shelving puts your dinnerware on display. Set aside space in the kitchen for a small office for making lists, a landing area for phones and keys, or craft and hobby storage. Keep your favorite wine vintages on hand in the kitchen with a built-in rack. The lazy Susan, the grand dame of kitchen storage devices, turns dead corners in base cabinets into usable storage areas.

base cabinet

THIS FINELY CRAFTED BASE CABINET could easily be the basic building block of any kitchen remodel. It is designed to go with the wall cabinet featured on page 155. As with that project, you may decide to use a different style of cabinet door rather than the overlay frame-and-raised-panel door shown.

The Materials List provided is for a cabinet that is 18 inches wide, a standard cabinet width. You'll probably want to gang several cabinets together for the counter length you need. Size the cabinets to fit your space exactly.

Make the cabinets from plywood. Use hardwood plywood for side panels that will show and AC grade fir plywood for side panels that abut other cabinets or walls. Make the face frames, doors, drawer fronts, and edge trim from hardwood to match the hardwood plywood. The kick plate can be solid wood or plywood. The drawer sides and backs can be matching hardwood or clear pine.

The plans presented here call for a countertop of particleboard covered with plastic laminate. The counter edging and backsplash are solid wood. Make the countertop as long as you need to cover a run of cabinets. For other countertop options, refer to "Countertops," page 32.

BASE CABINET MATERIALS LIST

Difficulty Level: CHALLENGING

Qty	Part	Dimensions
Carcase and face frame		
2	Plywood sides	¾" x 23¼" x 35¼"
1	Plywood bottom	¾" x 22⅞" x 17"
1	Plywood back	¼" x 17¼" x 35¼"
1	Plywood shelf	¾" x 21¼" x 16"
1	Kick plate	¾" x 5" x 18"
1	Nailing cleat	¾" x 1½" x 16½"
3	Plywood crosspieces	¾" x 5" x 16¼"
2	Solid-wood guide hangers	¾" x 3¼" x 22⅞"
1	Solid-wood shelf edge	¾" x ¾" x 16"
2	Stiles	¾" x 1½" x 31"
3	Rails	¾" x 1½" x 15"
Door		
1		¾" x 15¾" x 23¼" (with ⅜" overlay)
Drawer		
2	Plywood sides	½" x 3" x 23½"
1	Front	¾" x 3" x 13½"
1	Back	¾" x 2½" x 13½"

Qty	Part	Dimensions
1	Plywood bottom	¼" x 13½" x 23⅛"
1	False front	¾" x 4¾" x 15¾"
Countertop		
1	Particleboard panel	¾" x 23⅜" x as needed
1	Sheet plastic laminate (rough size)	25" x as needed
1	Front edge strip	¾" x 1½" x as needed
2	Side edge strips	¾" x 1½" x 24⅞"
1	Solid-wood backsplash	¾" x 5" x as needed
Hardware		
	4d Finishing nails	
	6d Finishing nails	
4	Adjustable shelf pins	
1 pair	Side-mounted drawer slides	
	⅞" Brads	
1 pair	Overlay hinges	
2	Door/drawer pulls	
	#6 x 2" Flathead wood screws	
	#6 x 1¼" Flathead wood screws	

BUILDING THE CARCASE

1. Cut the plywood. Cut the sides, bottom, back, shelf, and kick plate to the dimensions in the Materials List. Cut a notch for the kick plate in each side panel as shown in *Side Panel Details*. Drill holes in the inside faces of both side panels as shown for the adjustable shelf pins. (See "Installing Shelf Pins," page 28, for instructions on making and using a shelf pin drilling template.)

2. Dado and rabbet the sides. Dado and rabbet the side panels as shown in *Side Panel Details*. The rabbet for the back is ⅛ inch deeper than the plywood thickness to create a fitting allowance for a less-than-perfect wall. Note that the drawing shows one cabinet side. Don't forget to make the other side in a mirror image. (For more information on cutting rabbets and dadoes, refer to "Dadoes, Grooves, and Rabbets," page 17.)

SIDE PANEL DETAILS

23¼"

⅜" x ⅜" Deep Rabbet

12"

2"

1½"

Shelf Peg Holes

35¼"

4"

¾" x ⅜" Deep Dado

4¼" High x 3" Deep Notch for Kick Plate

5"

OVERALL VIEW

Backsplash

#6 x 2" Flathead Wood Screws

Particleboard Panel

Plastic Laminate

Edge Strip

Back

Front Crosspieces

Nailing Cleat

Rear Crosspiece

Drawer Guide

Rail

Stile

Drawer Guide
Hanger

4"

Side

Shelf Edge

Drawer Slide

Bottom

¾" x ¾" Notch
for Sides

Kick Plate

Raised-Panel Door

3. Assemble the carcase. Use glue and 6d finishing nails to join the sides to the bottom shelf. Cut the nailing cleat and crosspieces to the dimensions in the Materials List. Glue and nail the nailing cleat to the sides. Glue the rear crosspiece to the nailing cleat, and nail it to the sides. Install the remaining crosspieces as shown in the *Overall View.* Note that the lower crosspiece is 4¾ inches below the top crosspiece. This will give you a 4-inch-high drawer opening.

4. Notch and install the kick plate. Notch the kick plate to fit around the sides as shown in the *Overall View.* Install the kick plate at the bottom front of the carcase using glue and 4d finishing nails.

5. Install the drawer guide hangers. The drawer guide hangers are necessary only if you plan to use side-mounted metal drawer slides. You won't need them for bottom-mounted slides, but for bottom-mounts you may have to shorten the drawer to make room for the hardware behind the drawer. Purchase your slide hardware before you build the drawer.

Cut the drawer guide hangers to the dimensions in the Materials List. The top of the hangers will fit under the nailing cleat while the bottom of the hangers will rest on the lower front crosspiece. Glue and screw the hangers to the cabinet sides. Use #6 x 1¼-inch flathead wood screws.

6. Install the back. Use a framing square to make sure the sides are square with the upper crosspiece. Apply glue to the rabbets in the side panels; lay the back in place; and secure it with ⅞-inch brads.

7. Make the shelf. Cut the shelf edge to the dimensions in the Materials

List. Glue and clamp it to the front edge of the shelf. Install the shelf.

8. Cut and attach the stiles and rails. The rail dimensions in the Materials List will make the stiles flush to the sides of the cabinet. This looks best for a freestanding cabinet. However, if you are building a run of cabinets, you may want to add ¼ inch to the rail lengths. This way the stiles will extend ⅛ inch past each side of the cabinet. This will allow for warped cabinet sides or irregular walls. If you do this, you'll need to adjust the door widths accordingly. Cut the stiles, and fasten them using glue and 6d finishing nails. Then cut the rails to fit between, and fasten them the same way.

9. Make and hang the door. The door dimensions in the Materials List are for a door that overlays the stiles and rails by ⅜ inch on all sides. (See "Making Cabinet Doors," page 22.) To hang the door, fasten a pair of overlay hinges 2 inches from each end of a stile. (See "Installing Overlay Doors," page 27.) Hold the door over the face frame, aligning door edges squarely and evenly with the face frame. Use an awl to mark centers for hinge screws. Drill pilot holes, and attach the door using the screws provided.

10. Make the drawer. The drawer shown is a simple box with a false front that overlays the drawer opening by ⅜ inch on all sides. Cut the parts to the dimensions in the Materials List. (Make the drawer as described in "Drawer Construction," page 29.)

11. Finish and install the cabinet or cabinets. Apply finish to the cabinets. Install drawer pulls using screws provided. (See "Installing Cabinets and Built-ins," page 34.)

MAKING & INSTALLING THE COUNTERTOP

1. Cut the particleboard. Cut particleboard to the width in the Materials List and ⅛ inch longer than the run of cabinets. For a single cabinet, cut it 18⅛ inches long.

2. Cut and attach the hardwood edging. Cut edging strips to the thickness and width in the Materials List and to length as needed (18¾ inches for a single cabinet). Cut pieces to length with mitered joints at the corner and square cuts to meet the walls. Attach the edging using glue and 6d finishing nails.

3. Install the laminate top. Install the laminate with contact adhesive. Use a router and flush-trimming bit to trim all four edges of the laminate flush with the sides of the solid-wood edging. The laminate will cover the top of the edging.

4. Chamfer the side and front edges. Use a chamfering bit in the router to complete the countertop's edge detail. Stop the chamfer 1½ inches from each back corner of the countertop.

5. Install the backsplash. Cut the backsplash to the dimensions in the Materials List. Drill four equally-spaced countersunk pilot holes from the underside of the countertop for the installation screws. Attach the backsplash using four 2-inch flathead wood screws in countersunk holes.

6. Install the countertop. Secure the countertop to the cabinet using four 1¼-inch flathead wood screws, driven up through the top crosspieces into the underside of the particleboard.

wall cabinet

BASE CABINETS are the foundation of a kitchen re-model, but well-designed wall cabinets make the first impression. Because they are at eye level, wall cabinets are often the first thing people see in a kitchen. This wall cabinet is designed to go with the base cabinet on page 151. Both cabinets feature overlay frame-and-raised-panel doors, but you may decide on a different style.

Like the base cabinet it matches, this cabinet is 18 inches wide, a standard cabinet width, and the Materials List reflects this. However, you can modify the dimensions. For example, you can resize upper cabinets to fit around a range hood or over a refrigerator. Because this cabinet has no fixed shelves, it is particularly easy to modify for height; simply shorten the sides, face frame, and door by the same amount.

Similarly, if you have a wider expanse to cover, you can widen the cabinets and install double doors. If you do this, you'll need to add a center stile to the face frame. Make the center stile twice as wide as the side stiles.

To make the basic wall cabinet, use hardwood plywood for the side panels that will show and AC grade fir plywood for the side panels that abut other cabinets or walls. Face frames, doors, and edge trim should all be hardwood to match the hardwood plywood you use.

WALL CABINET MATERIALS LIST

Difficulty Level: CHALLENGING

Qty	Part	Dimensions	Qty	Part	Dimensions
Carcase and face frame			**Door**		
1	Plywood top	¾" x 11¼" x 17¼"	1		¾" x 15¾" x 26¼" (with ⅜" overlay)
2	Plywood sides	¾" x 11¼" x 30"			
1	Plywood bottom	¾" x 11" x 17¼"	**Hardware**		
2	Plywood shelves	¾" x 10¼" x 16¼"	12	Adjustable shelf pins	
1	Plywood back	¼" x 17¼" x 29⅝"		6d Finishing nails	
2	Nailing cleats	¾" x 1½" x 16½"		⅞" Brads	
2	Stiles	¾" x 1½" x 30"	1 pair	Overlay hinges	
2	Rails	¾" x 2¼" x 15"	1	Door pull	
2	Solid-wood shelf edges	¾" x ¾" x 16¼"		3" Drywall screws	

BUILDING THE CARCASE

1. Cut the plywood. Cut the top, sides, bottom, shelves, back, and nailing cleats to the dimensions in the Materials List. Drill holes for the adjustable shelf pins in the inside faces of both side panels as shown in *Side Panel Details*. (See "Installing Shelf Pins," page 28, for instructions on making and using a shelf pin drilling template.)

2. Dado and rabbet the sides and top. Dado and rabbet the side panels as shown in *Side Panel Details*. The rabbets for the back are ⅛ inch deeper than the thickness of the back to create a fitting allowance for less-than-perfect walls. Note that the drawing shows one cabinet side. Don't forget to make the other side in a mirror image. (See "Dadoes, Grooves, and Rabbets," page 17.)

3. Assemble the carcase. Use glue and 6d finishing nails to join the sides to the bottom and top. Glue and nail the nailing cleats in place as shown in the *Overall View*.

4. Install the back. Use a framing square to make sure the sides are square with the top and bottom. Apply glue to the rabbets in the side panels and top panel; lay the back in place; and secure it using ⅞-inch brads.

5. Cut and attach the stiles and rails. The rail dimensions in the Materials List will make the stiles flush to the sides of the cabinet. This looks best for an individual cabinet. However, if you are building a run of cabinets, you may want to add ¼ inch to the rail lengths to allow for warped cabinet sides or irregular walls. Cut the stiles, and fasten them using glue and 6d finishing nails. Then cut the rails to fit between, and fasten them the same way.

SHELVES, DOOR, AND INSTALLATION

1. Make the shelves. Cut the shelf edges to the dimensions in the Materials List. Glue and clamp them to the front edges of the shelves.

2. Make and hang the door. The door dimensions in the Materials List are for a door that overlays the stiles and rails by ⅜ inch on all sides. (See "Making Cabinet Doors," page 22.) To hang the door, fasten a pair of overlay hinges 2 inches from each end of a stile. (See "Installing Doors and Hinges," page 25.) Fasten the hinges to the stiles, and hang the door, making sure it is square with the face frame.

3. Finish and install the cabinet or cabinets. Apply finish to the cabinet (polyurethane is a good, durable choice). Install the door pull with screws provided. Use 3-inch drywall screws through the top and bottom nailing cleats to hang the cabinet. Hanging a wall cabinet can be tricky since it must be supported until it is secured. (See "Installing Cabinets and Built-ins," page 34.)

SIDE PANEL DETAILS

3"

¾" x ⅜" Deep Rabbet for Top

⅜" x ⅜" Deep Rabbet for Back

1½"

30"

2"

¾" x ⅜" Deep Dado for Bottom

8"

2¼"

11¼"

OVERALL VIEW

⅜" x ⅜" Rabbet

Back

Top

Nailing Cleat

Shelf Edge

Shelf

Shelf Edge

Side Panel

Bottom

Nailing Cleat

Stile

Rail

Raised-Panel Door

pantry cabinet

AMONG THE BEST FEATURES of many older houses and a few newer ones is a tremendously practical storage area known as a pantry. Pantries come in many sizes and configurations, ranging from small shelved closets to good-sized rooms.

Pantries are ideal for storing canned foods, dry goods, and staples of all kinds. They're also good places for keeping bulky cooking and canning equipment, as well as appliances and accessories that don't see everyday use.

The spacious cabinet featured here has one fixed shelf and four adjustable shelves that rest on supports attached to metal standards. Cut the standards needed for this pantry from eight 42-inch or four 84-inch pieces.

This unit matches existing cabinets where the distance from floor to ceiling or soffit is 7 feet. In the absence of a soffit, you can build the cabinet to match existing cabinets or extend it all the way to the ceiling. To facilitate cabinet placement, allow ½ inch of clearance between the cabinet top and soffit; then conceal the gap with molding.

PANTRY CABINET MATERIALS LIST

Qty	Part	Dimensions		Qty	Part
Carcase, shelves, and doors				**Hardware**	
2	Plywood side panels	¾" x 23¼" x 83½"			4d Finishing nails
3	Plywood top, bottom, and fixed shelf	¾" x 23" x 31¼"			⅞" Brads
4	Plywood shelves	¾" x 22⅛" x 30¼"			6d Finishing nails
1	Plywood back	¼" x 31¼" x 76¾"			#10 x 3½" Wood screws
2	Solid-wood nailing cleats	¾" x 3½" x 31¼"		4	37⅞" Metal shelf standards
1	Solid-wood kick plate	¾" x 5" x 32"		4	38⅛" Metal shelf standards
2	Solid-wood face frame stiles	¾" x 1½" x 79¼"		16	Metal shelf supports
3	Solid-wood face frame rails	¾" x 1½" x 29"		4	Door pulls
4	Solid-wood shelf edges	¾" x ¾" x 30¼"		8	Self-closing hinges
4	Doors (with ⅜" overlay)	¾" x 14¹³⁄₁₆" x 38⅛"			

BUILDING THE CARCASE

1. Cut the parts. Cut the sides, top, bottom, shelves, back, nailing cleats, and kick plate to the dimensions in the Materials List. Then cut the kick plate notches in the bottom edge of each side panel, as shown in *Side Panel Details*.

2. Cut the dadoes. Cut dadoes across the inside surfaces of the side panels positioned as shown in *Side Panel Details*. (See "Dadoes, Grooves, and Rabbets," page 17.)

3. Cut grooves for the standards. Rout ³⁄₁₆-inch-deep and ⅝-inch-wide grooves in the side panels. Locate these grooves as shown in *Side Panel Details*. Note that the drawing shows one cabinet side. Don't forget to make the other side in a mirror image. (See "Making Dadoes and Grooves with the Table Saw," page 17.)

4. Cut the rabbets. Cut a ⅜ x ⅜-inch rabbet along the rear inside edge of each side panel as shown in *Side Panel Details*. These rabbets are ⅛ inch deeper than the back panel thickness to create a fitting allowance for less-than-perfect walls. Then use a straight

SIDE PANEL DETAILS

⅝" x ³⁄₁₆" Deep Grooves

¾" x ⅜" Dado Located ¼" from Top

1⅛" x 3½" Stopped Rabbet

38⅞"

⅜" x ⅜" Rabbet

Shelf Standards

¾" x ⅜" Deep Dadoes

5"

14"

1⅛" x 3½" Stopped Rabbet

5"

4¼" High x 3" Deep Notch for Kick Plate

bit to widen the rabbet to 1 inch for 3½ inches below the top dado and 3½ inches above the bottom dado. This accommodates the 1x4 nailers. Square off these widened areas using a chisel.

5. Assemble the cabinet. Assemble the top, bottom, and fixed shelf to the sides using glue and four 4d finishing nails into each dado. (See "Squaring a Carcase," page 21.)

6. Notch and attach the kick plate. Notch the kick plate to fit around the sides as shown in the *Overall View*. Attach the kick plate to the sides using glue and two 4d finishing nails at each end.

159

OVERALL VIEW

Nailing Cleat

Metal Shelf Standards

Back

Side Panel

Rail

Fixed Shelf

Doors

Nailing Cleat

Stile

¾" x ¾" Notches for Sides

Kick Plate

Note: Adjustable
shelves are not shown.

Here are two pantry design ideas: add shelving to a closet to store kitchen items, left; install a ready-made pantry, right.

7. Attach the nailing cleats. Apply glue to the widened rabbets in the rear of the side panels; position the nailing cleats between the rabbets; and drive two 4d finishing nails through the side panels into each end of each nailing cleat.

8. Attach the back panel. Apply glue to the rabbets in the rear edges of the side panels, the rear edges of the horizontal panels, and the rear surfaces of the nailers. Lay the back panel in place with its top edge flush to the top of the top panel. Secure the back using ⅞-inch brads.

BUILDING THE FACE FRAME AND SHELVES

1. Cut and attach the stiles and rails. Cut the face frame stiles to the dimensions in the Materials List, and fasten them to the cabinet with glue and 6d finishing nails. Cut the rails to fit between, and then glue and nail them with their tops flush to the tops of the sides, fixed shelf, and bottom.

2. Complete the adjustable shelves. Cut the solid-wood shelf edges to the dimensions in the Materials List. Glue and clamp the edges to the front of the adjustable shelves.

3. Install the cabinet. Before installation, sand the solid-wood parts, and apply the finish of your choice. Set the cabinet in place against the wall. Make sure the unit is plumb and level, and shim it as necessary beneath the side panels and kick plate. Then attach the cabinet to the wall by driving two #10 x 3½-inch wood screws through each nailer into each stud (four screws per nailer). (For more on installation techniques, see "Installing Cabinets and Built-ins," page 34.)

4. Install the shelves. Use a hacksaw to trim the metal shelf standards to length. Make all the cuts from the top ends of the standards to keep them in perfect register.

Then set the standards in place inside the grooves in the side panels, and secure them with the nails provided. Snap a metal shelf support into each standard for each shelf; then lay the shelves atop the supports.

BUILDING AND FINISHING THE DOORS

1. Build the doors. The dimensions in the Materials List are for doors that overlay the cabinet by ⅜ inch all around. (See "Making Cabinet Doors," page 22.)

2. Finish the doors. Finish the doors to match the cabinet carcase. Attach door pulls and self-closing hinges using screws provided. Then hang the doors on the cabinet. (See "Installing Doors and Hinges," page 25.)

rollout shelf

SOME BASE CABINETS can be a pain in the back, especially when you try to reach pots, pans, or other items stored in them—invariably, whatever you're reaching for is at the very back of the cabinet. If you're tired of being a kitchen contortionist and unloading cabinets just to reach a sauce pan or to lift out a heavy food processor, this rollout shelf is the prescription for your relief. You'll probably want to make and install several of them.

The shelf featured here is sized to fit into a cabinet that is 18 inches wide and 24 inches deep. It's designed to work with the base cabinet on page 151. The base cabinet is built of ¾-inch-thick plywood with 1½-inch-wide face frames. As a result, the rollout shelf uses ¾-inch-thick wood slide hangers to allow the shelf to slide past the face frames. If you are installing the rollout shelf in cabinets that have a ¾-inch-wide face frame or no face frame at all, omit the slide hangers.

The rollout shelf uses side-mounted metal drawer slides. Typically, these slides require ½ inch of clearance on each side. This leaves you with an overall shelf width of 20 inches. To accommodate wider or narrower openings and deeper or shallower cabinets, adjust shelf dimensions to suit your needs.

ROLLOUT SHELF MATERIALS LIST

Difficulty Level: EASY

Qty	Part	Dimensions	Qty	Part
2	Solid-wood sides	¾" x 3" x 22½"		*Hardware*
1	Solid-wood back	¾" x 3" x 14"		¾" Brads
1	Plywood bottom	½" x 13¼" x 22½"		#6 x 1¼" Wood screws
2	Guide hangers	¾" x 4" x 22⅞"	1 set	22" Side-mounted metal drawer slides

OVERALL VIEW

Bottom

Back

¾" x ⅜" Rabbet

Side

22½"

1¼"

13¼"

½" x ⅜" Grooves

Drawer Guide

Drawer Slide

BUILDING THE SHELF

1. Cut the parts. Cut sides, back, bottom, and slide hangers to the dimensions in the Materials List. Then cut off the top front corner of each side. Make the cut at a 45-degree angle, 1¼ inches up from the bottom front corner.

2. Groove and rabbet the sides and back. Cut grooves in the sides and back as shown in the *Overall View*. Then cut rabbets into the ends of the back panel. (See "Making Dadoes and Grooves with a Table Saw," page 17; and "Making Rabbets with a Table Saw," page 18.)

3. Assemble the shelf. Sand all parts before assembly. Assemble the shelf using glue and ¾-inch brads. Clamp it using bar or pipe clamps, and let it stand until the glue sets.

4. Apply the finish. Sand the shelf, and apply the finish of your choice. Allow the finish to dry.

INSTALLING THE SLIDES AND SHELF

1. Install the guide hangers. If the rollout shelf will be installed directly over an existing fixed shelf, simply attach the slide hangers directly on top of the shelf using glue and countersink 1¼-inch wood screws into the cabinet sides as shown in *Shelf Installation*. Otherwise, draw level lines where you want the shelf to go, and attach the hangers along those lines.

2. Attach the slides and glides. Following the manufacturer's directions, attach drawer slides to the rollout shelf using the screws provided. Fasten the drawer guides to the cabinet side panels using the screws provided. Make sure the guides are level both front to back and with each other.

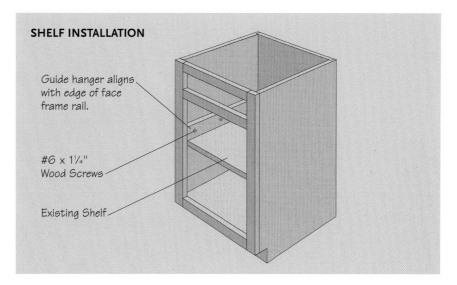

SHELF INSTALLATION

Guide hanger aligns with edge of face frame rail.

#6 x 1¼" Wood Screws

Existing Shelf

163

door-mounted shelves

MOST HOMES have an abundance of potential storage space that goes to waste, some of which is no farther than the nearest cabinet door. Wherever cabinet doors have no shelves behind them or have shelves that lie at least four inches from the door, you can add shallow shelving to the doors themselves.

Door-mounted shelves are ideal for under-sink cabinets in kitchens, bathrooms, and utility rooms, where they store and organize soaps, cleansers, and cleaning paraphernalia. Other good prospects for this project are pantry, work-shop, and hobby-room cabinets.

This plan is for a shelf unit designed to fit on the door of a standard 18-inch-wide single-door cabinet or 36-inch-wide two-door cabinet. Adjust the dimensions to fit your needs, but make sure the shelf unit is mounted at least $1/2$ inch inside all door edges to allow adequate clearance of the face frame.

DOOR-MOUNTED SHELVES MATERIALS LIST

Difficulty Level: EASY

Qty	Part	Dimensions	Part
1	Plywood support panel	¾" x 12½" x 19¼"	*Hardware*
3	Solid-wood shelves	½" x 3" x 13"	4d Finishing nails
2	Solid-wood sides	¾" x 3½" x 19¼"	#8 x 1¼" Wood screws
3	Shelf stops	¼" x 1⅛" x 14"	

OVERALL VIEW

Corners Cut Off at 45°

Side

1"

Cabinet Door

Support Panel

12½"

5³⁄₄"

19¼"

5³⁄₄"

½" × ¼"
Dadoes

5³⁄₄"

Shelf Stop

Shelf

4d Finishing
Nails

½"

Side

½"

CONSTRUCTING SUPPORTS & SIDE PANELS

1. Cut and sand the parts. Cut the support panel, shelves, sides, and shelf stops to the dimensions in the Materials List. Then cut off the top front corners of the sides at 45 degrees. Start the cuts 1 inch down from the top edge of the sides as shown in the *Overall View.* Lightly sand all parts.

2. Dado support and side panels. Cut dadoes in the support panel and sides as shown in the *Overall View.* You can use the shelf spacing shown

or adjust the spacing to suit your needs. (See "Dadoes, Grooves, and Rabbets," page 17.)

3. Assemble the shelf unit. Put glue in the support panel dadoes. Affix the support panel to the shelves using 4d finishing nails through the back of the panel. Put glue in the side panel dadoes. Attach the side panels to the shelves using 4d finishing nails. Check that the assembly is square.

4. Attach shelf unit to the cabinet door. Center the unit on the inside

surface of a cabinet door, and attach the panel to the door using four 1¼-inch wood screws.

5. Attach shelf stops. Apply a small amount of glue to each end of each shelf stop. Position each stop about an inch above its respective shelf, and attach the stop using one 4d finishing nail at each end.

6. Apply the finish. Sink all nails with a nail set, and fill holes with wood putty. Lightly sand as required, and apply the finish of your choice.

cutting board with knife storage

WHY NOT STORE your knives right where you use them? If this reasoning makes sense to you, you'll enjoy making and using the project shown here. Beneath the hefty hardwood cutting board, there's a compartment that holds a drawer for storing your cutlery. Because cutting boards need regular cleaning, this one is designed to separate easily from the storage compartment.

Maple is the hardwood most commonly used for cutting boards and butcher blocks because it is a particularly hard and tight-grained wood that stands up to use and washing. It's also widely available. Other good choices are birch, cherry, and myrtlewood (also known as California laurel).

Regardless of the species you choose, be sure to use a water-resistant glue when laminating the board. You can make the drawer front of matching hardwood, or choose another wood to correspond with the decor of your kitchen. The other solid-wood components can be hardwood or a softwood, such as pine.

Kitchen cutting boards range in thickness from $\frac{3}{4}$ inch to 2 inches or more. These plans call for a thickness of $1\frac{1}{2}$ inches simply because you may be able to find maple or other suitable hardwood available in nominal 1x2 ($\frac{3}{4}$ by $1\frac{1}{2}$ inches), finished on all four sides. If that stock isn't locally available, you can rip your own from any suitable $\frac{3}{4}$-inch-thick stock; then run the sawn edges through a jointer. If you don't own a jointer, you can hand-plane the edges or use a portable belt sander to rough-sand the assembled board. In any event, for visual purposes, plan for the finished board to be between 1 and $1\frac{1}{2}$ inches thick.

CUTTING BOARD WITH KNIFE STORAGE MATERIALS LIST

Difficulty Level: CHALLENGING

Qty	Part	Dimensions	Qty	Part	Dimensions
	Cutting board		1	Solid-wood false front	¾" x 2½" x 11"
16	Solid-wood strips	¾" x 1½" x 18" (rough length)	2	Solid-wood runners	⅜" x 1¹⁄₁₆" x 14⅜"
	Compartment			*Hardware*	
2	Solid-wood sides	¾" x 3" x 15"		6d Finishing nails	
1	Plywood back	½" x 2¼" x 10¼"		4d Finishing nails	
1	Solid-wood bottom	¾" x 10¼" x 15"	4	¼" x 1" Wooden dowels	
	Drawer			¾" Brads	
2	Solid-wood sides	¾" x 2⅛" x 14⅜"		⅝" Drywall screws	
1	Plywood bottom	¼" x 8⅝" x 14⅜"		1" Drywall screws	
2	Plywood front & back	½" x 1⅞" x 8⅝"	1	Wood knob	
			4	Self-adhesive, nonskid furniture cushions	

MAKING THE CUTTING BOARD

1. Cut the strips. If necessary, rip the solid-wood strips from ¾-inch stock; then cut them to a rough length of 18 inches.

2. Glue the strips. Tape waxed paper or coated freezer paper to the top of your work surface. Use a small brush or roller applicator to apply an even coat of glue to all broad surfaces, except the outer ones, of all the strips. Clamp them together using a pair of bar or pipe clamps, keeping all the strips aligned as you slowly tighten the clamps. Let the strips stand overnight with the clamps in place.

3. Trim and sand the cutting board. After removing the clamps, scrape off the hardened glue. Trim one end of the board square and even; then cut the other end to the board's finished length of 16¾ inches. Use a router and roundover bit to roundover all edges and corners.

MAKING THE COMPARTMENT

1. Cut the parts. Cut the compartment sides, back, and bottom to the dimensions in the Materials List.

OVERALL VIEW

Cutting Board

Dowel

Compartment

Drawer Runner

Drawer

Note: This is also a good time to cut all the drawer parts to save the time and trouble of removing and then replacing the dado cutter later on.

2. Rabbet the sides. Mill a ½-inch-wide, ⅜-inch-deep rabbet in the back end of each side panel as shown in *Compartment Construction,* page 168. Then mill a ¾-inch-wide, ⅜-inch-deep rabbet along the bottom inside edge of each side panel. (See "Dadoes, Grooves, and Rabbets," page 17.)

3. Groove the sides. Mill a ¾-inch-wide, ⅜-inch-deep groove in the inside surface of each side panel ¾ inch from the top edge. (See "Making Dadoes and Grooves with a Table Saw," page 17.)

4. Assemble the compartment. Using 6d finishing nails and glue, attach the bottom to the sides with the back edges flush. Then attach the back panel using glue and 4d finishing nails, as shown in *Compartment Construction,* page 168.

COMPARTMENT CONSTRUCTION

Back
½" x ⅜" Rabbet
¾" x ⅜" Groove for Drawer Runner
¾"
2"
Dowel
2"
Side
Bottom
¾" x ⅜" Rabbet

DRAWER CONSTRUCTION

Bottom
Side
Back
½" x ⅜" Rabbet
¼" x ⅜" Rabbet in Bottom of Sides
⅜" x ¹⁄₁₆" Wood Runner
Front
Wood Knob
False Front

5. Install the dowels in the compartment sides. Lay out the center points for the four dowels in the compartment sides as shown in *Compartment Construction*. Drill the ¼-inch-diameter holes ½ inch deep, and glue a dowel in each.

6. Locate the dowel centers on the cutting board. Turn the compartment upside down, and position it on the bottom of the cutting board so that the board will overlap the sides and back by ½ inch and the front by 1¼ inches. Put a piece of scrap wood on the compartment, and rap the scrap once with a hammer so that the dowels will mark the cutting board.

7. Drill the dowel holes in the cutting board. Drill ⁵⁄₁₆-inch-diameter holes ⅝ inch deep at the marks on the cutting board.

MAKING THE DRAWER

1. Cut the parts. If you haven't already done so, cut the drawer sides, bottom, front, back, false front, and runners to the dimensions in the Materials List. Rip down the solid-wood

drawer runners so that they are slightly less than ¾ inch wide.

2. Rabbet the sides. Mill a ½-inch-wide, ⅜-inch-deep rabbet in the ends of each side panel. Make a ¼-inch-wide, ⅜-inch-deep rabbet in the bottom inside edge of each side panel.

3. Assemble the drawer. Use glue and ¾-inch brads to fasten the sides to the back. Make sure the assembly is square, and attach the bottom using glue and ¾-inch brads.

4. Attach the solid-wood runners. Center the runners along the sides, as shown in *Drawer Construction*. Clamp each runner in position, and install them by driving three ⅝-inch drywall screws in holes that have been counterbored about ⅛ inch. This will keep the screw heads just below the wood surface. Use a block plane to chamfer the two long edges on each runner.

5. Install the false front. Clamp the false front against the plywood drawer front so that their top edges are flush

and the front overlaps the drawer sides evenly. Install the front by driving four 1-inch drywall screws from inside the drawer. Soften the corners of the drawer front by chamfering or sanding.

6. Install the knob. Center the knob's installation hole in the front, and screw the knob in place.

FINISHING UP

The cutting board requires a nontoxic finish. Don't use corn oil or other vegetable oils that can soon turn to a rancid, sticky varnish. The best choices are mineral oil or products formulated specifically for wood surfaces that will come in contact with food.

Use a polyurethane varnish on the compartment and drawer. Apply two or three coats. Once the finish has dried, install the nonskid furniture cushions on the bottom corners of the compartment. These give the unit a firm footing, preventing it from sliding around when you're cutting.

Rub some candle wax or beeswax along the runners to ensure that the drawer runs smoothly.

spice rack

ANY COOK who has tried storing jars of spices and herbs in a kitchen cabinet knows how difficult it can be to organize and locate the small jars. By simply adding a spice rack, this problem can be easily solved. However, the trouble with most commercially made spice racks is that they're too small and usually hold only one jar size.

This ample and handsome rack will provide all the room you need to store and organize your dried herbs and spices, as well as jars and tins of pasta, grains, legumes, teas, flavored vinegars, salt and pepper shakers, and more.

Beyond its utilitarian value, the rack has been designed to complement any kitchen design. The use of picture-frame molding and the arrangement of shelves and partitions combine to create a shadow box with the appeal of a still-life painting. There's even a tall compartment that can house a small vase of fresh-cut or dried flowers.

Plans call for the rack to be made using ½ x 3½-inch stock, which you'll need to rip to a 3¼-inch width for the shelves and partitions. Nice, clear ½-inch stock is available at most lumberyards as "door stop."

You can paint the rack or finish it naturally and choose picture-frame molding to complement any decor. The plans call for 1¼-inch-wide molding, but you can use any size molding as plain or ornate as you wish.

Attach the unit directly to studs. If you must mount it on a hollow or masonry wall, substitute the appropriate anchors for the oval-head screws.

SPICE RACK MATERIALS LIST

Difficulty Level: CHALLENGING

Qty	Part	Dimensions
Carcase		
2	Solid-wood top and bottom	½" x 3½" x 45"
2	Solid-wood sides	½" x 3½" x 33½"
1	Plywood back	¼" x 33½" x 44½"
Shelves and Partitions		
1	Solid-wood shelf (S-1)	½" x 3¼" x 44½"
2	Solid-wood shelves (S-2, S-4)	½" x 3¼" x 8½"
1	Solid-wood shelf (S-3)	½" x 3¼" x 29½"
1	Solid-wood shelf (S-5)	½" x 3¼" x 17½"
1	Solid-wood shelf (S-6)	½" x 3¼" x 32½"
1	Solid-wood shelf (S-7)	½" x 3¼" x 12"
2	Solid-wood partitions (P-1, P-2)	½" x 3¼" x 16½"
1	Solid-wood partition (P-3)	½" x 3¼" x 20½"

Qty	Part	Dimensions
Frame		
2	Picture-frame molding	¾" x 1¼" x 36"
2	Picture-frame molding	¾" x 1¼" x 47"
Hardware		
	1" Brads	
	4d Finishing nails	
4	1½" x #10 Oval-head wood screws	
4	#10 Finishing washers	

OVERALL VIEW

LAYING OUT DADOES

Left Surface of
P-1 and Right
Surface of P-2

Left Surface
of P-3

Right Surface
of P-3

¼" x ¼" Rabbet for Back

¼" x ¼" Rabbet for Back

Left Side

Right Side

Note: All
dadoes are
½" wide and
¼" deep.

Bottom of S-1

Bottom of S-3

Top of S-6

½" x ¼"
Rabbet

Top of
Bottom
Piece

½" x ¼"
Rabbet

MAKING THE CARCASE PARTS

1. Cut the outer parts. Cut the top, bottom, and sides from clear stock to the dimensions in the Materials List. Cut the back panel from ¼-inch plywood.

2. Cut and label the shelves and partitions. Rip enough clear stock to 3¼ inches to make the shelves and partitions. Cut the shelves and partitions to the lengths in the Materials List. As you make the length cuts, mark each piece with the designations in the Materials List—S-1, S-2, P-1, P-2, and so on.

3. Mill the rabbets. Use a router to rabbet the ends of the top and bottom pieces as shown in the *Overall View*. (See "Making Rabbets with a Router," page 20.)

Use the router to rabbet the rear inside edge of the top, bottom, and sides as shown in the *Overall View*.

4. Mill the Dadoes. Lay out the ½-inch x ¼-inch dadoes as shown in *Laying Out Dadoes,* page 171. Cut the dadoes. (See "Making Dadoes with the Router," page 19.)

ASSEMBLING THE SPICE RACK

1. Assemble the Carcase. Assemble the sides into the rabbets in the top and bottom using glue and two 1-inch brads at each joint as shown in the *Overall View.* Before the glue sets, install the back using glue and 1-inch brads every 8 inches. Check that the carcase is square. (Installing the back will help square the carcase.)

INSTALLING THE SHELVES & PARTITIONS

1. Make a subassembly. If you have corner clamps, they'll be handy for assembling the partitions and shelves. Using glue and two 1-inch brads at each dado joint, assemble shelves S-1 and S-6 to partitions P-1 and P-2. Then attach shelf S-5 and partition P-3.

2. Install the subassembly. Apply glue to the rear edges of the subassembly and to the ends of shelf S-1, the left end of shelf S-6, the bottom end of partition P-3, and to the corresponding dadoes in the carcase. Slide the subassembly into the carcase, and secure it using two 1-inch brads, at each joint.

3. Install the remaining shelves. Glue the remaining shelves in place, and secure the ends using brads wherever there's room to swing a hammer. Where there isn't sufficient space, use bar or pipe clamps to pull joints together. Wipe away seeping glue using a damp sponge.

ATTACHING THE PICTURE-FRAME MOLDING

C-Clamps

Mounting-Screw Holes

Picture-Frame Molding

ATTACHING THE PICTURE-FRAME MOLDING

1. Cut and attach the top molding piece. Picture-frame molding is used for this project because it comes with a rabbet in the back, which is usually used to contain a picture. Use a miter box and backsaw to miter-cut a piece of molding to the dimensions in the Materials List. Apply glue to the rabbet in the molding, and hold the piece in place with several cushioned C-clamps as shown in *Attaching the Picture-Frame Molding.*

2. Cut and attach the remaining molding pieces. Miter-cut the right-side molding to the dimensions in the Materials List. Apply glue to the rabbet in the molding, to the top mitered end, and the right mitered end of the top piece. Clamp the piece to the carcase side, and secure the top right corner using a 4d finishing nail. Cut and attach the other two pieces the same way.

COMPLETING THE PROJECT

1. Drill the mounting-screw holes. Drill four ¹¹⁄₆₄-inch mounting-screw holes, locating them as shown in *Attaching the Picture-Frame Molding.*

2. Apply the finish. After filling nail-holes, scraping away any visible dried glue, and doing any necessary sanding, apply the finish of your choice.

3. Hang the spice rack. Find the studs from which you intend to hang the rack. Place the rack against the wall; level it; and then use the holes in the rack as guides to mark for the screw holes. Drill ⁷⁄₆₄-inch pilot holes into the studs; then secure the rack with four #10 x 1½-inch screws and finishing washers.

wall-hung shelf unit

EVEN A WELL-DESIGNED KITCHEN can eventually run out of storage space, and many kitchens are poorly planned from the outset. One possible solution to a lack of sufficient shelf space is an easy-to-build wall-hung shelf unit like the one presented here. This piece would be at home with most kitchen plans. Its open access makes it handy for dishes, glass-ware, or frequently used food items; it is designed to be painted, but you could also apply a stained or clear finish to match existing cabinets or architectural trim.

The shelf plans call for clear pine lumber as the solid-wood material and ply-wood panels for the top and back. You could use single 1x12 boards for the shelves and sides, but wide boards some-times have a tendency to twist, cup, or warp. If you find this to be the case when you go to shop for lumber, an alternative approach would be to glue up these parts from narrower stock selected to reduce these defects. As an alternative approach, you could also use ³⁄₄-inch-thick plywood panels for the sides and shelves instead of using solid pine.

WALL-HUNG SHELF UNIT MATERIALS LIST

Difficulty Level: EASY

Qty	Part	Dimensions	Qty	Part	Dimensions
Face Frame			2	Bed molding	⁹⁄₁₆" x 1¾" x 13⅛"
2	Solid-wood stiles	¾" x 1½" x 29⅞"	2	Bed molding	⁹⁄₁₆" x 1¾" x 32⅛"
2	Solid-wood rails	¾" x 1½" x 27"	1	Birch plywood top panel	¾" x 12⅞" x 31⅝"
1	Solid-wood top rail	¾" x 2⅛" x 27"		before edging	
				finished size after edging	¾" x 13⅝" x 33⅛"
Carcase			1	Birch plywood back panel	½" x 29⅜" x 29¹¹⁄₁₆"
2	Solid-wood sides	¾" x 11¼" x 29⅞"	**Hardware and Miscellaneous Supplies**		
	1x12 boards or glue up		12	¼" x 1½" wood dowels	
	narrow stock			#8 x 2" oval head wood screws for wall mounting	
2	Solid-wood shelves	¾" x 10¾" x 28⅞"		#8 finishing washers	
1	Solid-wood bottom cleat	½" x ¹¹⁄₁₆" x 29⅜"		4d finishing nails	
2	Solid-wood edging strip	¾" x ¹³⁄₁₆" x 13⅝"		1" brads	
1	Solid-wood edging strip	¾" x ¹³⁄₁₆" x 33⅛"			

173

OVERALL VIEW

Blind ½" x ½" Rabbet for Back

Top

Edging Strip with ³⁄₈" Rad. Cove

½" x ½" Rabbet

Side

Top Rail

Bed Molding

Back

Notch stile to fit bed molding.

¼" x ³⁄₄" Dado

Shelf

4d Finishing Nail

4d Finishing Nail

Cleat

Bottom Rail

Stile

¼" x 1½" Dowel

BUILDING THE CASE

1. Cut the parts. Rip and crosscut the side and shelf panels to finished dimensions listed in the Materials List.

2. Cut rabbets and dadoes in the side panels. Use either dado blades in the table saw or the router with a straight bit to make these cuts as shown in the *Overall View*. (See "Dadoes, Grooves, and Rabbets," pages 17 to 20.)

3. Assemble shelves and sides. Apply glue to the dadoes in case sides, and then insert the shelf ends

into the dadoes. Use 4d finishing nails to pin the parts together. Use a nail set to drive the nailheads below the wood surface. Check that the case is square.

BUILDING THE FACE FRAME

1. Cut the parts. Rip and crosscut the face frame parts to size as shown in the Material List.

2. Bore dowel holes. Use a doweling jig to bore ¼-inch-diameter holes in the ends of the rails and in the edges of the stiles.

3. Assemble the face frame. Apply glue to the dowel holes, and brush a small amount on each dowel before inserting it in place. Join the rails to the stiles using bar clamps to pull the joints tight. Check that the assembly is square by comparing opposite diagonal measurements. If the measurements are equal, the face frame is square.

JOIN THE FACE FRAME TO THE CASE

1. Apply glue. Lay the case on its back on a worktable or a set of saw horses. Spread a light coating of glue on the front edges of the case sides and shelves using a wood shim or small brush.

2. Position the face frame over the case. Adjust the position as shown in the *Overall View*.

3. Fasten the face frame. Use 4d finishing nails to pin the face frame to the sides and shelves. Set the nailheads below the surface of the wood.

BUILDING THE CASE TOP

1. Cut the panel and edging. Cut a piece of ³⁄₄-inch-thick plywood to size for the case top. Rip edging stock from solid pine, leaving the strips a few inches longer than finished dimension. Note that the edging strips are slightly thicker than the plywood stock to make the application easier.

2. Cut edging to size. Use a miter saw to cut the edging to length. Note that 45-degree miter joints are required at the front corners.

3. Apply edging. First spread glue on the front edge of the plywood panel; then position the edging so that it

SIDE SECTION

Edging

Top

7/8" Front and Sides

3/4"

Top
Rail

Note: Top of
edging is flush
with top panel;
rails extend 1/16"
above shelves;
stiles extend 1/16"
beyond sides.

12⅜"

Back

30⅝"

Rail

Shelves

12⅜"

13¼"

Rail

Cleat

13/16"

slightly overlaps the plywood on both faces. Use clamps or masking tape to pull the joint tight, checking to make sure that the short point of the end cuts perfectly align with the ends of the panel. (See "Working With Plywood, Finishing Edges," page 12.) After the glue has set for at least 30 minutes, remove the clamps, and apply the end pieces using the same technique.

4. Trim the edging. Use a sharp block plane and a sanding block to trim the edging until it is flush with the panel surfaces.

5. Shape the panel edge. Install a ⅜-inch-radius cove bit in the router, and use it shape the edge profile on the case top.

6. Install a straight bit in the router, and use an edge guide to cut the rabbet for the back panel in the top panel. Note that the rabbet is stopped at both ends of the panel, so stop the router cut about ⅛ inch from

the stop line. Use a sharp chisel to complete the rabbet, squaring the ends of the cut.

INSTALL THE TOP

1. Position the top. Place the top on the case, adjusting its position for the proper overhang on the front and both ends.

2. Fasten the top. Bore 1/16-inch-diameter pilot holes through the panel; then use 4d finishing nails to fasten the panel to the case sides and face frame. Set all nailheads.

APPLY THE BED MOLDING

1. Cut molding to length. Use a miter saw to trim the bed molding to length as specified in the plan.

2. Install the molding. Use 1-inch brads and 4d finishing nails to install the molding to the front and sides of the case. Because the face frame overhangs the sides of the case by 1/16 inch, notch the edges of the face frame to allow the bed molding to sit tight to the side panels. Mark the height of the bottom edge of the molding, and use a sharp chisel to remove the stock. Use a nail set to set the nailheads.

INSTALL THE CASE BACK

1. Cut the panel. Cut ½-inch-thick plywood to specified dimensions.

2. Install the back. Lay the case face down on a padded worktable or pair of saw horses. Place the back in position so that it fits into the rabbets on the case sides and top. Fasten the back by nailing it to the edges of the back, sides, and shelves using 4d finishing nails.

3. Cut the bottom cleat. Cut a strip of pine for the bottom cleat. This piece

will hide the raw edge of the back panel, providing a finished appearance.

4. Install the cleat. Apply glue to the top edge of the cleat, and place it in position. Use 1-inch brads to pin it to the bottom edge of the back panel.

SAND & FINISH THE PIECE

1. Fill nailholes. Apply wood filler to all nailholes, allowing the material to mound up slightly over the hole to allow for shrinkage while it dries.

2. Sand and paint. Sand all surfaces using 180-grit sandpaper; remove all dust before priming and painting.

INSTALLATION

1. Determine the location of the unit. Decide on the exact position of the shelving unit on the wall; mark outside edges of the side panels.

2. Locate the wall studs. Use an electronic stud finder to locate the wall studs behind the shelf unit. Mark the stud centers on the wall.

3. Bore pilot holes for mounting. Measure from the edge marks to the stud centers, and transfer those measurements to the back panel of the shelving unit. Bore pilot holes for mounting screws through the back. Plan on two screws near the top and two near the bottom.

4. Install the case. Have an assistant help you support the case, aligning the outside edges with your marks. Using oval-head screws and finishing washers, drive one screw into a wall stud; then use a spirit level to check the case for plumb and level. Drive the rest of the screws to hold the unit to the wall.

wine rack

IN AMERICA, INTEREST IN WINE was once widely considered to be largely an upper-class pursuit or something associated with European culture, where wine has always been an integral part of daily life. Now, however, both wine consumption and production in the United States have grown tremendously—especially in light of research showing the medical benefits of moderate use. As a result, it has become much more common for people to enjoy a glass of wine with dinner. And part of the fascination with wine comes in exploring its many varieties— comparing the products of different regions, grape species, and vintages.

If you begin to pursue wine as a hobby, as well as a beverage, it is likely that you will accumulate a small collection that needs storing. Most of us cannot justify the construction of a dedicated wine cellar, but a realistic alternative is to build a small wine rack. Our design will hold 42 bottles, allowing you to easily store and display a variety of wines. The open frame design of the sides and partitions will allow you to better view the individual bottles, making it easy to find a particular wine in your collection. The rack is simple to build, but attractive enough that you can proudly place it in your dining room or kitchen.

WINE RACK MATERIALS LIST

Difficulty Level: CHALLENGING

Qty	Part	Dimensions	Qty	Part	Dimensions
Top (¾" x 29¼" x 14¾")			1	Plywood back	¼" x 27¼" x 32"
1	Plywood panel	¾" x 27¼" x 13¾"	72	Support strips	¾" x ¾" x 13"
1	Edging	¾" x 1" x 29¼"	1	Blocking (2 x 4 lumber)	1½" x 3½" x 27¾"
2	Edging	¾" x 1" x 14¾"	2	Blocking (2 x 4 lumber)	1½" x 3½" x 10½"
			1	Baseboard	¾" x 4" x 29¼"
2 Sides (¾" x 14" x 31½")			2	Baseboard	¾" x 4" x 14¾"
4	Solid-wood stiles	¾" x 2½" x 31½"			
2	Solid-wood rails	¾" x 3¾" x 9"	**Hardware and Miscellaneous Supplies**		
2	Solid-wood rails	¾" x 4½" x 9"		1" brads	
2	Solid-wood mullions	¾" x 2½" x 23¼"		#20 joining plates	
				¼" x 1½" wood dowels	
5 Partitions (¾" x 13¾" x 30¾")				#8 x 2" flathead wood screws	
5	Solid-wood stiles	¾" x 2¼" x 30¾"		#8 x 1½" flathead wood screws	
5	Solid-wood stiles	¾" x 2½" x 30¾"		#8 x 1¼" flathead wood screws	
10	Solid-wood rails	¾" x 3¾" x 9"		4d finishing nails	
5	Solid-wood mullions	¾" x 2½" x 23¼"			
Bottom panel (¾" x 13¾" x 26¼")					
1	Plywood panel	¾" x 13" x 26¼"			
1	Edging	¾" x ¾" x 26¼"			

OVERALL VIEW

¼" x ½" Rabbet, Back Edge of Top and Side Frame

Top

³⁄₈" Rad. Half-Round Edging

¾" Overhang at Front and Sides

No. 20 Joining Plate, Three per Joint

Partition Frame

¼" x 1½" Dowel

1" Brad

Back

30° Bevel

Support Strip

Side Frame

3¾"

3¾"

3¾"

4½" (Bottom Side Only)

#8 x 1¼" Screw

Mullion

Rail   Stile   Bottom

Bottom Edging

BUILDING THE SIDES AND PARTITIONS

1. Cut the parts. Cut the rails, stiles, and mullions to the dimensions in the materials list. Label the parts for the sides and partitions to avoid confusion in assembly. Use a doweling jig to drill ¼-inch-diameter holes in the parts for the dowel joints. (See "Reinforcing Joints with Dowels," page 15.) Note that the holes are slightly deeper than the overall dowel length to allow space for extra glue at the bottom.

2. Assemble the frames. Begin with the rail/mullion joints. Apply a small amount of glue to the walls of the dowel holes and also on the dowels; then insert them into the holes in the mullion ends; and assemble the mullions to the top and bottom rails. Use clamps to pull the joints tight, and

check that the assembly is square by comparing opposite diagonal measurements. Allow the glue to set for at least one hour; then join the stiles to the rails using the same techniques.

3. Cut frame joints. Use a router with a straight bit or the table saw with dado blades to cut the rabbets in the back stiles of the side frames as shown in the plans. (See "Making Rabbets with a Table Saw," page 18, and "Making Rabbets with a Router," page 20.) Next, use the plate joiner to cut the slots in the sides and partitions for attaching the bottom and top panels. (See "Reinforcing Joints with Biscuits," page 16.)

4. Cut and install the bottle support strips. Cut the support strips to size as shown in the Materials List. Use a miter saw to make the angled

cut on the front end of each strip; then drill and countersink pilot holes for screwing the strips to the frames. Note that the screw-hole locations need to be offset slightly on the strips that mount to opposite sides of the same partition.

Lay out the positions of the strips on the side and partition frames; then screw them in place.

BUILDING THE TOP AND BOTTOM PANELS

1. Cut the parts. Cut plywood panels and edging strips to the dimensions shown in the Materials List. Use a miter saw to cut the 45-degree end joints on the top edging strips.

2. Rabbet the top plywood panel. Use the router or table saw to cut the rabbet in the back edge of the top panel. (See "Making Rabbets with a Table Saw," page 18, and "Making Rabbets with a Router," page 20.)

3. Apply edging. Spread glue on the edges of the plywood panels and also on the edging strips; then apply the edging using masking tape to clamp the strips to the panel. As an alternative, you can use small bar clamps to hold the strips in position.

4. Cut joining plate slots. Use the plate joiner to cut the slots for joining plates in the top and bottom panels as shown in the plans. Drill and countersink pilot holes in the bottom panel for screws to fasten the partition frames. Note: the joints between the bottom panels and partition frames use a combination of joining plates and screws. The plates serve as a means of locating the partitions while the screws hold the joints tight, eliminating the need to apply glue or to clamp these joints.

BASE DETAILS

BASE DETAIL FRONT

BASE DETAIL TOP

5. Shape the top edge. Install a $\frac{3}{8}$-inch-diameter roundover bit in the router, and use it to shape the front and sides of the top panel. In order to form the half-round shape of the top, first cut the quarter-round shape on one surface; then flip the panel over to cut the second half of the profile. Because the profile encompasses the entire thickness of the edge, you will need to use an accessory edge guide with the router instead of relying on the ball-bearing pilot on the bit.

ASSEMBLE THE CASE

1. Join the partitions to the bottom. Insert joining plates in the slots in the bottom panel, then place the partition frames over the plates—there is no need to use glue on these joints. Drive #8 x 1$\frac{1}{2}$-inch flathead screws through the bottom to fasten the partitions.

2. Join the sides to the bottom. Apply glue to joining plate slots in the side frames and also to the end slots in the bottom panel. Insert joining plates in the slots, and then assemble the sides to the bottom. Use clamps to pull the joints tight, leaving them in place until the glue sets—at least one hour.

3. Install the top and back panels. Apply glue to the joining plate slots in the top panel and on the top ends of the side and partition frames. Insert joining plates into the slots, and place the top into position. Use clamps to pull the joints tight. If you do not have sufficient clamps to do the job, you can place heavy weights on the top to close the joints. Cut the back panel to finished size as shown in the Materials List; then install it to the back of the case. Use 1-inch brads to fasten the back, nailing it to the sides, top, bottom, and partitions.

ADD BASE MOLDING

1. Cut molding. Rip stock to width for the base molding, leaving the pieces several inches longer than finished dimension. Use a $\frac{1}{2}$-inch-radius cove bit in the router to shape the top edge of the molding stock as shown in the plan. Trim the molding to length with a miter saw with 45-degree bevel joints at the front corners and square cuts at the back edge of the case.

2. Install the base molding. Cut 2x4 stock to length for blocking. Drill and countersink pilot holes, and then fasten the blocking to the bottom of the

case using #8 x 2-inch flathead screws. Nail the base molding in place using 4d and 6d finishing nails. Remember to apply glue to the mating faces of the corner bevels to ensure tight, permanent joints.

SAND AND FINISH THE CASE

1. Set nails and fill holes. Use a nail set to drive all nailheads below the wood surface; then fill the holes with matching wood filler. Allow the filler to dry thoroughly; then sand the case, easing all sharp edges. (See "Preparing Wood," page 57.)

2. Apply stain and finish. If you would like to stain the case, follow the manufacturer's directions for proper application; then let the stain dry before applying the clear top coat of your choice. (See "Wood Finishing," pages 62 to 71.)

For a painted finish, first prime all surfaces; then when dry, lightly sand the primer before applying the finish coats of paint. (See "Priming and Sealing Wood," page 65, and "Types of Paint," page 72.)

9 bathroom

MAKE THE MOST OF EVERY INCH OF AVAILABLE STORAGE SPACE

bathroom storage ideas

Clockwise (from top right) Open shelves provide personal storage for two people. Pullout shelves keep toiletries neat and easy to reach. Gain a little personal space as well as storage by placing a cabinet between two vanity sinks. Stand-alone open shelves supplement medicine and vanity cabinet storage.

medicine cabinet

A MEDICINE CABINET WITH A MIRROR is a standard bathroom fixture, but it needn't be standard fare. This attractive built-in model will grace any bathroom and is a good project to consider if you're planning to add a bath or remodel an existing one. Depending on the decor of your bathroom, you can build the cabinet from hardwood and finish it with or without stain, or you can build it using pine and paint it.

The plans call for three adjustable shelves, which you can make from 1x4 stock if you wish, but shelves of $\frac{1}{4}$-inch glass also add a nice touch and don't cost much. When you order your shelves cut to size, ask for used or reclaimed plate glass, which is salvaged from broken store windows and is usually available at about half the price of new glass. Have the glass shop seam or sand one of the edges of each shelf to remove the sharp edges.

This cabinet is designed to fit between studs that are on 16-inch centers, so you'll have to cut a hole in the wall where the cabinet will go. Use a stud finder to locate the studs. Then use a level to scribe horizontal lines for the top and bottom of the hole. Scribe one line at 51 inches and the other at 75 inches from the floor. Use a hammer and a 6d finishing nail to poke holes in the wall until you find the inside edge of each stud. You can also use a drill with a small bit for this job. Use the level to draw plumb lines along the inside edges. Connect the level lines and form a box measuring $14\frac{1}{2}$ by 24 inches. Now remove the wall material inside the box. (See "Removing Wallboard," page 34.) Measure to make sure the distance between the two studs is $14\frac{1}{2}$ inches. If the stud spacing is a little off, you'll want to adjust the cabinet dimensions to fit.

MEDICINE CABINET MATERIALS LIST

Difficulty Level: CHALLENGING

Qty	Part	Dimensions	Qty	Part	Dimensions
Carcase, frame, and door			**Hardware**		
2	Solid-wood cabinet sides	¾" x 3½" x 24"		6d Finishing nails	
2	Solid-wood top/bottom panels	¾" x 3½" x 13½"		1¼" Drywall screws	
1	Plywood cabinet back	¼" x 14½" x 23½"		⅞" Brads	
4	Solid-wood rails	¾" x 1½" x 16"		4d Finishing nails	
4	Solid-wood stiles	¾" x 1½" x 25"		#8 x 1½" Flathead wood screws	
1	Plywood mirror back	¼" x 13⅞" x 22⅞"	1 pair	¾" x 2" Butt hinges	
2	Horizontal retaining strips	⅛" x ½" x 14³⁄₁₆"		#4 x ½" Brass flathead wood screws	
2	Vertical retaining strips	⅛" x ½" x 23³⁄₁₆"		#10 x 2" Oval-head wood screws	
Glass				#10 Finishing washers	
3	Shelves	¼" x 3½" x 12⅞"	1	Small cabinet doorknob	
1	Mirror	⅛" x 13⅞" x 22⅞"	1	Magnetic latch	
			12	Adjustable shelf pins	

OVERALL VIEW

SIDE PANEL LAYOUT

BUILDING THE CABINET CARCASE

1. Cut the parts. Cut the cabinet sides, top, bottom, and plywood back to the dimensions in the Materials List.

2. Dado the sides. Dado the side panels as shown in the *Side Panel Layout*. (See "Dadoes, Grooves, and Rabbets," page 17.)

3. Drill the sides. Drill attachment hole and shelf pin holes in the cabinet sides as shown in *Side Panel Layout*. Use a template to drill the shelf pin holes. (See "Installing Shelf Pins," page 28.)

4. Assemble the carcase. Assemble the top and bottom panels into the dadoes in the side panels using glue and two 1¼-inch drywall screws at each connection. Install the back panel using glue and ⅞-inch brads.

BUILDING & INSTALLING THE CABINET FRAME

1. Cut the parts. The cabinet frame and the door frame have the same dimensions. Cut both sets of rails and stiles.

2. Attach the cabinet frame. Put glue along one front vertical edge of the cabinet. Put one stile in place over the glue, flush to the inside of the cabinet, and secure it using 4d finishing nails. Put glue on the top mitered end of the stile and on the top front edge of the cabinet. Nail the top rail in place. Repeat this process for the other stile and the last lower rail. Secure each miter joint using two $7/8$-inch brads.

3. Make the hinge mortises. Cut hinge mortises in the frame as shown in *Cabinet Frame Details*. (See "Installing Doors and Hinges," page 25.)

BUILDING THE CABINET DOOR

1. Cut the parts. Cut the mirror back from $1/4$-inch plywood. Cut the retaining strips to the dimensions in the Materials List with a 45-degree miter on each end.

2. Rabbet the rails and stiles. These stepped rabbets are shown in *Door Details*. First, cut a $1/8$-inch-deep, $3/4$-inch-wide rabbet for the retaining strip; then mill the second rabbet to $1/2$ x $3/8$ inch for the mirror and back, which will modify the first rabbet to $1/4$ x $1/8$ inch.

3. Assemble the door frame. Use corner clamps to clamp the frame together without glue. At each miter joint, counterbore through the top of the top rail and the bottom of the bottom rail, through the rail into the stile for one #8 x $1\frac{1}{2}$-inch flathead wood screw at each location, as shown in *Overall View*. Locate the screws no more than $1/2$ inch

CABINET FRAME DETAILS

Brads

2"

4d Finishing Nails

DOOR DETAILS

Door Back

Mirror

Retaining Strip

Mirror Frame

$1/4$" x $1/8$" Rabbet

$1/2$" x $3/8$" Deep Rabbet

from the corners so they won't interfere with the rabbets. Put glue on the mitered ends; assemble the frame in corner clamps; then insert the screws. Plug the screw holes.

4. Mortise the door frame. Lay the cabinet frame faceup. Align the door frame immediately to the left, facedown. Using the hinges as templates, mortise the door frame.

5. Drill the hinge and knob holes. Using the hinges as templates, mark the cabinet and door frames for hinge-screw holes. Drill small pilot holes for the hinge screws, and temporarily install the hinges. Drill the doorknob hole 6 inches up from the bottom right corner.

6. Sand the cabinet and door frames. It's important to sand these frames together, so they'll mate perfectly when finished. With the door and frame clamped in the closed position, sand the top, bottom, and right surfaces using 120- and 220-grit sandpaper, gently easing the sharp edges and corners as you proceed. Remove clamps and hinges; reclamp the frames; and sand the left sides. Then sand the face of the door frame.

7. Complete the door. Sand and varnish or paint the door frame before you install the mirror. When dry, lay the door frame facedown; then lay the mirror and door back in place. Attach the retaining strips using #4 x $1/2$-inch brass flathead wood screws driven through countersunk pilot holes.

FINISHING AND INSTALLING THE CABINET

1. Finish the cabinet. Do any necessary sanding. Apply the finish of your choice to the cabinet and the back of the door.

2. Install the cabinet. Make sure the cabinet is level in the opening. Attach it to studs using four oval-head wood screws with finish washers.

3. Hang the door, and attach the knob and magnetic latch. Attach the hinges and the knob. Attach the magnetic portion of a magnetic latch to the inside of the unhinged frame stile. Put the little metal latch plate opposing it on the inside of the door.

4. Install the shelves. Install each shelf using four metal shelf supports.

183

vanity

A VANITY is an attractive and useful addition to any bathroom. You can buy a vanity, but by building your own you can create a unit that perfectly fits your space and decor.

The handsome vanity shown here is designed for a large bathroom where there is 7 feet of wall space available, but you can easily adapt the design and dimensions to your own situation.

This vanity provides a spacious countertop and plenty of storage in its six drawers and behind its three cabinet doors. It uses a post-formed plastic-laminate countertop—available at home centers—in standard width with the length cut to order. (See "Countertops," page 32.)

Space beside the bank of drawers on the right is for a chair or stool. Install a well-lit mirror, and this becomes the perfect place for applying makeup.

VANITY MATERIALS LIST

Difficulty Level: DIFFICULT

Qty	Part	Dimensions
Carcase and face frame		
2	Plywood side panels	¾" x 20¼" x 31¼"
1	Plywood bottom panel	¾" x 17" x 20"
1	Plywood bottom panel	¾" x 40½" x 20"
2	Plywood partitions	¾" x 20" x 31¼"
1	Plywood back panel	¼" x 31¼" x 83¼"
1	Solid-wood nailer	¾" x 3½" x 83¼"
1	Solid-wood kick plate	¾" x 4¼" x 18"
1	Solid-wood kick plate	¾" x 4¼" x 41½"
1	Solid-wood rail	¾" x 1½" x 81"
1	Solid-wood rail	¾" x 1½" x 38½"
1	Solid-wood rail	¾" x 1½" x 24½"
1	Solid-wood rail	¾" x 1½" x 22"
5	Solid-wood rails	¾" x 1½" x 15"
2	Solid-wood stiles	¾" x 1½" x 27¾"
2	Solid-wood stiles	¾" x 1½" x 26¼"
1	Solid-wood short stile	¾" x 1½" x 24¾"
4	Plywood corner blocks	¾" x 3½" x 3½" x 5"
1	Preformed countertop	¾" x 22½" x 85"
1	Solid-wood fixed panel	¾" x 5" x 22¾"
Drawers (with ⅜" overlay)		
For 4¼" x 15" openings:		
8	Sides	¾" x 3¾" x 19"
4	Fronts	¾" x 3¾" x 14"
4	Backs	¾" x 3⅛" x 14"
4	Bottoms	¼" x 13½" x 18½"
4	False fronts	¾" x 5" x 15¾"

Qty	Part	Dimensions
For 4¼" x 24½" opening:		
2	Sides	¾" x 3¾" x 19"
1	Front	¾" x 3¾" x 23"
1	Back	¾" x 3⅛" x 23"
1	Bottom	¼" x 18½" x 23"
1	False front	¾" x 5" x 25¼"
For 7½" x 15" opening:		
2	Sides	¾" x 7" x 19"
1	Front	¾" x 7" x 14"
1	Back	¾" x 6⅛" x 14"
1	Bottom	¼" x 13½" x 18½"
1	False front	¾" x 8¼" x 15¾"
Doors (with ⅜" overlay)		
1	Door	¾" x 15¾" x 19¾"
2	Doors	¾" x 11⁵⁄₁₆" x 19¾"
Hardware		
	4d Finishing nails	
	⅞" Brads	
	¼" x 1¼" Dowels	
	#10 x 3½" Wood screws	
	#10 x 1¼" Wood screws	
	Bottom-mounted metal drawer slides	
3	Doorknobs	
6	Drawer pulls	
	Self-closing hinges	

OVERALL VIEW

Side Panel

Partitions

Nailer

Face Frame

Bottom Panel

Nailer Notch

Back Panel

¾" x ¾" Notches for Sides

Bottom Panel

Kick Plate Notch 3½" x 3" Deep

Kick Plate

Kick Plate

BUILDING THE CARCASE

1. Cut the parts. Cut side and bottom panels, partitions, back panel, nailer, and kick plates to the dimensions in the Materials List. Then cut kick plate notches in the bottom front edge of each side partition. Cut nailer notches in the top rear edge of both partitions. These details are shown in *Side Panel Layout* and *Partition Layout*.

2. Rabbet and dado the panels. Rabbet the back of the side panels as shown in Side Panel Layout. (See "Dadoes, Grooves, and Rabbets," page 17.) Then widen the top of the rabbets to 1 inch to accept the nailer. Square off the nailer rabbet using a

1-inch chisel. Dado side and partition panels as shown in *Side Panel Layout* and *Partition Layout*. Note that these drawings show only one side panel and one partition. The other side panel is a mirror of the one shown. The other partition gets dadoes on the other face. See the *Overall View*.

3. Install the bottoms. Secure the bottom panels into the dadoes in the side panels and partitions using glue and 4d finishing nails.

4. Attach the nailer and back. Attach the nailer to the side panels and partitions using glue and 4d finishing nails. Set the back panel in place, and secure using ⅞-inch brads.

5. Notch and attach kick plates. Notch the kick plates as shown in the *Overall View*. Attach the kick plates in their notches using glue and 4d finishing nails.

BUILDING & INSTALLING THE FACE FRAME

1. Cut the parts. Cut all face-frame rails and stiles to the dimensions in the Materials List.

2. Assemble the face frame. Assemble using glue and two dowels at each joint, locating the parts as shown in *Face Frame Construction*. (See "Reinforcing Joints with Dowels," page 15.)

3. Install the face frame. Fasten the face frame to the carcase using glue and 4d finishing nails, spaced about 12 inches apart.

INSTALLING & FINISHING THE VANITY

1. Cut plumbing holes. With the vanity near the rear wall, measure the distance from the wall and floor for the plumbing pipes. Use a drill and saber saw to cut pipe holes in the vanity back, allowing about an inch of clearance around each pipe.

SIDE PANEL LAYOUT

20¼"

1" x ⅜" x 3½" Rabbet

¼" x ⅜" Rabbet

¾" x ¼" Dado

5"   3½" High x 3" Deep Notch for Kick Plate

PARTITION LAYOUT

¾" x 3½" Notch for Nailer

¾" x ¼" Dado

5"   3½" High x 3" Deep Notch for Kick Plate

FACE FRAME CONSTRUCTION

Fixed Panel

⅜" x ⅜" Rabbet

¼" Dowel

4¼"

24½"

15"

22"

4¼"

4¼"

7½"

Rail

Stile

Short Stile

INSTALLING THE VANITY

Countertop

Level Line

Corner Block

Stud

31¼"

Centered Hole
(Drill with ³⁄₁₆" Bit)

15" Rail

15" Rail

22" Rail

24½" Rail

2. Install the vanity. Scribe a level line along the rear wall 31¼ inches from the high point in the floor as shown in *Installing the Vanity*. Slide the vanity in place, and level it using shims as necessary. Then drive two #10 x 3½-inch wood screws through the nailer into each stud. (See "Installing Cabinets and Built-ins," page 34.)

3. Finish the vanity. Before installing the countertop, fill nailholes with wood putty. Sand as necessary, and apply the finish of your choice.

INSTALLING THE COUNTERTOP

1. Cut and install corner blocks. Cut four triangular plywood corner blocks to the dimensions in the Materials List. On each block, apply glue to the two edges forming the 90-degree angle; press one in place in each top corner;

and secure using 4d finishing nails. Drive nails from inside the vanity, being careful to avoid driving them through the vanity exterior. Let the glue dry.

2. Install the countertop. With a ³⁄₁₆-inch bit, drill a centered hole through each corner block. Lay the countertop in place, and attach it from the underside using four #10 x 1¼-inch wood screws through the corner blocks.

BUILDING & INSTALLING DRAWERS AND DOORS

1. Make the drawers and doors. The cabinet shown has plain, solid-wood drawer fronts and raised-panel doors for a traditional look. The dimensions in the Materials List are for inset doors that overlay the face frame by ⅜ inch on all sides. You may build drawers and doors to suit your decor. The drawers use bottom-mounted metal slides, so be sure to

leave enough room between the bottom panel and the drawer bottom to accommodate the slides that you purchase. (See "Building Drawers," page 28 and "Making Cabinet Doors," page 22.)

2. Make and install the fixed panel. Because of plumbing, there is no room for a drawer under the sink. Instead, make a fixed panel to match the false drawer fronts. If you are making inset drawers, rabbet the panel all around as you did for the drawers. Glue and clamp the panel over the opening.

3. Finish drawers and doors, and install hardware. Finish drawer faces and doors to match the vanity. Then install pulls and slide hardware. Attach self-closing hinges to doors and face frames. (See "Installing Doors and Hinges," page 25 and "Installing Drawer-Slide Hardware," page 31.)

clothes hamper

THIS HAMPER IS SO HANDY that your family might even be encouraged to use it instead of leaving dirty clothes around the house. It features a double-bin design to separate clothes into "lights" and "darks," and the self-closing door couldn't be easier to operate.

The laundry baskets in this project are actually a pair of plastic, kitchen-size trash receptacles. You'll find these durable containers at just about any hardware store or home center. If you'd prefer a hamper with just one container, or if your containers are a different size than those shown here, you can adjust the project's dimensions ac-

cordingly. The design and construction basics will remain the same.

Your choice of wood and plywood depends largely on how you want to finish the unit. If you plan to paint your finished project, pine or poplar are two economical choices for the solid-wood parts.

The easiest way to make the top is to cut it from commercially available edge-glued stock, but if you can't find suitable stock, it's not much harder to glue up your own from clear nominal 1-inch stock. (See "Edge-Gluing Stock," page 14.)

CLOTHES HAMPER MATERIALS LIST

Difficulty Level: CHALLENGING

Qty	Part	Dimensions	Qty	Part	Dimensions
Carcase			*Top*		
2	Plywood sides	¾" x 11¾" x 29⅝"	1	Solid-wood top	¾" x 13¼" x 36½"
1	Tempered pegboard back	¼" x 29⅝" x34¼"	*Hardware*		
2	Solid-wood front edge strips	¾" x ¾" x 29⅝"		4d Finishing nails	
2	Solid-wood crosspieces	¾" x 2¾" x 33½"		#6 x 1½" Flathead wood screws	
2	Solid-wood top corner blocks	¾" x 3½" x 3½"		⅞" Brads	
2	Solid-wood stop blocks	¾" x 1½" x 1½"		#6 x 1¼" Flathead wood screws	
4	Solid-wood bottom corner block	1¼" x 1½" x 2¾"	20	⅜" Wood plugs	
2	Tilt-stop blocks	¾" x 1½" x 1½"		#6 x 1⅝" Flathead wood screws	
Door/platform assembly			4	¾" dia. Self-adhesive rubber or plastic cushions	
1	Plywood door	¾" x 25¼" x 31⅞"	1	Doorknob	
2	Solid-wood side edge strips	¾" x ¾" x 25¼"	2	2½" Butt hinges	
1	Solid-wood top edge strip	¾" x ¾" x 33⅜"	2	Garbage bins	
1	Plywood platform	¾" x 11" x 33⅜"			
2	Plywood braces	¾" x 10¼" x 10¼"			

OVERALL VIEW

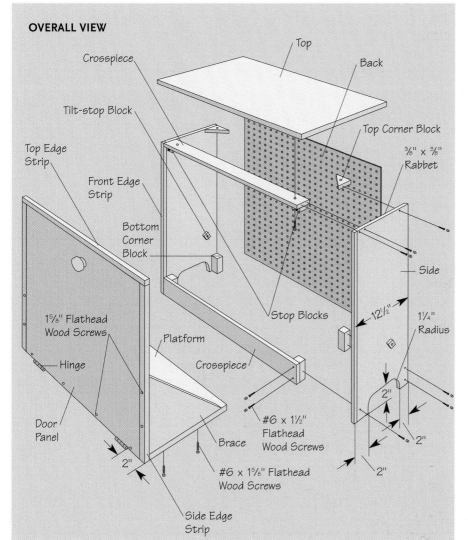

BUILDING THE CARCASE

1. Cut the parts. Cut the sides from ¾-inch plywood, the back from tempered pegboard, and all the other carcase parts from solid wood to the dimensions in the Materials List. Rabbet the side panels for the back as shown in the *Overall View*. (See "Dadoes, Grooves, and Rabbets," page 17.)

Use a saber saw to cut out the curved openings at the bottom of each side panel.

2. Attach the edge strips. Apply glue to the rear edge of each edge strip. Attach the strips to the front edge of each side panel using 4d finishing nails.

3. Counterbore screw holes. Use a counterbore bit or a combination of ⅜-inch and ³⁄₁₆-inch bits to drill and counterbore screw holes in the crosspieces as shown in the *Overall View*. (See "Countersink and Counterbore Bits," page 42.)

189

4. Attach the crosspieces and back panel. Glue and screw the bottom corner blocks onto both ends of the bottom crosspiece so that they are flush with the ends. Use #6 x 1½-inch flathead wood screws. Next, attach the top and bottom crosspieces to the side panels using glue and 1½-inch wood screws, as shown in the *Overall View*.

Apply glue to both rabbets in the back of the side panels, and position the pegboard back in place. Attach the back with ⅞-inch brads nailed into the rabbets.

5. Attach the top corner blocks. Cut the top corner blocks into a triangular shape; then glue and screw them in place as shown in the *Overall View*. Use two 1¼-inch screws for each block.

6. Plug the screw holes. Fill the counterbored holes with glued wood plugs, and sand flush.

7. Make the top. Rip three pieces of stock to 5½ inches, and cut them to a rough length of 38 inches. Apply glue to the edges of the boards to be joined, and clamp them together with three bar or pipe clamps. (See "Edge-Gluing Stock," page 14.)

After the glue has dried, scrape away any squeeze-out, and cut the top to the finished size given in the Materials List. To finish the edge of the top, use a router equipped with a chamfering bit. Chamfer only the bottom edges.

8. Install the top. Using a ³⁄₁₆-inch bit, drill two holes in the top crosspiece and one in each rear top-corner block, as shown in the *Overall View*. Because a solid-wood top will expand and contract in response to changes in relative humidity, it is important to allow it some room to move. You can

allow for this simply by wiggling the drill bit perpendicular to the length of the crosspiece. The oversized hole will provide adequate space for movement.

Position the top so that it overhangs both the sides and front by ¾ inch and is flush with the back panel. Attach the top to the crosspiece and corner braces using 1¼-inch flathead wood screws.

MAKING & INSTALLING THE DOOR/PLATFORM ASSEMBLY

1. Cut the parts. Cut the door, platform, and triangular braces from ¾-inch plywood to the dimensions in the Materials List. Cut the three edge strips from solid wood.

2. Build the door. Attach edge strips to the door panel top and sides using glue and 4d finishing nails. Secure the door panel to the door using four countersunk 1⅝-inch screws as shown in the *Overall View*.

Secure each triangular brace to the side edge strips and platform using two countersunk 1⅝-inch screws. Fill the screw holes with glued wood plugs, and sand the plugs flush.

3. Install the doorknob. Drill a centered hole for the knob screw 1½ inches from the door's top edge. Attach the knob using the screws provided.

4. Install the stop blocks. Glue and screw each stop block, with its rubber pad, against the cabinet side and top crosspiece, as shown in the *Overall View*. Make sure the pad surface is ¾ inch inside the front edge of the side panel. Use #6 x 1¼-inch flathead wood screws.

5. Hang the door. Position the hinges 2 inches inside the bottom corners of the door. Mortise the hinges in the door front. Then center the door in the cabinet opening, and mark the mortise location for each hinge. (See "Installing Doors and Hinges," page 25.)

6. Install tilt-stop block. Cut the tilt-stop blocks to the dimensions in the Materials List. Measure the width of your bins. Open the door enough so you will be able to take the bins in and out. Reach in with a pencil and mark where you want one of the tilt-stop blocks to be located. Attach one tilt-stop block to the marked location with glue and one 1¼-inch wood screw. Let the door tilt forward, and install the second block.

LOCATING TILT-STOP BLOCKS

Open door enough to remove bins.

Position tilt-stop block.

linen cabinet

FINDING SPACE to store towels and bed linen is a common problem. Although most home layouts do include a linen closet, these are often quite small and can quickly become inadequate as families grow and new purchases are made. And most linen closets end up serving as storage for other items as well—toiletries, cleaning supplies, and the like. To compound the problem, it is hard to find space in the typical home to add a full closet to act as a buffer. This linen cabinet was designed with these problems in mind. It is shallow enough that you could place it in areas you might otherwise consider unsuitable for storage. It can fit within a bathroom or bedroom without sacrificing valuable floor space, or you might even use it in a wide hallway or on a landing, providing there is enough room to meet building code safety requirements.

The construction details of the cabinet are intentionally very simple. It is designed to be built using paint-grade materials, such as birch plywood and poplar or pine lumber, although you could certainly substitute a more attractive hardwood species and apply a clear or stained finish if that better fits your decor. And you can personalize your cabinet somewhat by your choice of the applied panel molding that adorns the cabinet doors. While our model cabinet shows a simple molding profile, you will find a wide selection of possible moldings at any home center or lumberyard, and you can easily substitute one that appeals to you—it wouldn't even be necessary to adjust the dimensions shown in the Materials List.

LINEN CABINET MATERIALS LIST

Difficulty Level: CHALLENGING

Qty	Part	Dimensions	Qty	Part	Dimensions
Carcase			*Doors*		
2	Plywood sides	¾" x 11¼" x 83¼"	2	Upper doors	¾" x 16³⁄₁₆" x 44¼"
2	Plywood fixed shelves	¾" x 11" x 35"		2 Plywood door panels	¾" x 15³⁄₁₆" x 43¼"
1	Top	¾" x 13⅝" x 39¼"		4 Solid-wood edging	½" x ¾" x 16³⁄₁₆"
	1 Plywood top panel	¾" x 13½" x 38¼"		4 Solid-wood edging	½" x ¾" x 44¼"
	1 Solid-wood edging	½" x ¾" x 39¼"		4 Panel molding	⅝" x 1¼" x 10³⁄₁₆"
	2 Solid-wood edging	½" x ¾" x 13⅝"		4 Panel molding	⅝" x 1¼" x 38¼"
1	Plywood back	¼" x 35½" x 78⁵⁄₁₆"	2	Lower doors	¾" x 16³⁄₁₆" x 27⅝"
2	Solid-wood nailers	¾" x 5¼" x 35½"		2 Plywood door panels	¾" x 15³⁄₁₆" x 26⅝"
1	Bed molding	⁹⁄₁₆" x 1¾" x 38¼"		4 Solid-wood edging	½" x ¾" x 16³⁄₁₆"
2	Bed molding	⁹⁄₁₆" x 1¾" x 13⅛"		4 Solid-wood edging	½" x ¾" x 27⅝"
1	Solid-wood baseboard	¾" x 4" x 37½"		4 Panel molding	⅝" x 1¼" x 10³⁄₁₆"
2	Solid-wood baseboard	¾" x 4" x 12¾"		4 Panel molding	⅝" x 1¼" x 21⅝"
5	Adjustable shelves	¾" x 10⅞" x 34⅜"	*Hardware and Miscellaneous Supplies*		
	5 Plywood shelf panels	¾" x 10⅛" x 34⅜"	4 pr.	⅜" rabbet/overlay self-closing door hinges	
	5 Solid-wood edging	½" x ¾" x 34⅜"	4	door knobs	
1	Shoe molding (opt.)	½" x ¾" x 38½"	4	29¾" metal-shelf standards	
2	Shoe molding (opt.)	½" x ¾" x 13¼"	4	47⁵⁄₁₆" metal-shelf standards	
Face Frame			20	metal-shelf clips	
2	Solid-wood stiles	¾" x 2" x 83¾"	14	¼" x 1½" wood dowels	
1	Solid-wood top rail	¾" x 3½" x 32"		1" brads	
1	Solid-wood middle rail	¾" x 2⅝" x 32"		4d finishing nails	
1	Solid-wood bottom rail	¾" x 5¼" x 32"			

BUILDING THE CARCASE

1. Cut the parts. Cut plywood and solid stock to the dimensions shown in the Materials List for the sides, top, back, fixed shelves, and nailers.

2. Cut the dadoes and rabbets. Use a router with straight bit to cut the ¼-inch-deep dadoes in the case sides for the fixed shelves. (See "Making Dadoes with the Router," page 19.) Next, you can use the router with a straightedge guide to cut the rabbet along the back edge of each side panel to house the case back. Mark the limits of the stopped rabbet on the top panel; then use the router to cut that as well. Stop the router bit about ⅛-inch shy of the end marks, and use a sharp chisel to square the ends of the cut.

Mark the outlines of the wide rabbets for the top and bottom nailers in the side panels; then use the router to cut these recesses. Once again, stop the cut about ⅛-inch shy of the inside corner marks, and use a sharp chisel to finish the cuts.

Install a ⅝-inch-wide straight-cutting router bit into the router, and cut the grooves for shelf standards in the cabinet side panels.

3. Apply edging to the top. Cut the 45-degree miter joints on edging strips for the case top. Spread glue on the top panel edges, and apply the strips, using masking tape as a clamp to hold the strips in position while the glue sets. (See "Finishing Edges," page 12.)

4. Assemble the carcase. Spread glue in the shelf dadoes in the case sides; then join the sides to the shelves. Use 6d finishing nails to fasten these joints. Apply glue to the nailer rabbets, and slide the nailers into position. Drive finishing nails through the case sides to fix them in place. Next, spread glue on the top ends of the side panels, and place the top in position. Check that it overhangs equally on both ends; then fasten it using 6d finishing nails.

Lay the carcase on its face, and check that the assembly is square by comparing opposite diagonal measurements. (See "Squaring a Carcase," page 21.) Spread glue on the rabbets in the top and side panels and on the back edges of the shelves; then slide the back panel into position; and fasten it by nailing using 1-inch brads.

5. Build and install the face frame. Cut the stiles and rails to the dimensions shown in the Materials List. Mark the positions of dowels for the face frame joints; then use a doweling jig to bore the required holes. (See "Reinforcing Joints with Dowels," page 15.) Apply glue to the holes and also on each dowel; then assemble the face frame. Use bar clamps to pull the joints tight; then check that the frame is square by comparing opposite diagonal measurements; adjust the clamps if necessary to bring the assembly square.

6. Lay the carcase on its back, and spread glue on the front edges of the shelves and sides. Put the face frame into position, and nail it to the case parts using 6d finishing nails. You can also nail through the case top into the edge of the top rail.

7. Install the moldings. Cut the bed and base moldings to size with 45-degree angles for the front miter joints. Use 4d finishing nails to fasten the moldings in place—remember to apply glue to the mating surfaces of the miters to ensure that the joints stay tight.

8. Install the shelf tracks. Cut metal shelf tracks to length as shown in the Materials List. Install them in the dadoes in case sides using the screws or nails provided with the hardware.

BUILDING THE DOORS

1. Cut the parts. Cut door panels, edging strips, and panel moldings to the sizes shown in the Materials list. Use a miter saw to trim the ends of the edging strips and molding, which must be cut at 45-degree angles to form miter joints at the corners.

2. Apply the edging strips. Spread glue on the door panel edges; place the edging strips into position; and clamp them to the door using strips

OVERALL VIEW

Top Panel

Stopped Rabbet for Back

¼" x ⅝" Shelf Standard Grooves

⅜" Rad. Edge Molding

Nailer

Metal Shelf Standard

47⁵⁄₁₆"

½" Deep Nailer Notch

Back

Side

29"

Nailer

5⁷⁄₁₆"

½" x ¾" Shelf Dado

Fixed Shelves

¼" x ½" Stopped Rabbet for Back

of masking tape. (See "Molding and Solid Wood," page 12.) Allow the glue to cure for at least 30 minutes before removing the tape.

3. Rabbet the door edges. Use a router with a rabbeting bit, or table saw with dado blades, to cut the rabbets on three sides of each door panel as shown in the plans. (See also "Installing Inset Doors," page 27.) Remember that the edges of the doors that meet in the cen-

ter of the cabinet do not need to be rabbeted—only those edges that overlay the face frame.

4. Apply the panel molding. Mark the surface of the door to indicate the outer edges of the panel molding strips. Apply a small amount of glue to the back side of the molding; then use 1-inch brads to fasten it to the door panel. (See "Building a Slab Door," page 22.)

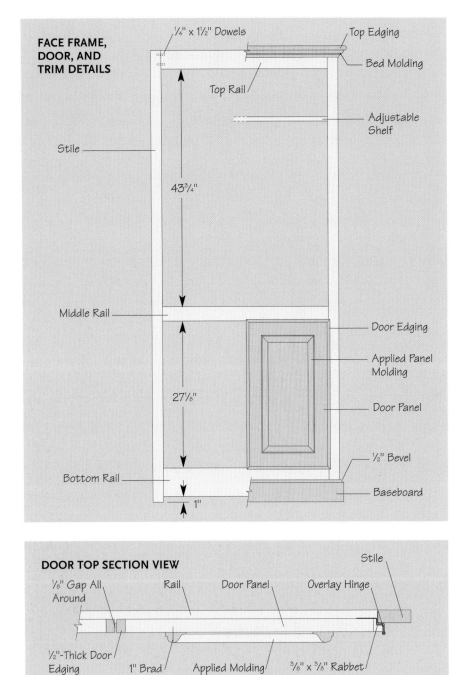

FACE FRAME, DOOR, AND TRIM DETAILS

¼" × 1½" Dowels

Top Edging

Bed Molding

Top Rail

Adjustable Shelf

Stile

43¾"

Middle Rail

Door Edging

Applied Panel Molding

27⅛"

Door Panel

½" Bevel

Bottom Rail

Baseboard

1"

DOOR TOP SECTION VIEW

Stile

⅛" Gap All Around

Rail

Door Panel

Overlay Hinge

½"-Thick Door Edging

1" Brad

Applied Molding

⅜" × ⅜" Rabbet

5. Install the doors. Mark the locations of screw holes for the hinges on each door; then drill pilot holes. Mount the hinges to the door panels using the screws provided. Hold the doors in position on the cabinet to mark the screw locations. Drill pilot holes, and mount the doors. Determine the location of door knobs; drill pilot holes; and mount the hardware.

MAKING THE ADJUSTABLE SHELVES

1. Cut the parts. Cut the plywood shelves and edging strips to the sizes listed in the Materials List.

2. Apply edging strips. Spread glue on the front edge of each shelf panel, and clamp the edging strips in place using masking tape.

FINISHING THE CABINET

1. Remove the shelves and doors. To make finishing easier, temporarily remove the doors and adjustable shelves from the cabinet.

2. Prep all parts. Set all nailheads below the wood surface, and fill the holes with drying wood filler. Mound the filler slightly over the surface to allow for shrinkage while it dries. Sand all cabinet parts using 120-, 150-, and 220-grit sandpaper, remembering to remove the sanding dust whenever you switch to a finer grit paper.

3. Apply the finish of your choice. Follow the manufacturer's directions for the product you choose. (See also "Wood Finishing," pages 55 to 72.)

4. Install the cabinet. Place the cabinet against the wall in the desired location. If there is baseboard molding on the wall, you will first need to remove it to allow the cabinet to fit flush to the wall surface. Use a spirit level to check that the cabinet is level and plumb. You can use small, tapered shingles to adjust the position of the cabinet if necessary. Drive screws through the top and bottom nailer strips inside the cabinet to fasten the case to the wall studs. Reinstall the baseboard molding to the wall on either side of the cabinet. If you placed shims under the cabinet to bring it level, you can now install shoe molding around the case to hide any gaps between the baseboard and finished floor surface.

Install the adjustable shelves, and remount the cabinet doors to complete the installation.

10 home office

TURNING UNUSED SPACE INTO WORK SPACE

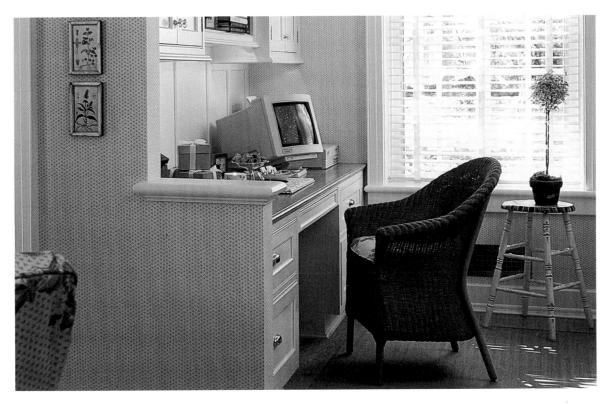

home office storage ideas

Clockwise (from top right) Tambour doors, similar to the ones used on kitchen cabinets, keep files and supplies out of sight. A wall-hung unit serves as a mini-workspace in a small office. For office space that is part of a kitchen, choose cabinets that complement the cabinetry used in the rest of the room. Traditional storage options are supplemented by the window-seat cabinet. Partners have plenty of room with this type of design.

short bookcase

HERE'S A LOVELY CLASSICAL BOOK-CASE that you can assemble in less than a day. Although its construction is simple, this bookcase will impress you with its pleasant proportions and its versatility. Its compact size and adjustable shelves serve well in a bedroom, family room, den, or study to display books or showcase your favorite momentos.

The cove and baseboard moldings give the piece a formal appearance, reminiscent of larger, built-in cabinets. The appearance is further enhanced by the solid-wood top with a quarter-round edge detail. If you choose, you can make the side panels of hardwood plywood to match the solid-wood top. Or you can emphasize the solid-wood top by painting the case.

SHORT BOOKCASE MATERIALS LIST

Difficulty Level: CHALLENGING

Qty	Part	Dimensions
Carcase		
2	Plywood side panels	¾" x 11¼" x 48"
2	Plywood top/bottom panels	¾" x 11" x 35¼"
1	Plywood back	¼" x 35¼" x 48"
Face frame		
2	Solid-wood stiles	¾" x 1½" x 48"
2	Solid-wood rails	¾" x 3½" x 33"
Top & Molding		
1	Solid-wood top	¾" x 13½" x 39"
1	Front base molding	¾" x 2½" x 37½"
2	Side base molding	¾" x 2½" x 12¾"

Qty	Part	Dimensions
1	Front cove molding	¾" x ⅞" x 37½"
2	Side cove molding	¾" x ⅞" x 12¾"
Shelves		
2	Plywood shelves	¾" x 10½" x 34¼"
2	Half-round shelf edge	⅜" x ¾" x 34¼"
Hardware		
	4d Finishing nails	
	#6 x 1¼" Flathead wood screws	
	1" Brads	
4	48" Metal shelf standards	
8	Metal shelf supports	

OVERALL VIEW

Cove Molding

Rail

Shelf Standards

Stile

Solid-Wood Top

Top

Back

Side Panel

Shelf

Half-Round Shelf Edge

Plywood Bottom

¾" x ⅜" Dado

Base Molding

BUILDING THE CASE

1. Cut the parts. Cut the side panels, top, and bottom from ³/₄-inch plywood and the back from ¹/₄-inch plywood to the dimensions in the Materials List.

2. Cut rabbets and dadoes. Rabbet and dado the side panels as shown in *Side Panel Layout.* Note that the drawing shows only one panel. Don't forget to make the other panel as a

mirror image. (See "Dadoes, Grooves, and Rabbets," page 17.)

3. Assemble the carcase. Assemble the top and bottom to the side panels using glue and 4d finishing nails. Install the back panel using glue and 4d finishing nails.

4. Make and attach the face frame. Cut the two stiles and the rails to the

dimensions in the Materials List. Attach the rails and stiles to the carcase using glue and 4d finishing nails.

MAKING THE SOLID-WOOD TOP

1. Edge-glue the boards. Make the top by edge-gluing several boards and then cutting the solid-wood panel to the final dimensions. (See "Edge-Gluing Stock," page 14.)

SIDE PANEL LAYOUT

2½"   2½"

¾" x ⅜" Rabbet

¼" x ⅜" Rabbet

¾" x ⅜" Dado

Grooves for Shelf Standards

3½"

INSTALLING THE TOP AND MOLDING

1. Cut and install the baseboard molding. Cut the front piece of base molding to its finished length, mitered at each end. Glue and nail it along the front edge. Use 4d finishing nails. Miter-cut one end of each side piece of base molding to rough length. Set each side piece in place; mark the rear of each; cut it to finished length; and install it using glue and 4d finishing nails.

2. Install the top. Turn the top upside down, and position the case upside down on the top. At each corner, predrill for 1¼-inch flathead wood screws into the top piece. Remove the top. Make the holes in the case oblong by inserting the drill in the holes and rocking from the front of the case to the back. (This will allow the solid-wood top to expand and contract with humidity changes.) Then counterbore the holes. Replace the top, and screw it in place.

2. Lay out the top. After sanding the solid-wood top using 220-grit sandpaper, decide which surface will be the bottom. Then mark layout lines on the bottom to indicate how the solid-wood top will be positioned on the case. The top should overhang the case by 1½ inches at the front and sides. The top and case should be flush at back.

3. Round-over the edge. Fit a router with a ½-inch roundover bit. Shape the bottom edges of the front and two sides of the solid-wood top, making several progressively deeper passes until the three bottom edges are rounded over ½ inch. Turn over the workpiece, and round the front and side edges using sandpaper.

3. Cut and install the cove molding. Cut the front piece of cove molding to rough length, mitered at one end. Test its fit beneath the overhanging top; mark the squared end; miter-cut it to finished length; and install it using 4d finishing nails. Test fit and install the side pieces as you did the base molding.

MAKING THE SHELVES

1. Cut the shelves. Cut the shelves to the dimensions in the Materials List. Cut two pieces of half-round molding to the length of the shelves. Attach the molding to the shelves using glue and 1-inch brads.

2. Install the shelves. Use a hacksaw to cut the shelf standards to fit between the top and bottom panels, and install the standards inside the grooves in the bookcase sides using the screws or nails provided or recommended. Install each shelf using four metal shelf supports. (See "Installing Metal Standards," page 27.)

INSTALLING MOLDING

Cove Molding

Miter

¾"   ¾"

¾"

¼"

⅞"

4d Finishing Nail

½" Roundover

Cove Molding

fold-down desk

IF YOU NEED A DESK for occasional paperwork, or a workbench for building models, tying flies, matting and framing pictures, making candles, wrapping gifts, or any of several dozen handicrafts, consider this practical project. This desk is easy to build, is attached to a wall, and folds up when not in use. For security, you can substitute a hasp and padlock for the hook and eye. The plans call for six drawers, but they're optional. Make as many as you want to suit your purposes, or you can omit them altogether. Because the drawers require no mounting hardware, you can also build the unit and add drawers later, as needs dictate.

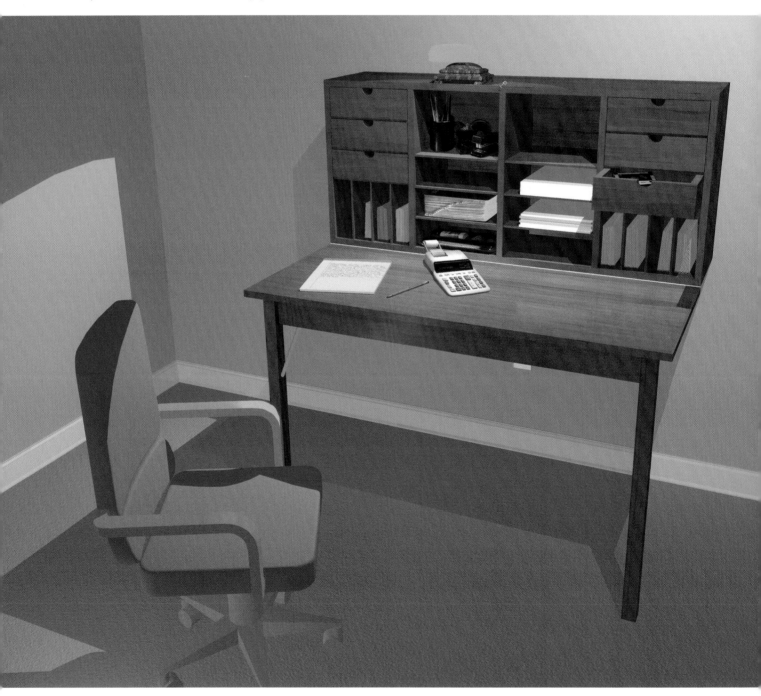

FOLD-DOWN DESK MATERIALS LIST

Difficulty Level: DIFFICULT

Qty	Part	Dimensions
Cabinet		
2	Plywood side panels	¾" x 11¼" x 20¼"
2	Plywood top/bottom panels	¾" x 11¼" x 46"
3	Plywood main partitions	¾" x 11" x 19½"
1	Plywood back panel	¼" x 19½" x 46"
4	Nailing cleats	¾" x 3" x 10³⁄₁₆"
12	Plywood shelves	¼" x 11¼" x 11"
6	Plywood envelope partitions	¼" x 7¾" x 11"
5	Solid-wood edging	¼" x ¾" x 18¾"
2	Solid-wood edging	¼" x ¾" x 46¾"
Desktop and legs		
1	Plywood desktop	¾" x 19¾" x 46¼"
2	Solid-wood legs	1½" x 1½" x 29¼"
1	Solid-wood leg rail	¾" x 3½" x 40¾"
2	Solid-wood edging	¼" x ¾" x 46¾"
2	Solid-wood edging	¼" x ¾" x 20¼"

Qty	Part	Dimensions
Drawers		
6	Solid-wood front panels	¾" x 3⁷⁄₁₆" x 10⅝"
6	Solid-wood rear panels	¾" x 2¹⁵⁄₁₆" x 9⅞"
8	Solid-wood side panels	¾" x 3⁷⁄₁₆" x 10⅞"
4	Solid-wood side panels	¾" x 3⁷⁄₁₆" x 10⅛"
4	Plywood bottom panels	¼" x 9⅞" x 10⅞"
2	Plywood bottom panels	¼" x 9⅞" x 10⅛"
Hardware		
	⅞" Brads	
	#6 x ¾" Flathead wood screws	
	#10 x 3½" Wood screws	
	½" Brads	
	1" Brads	
4	¼" x 1¼" Wood dowels	
1	Hook-and-screw-eye set	
2	48" Piano (continuous) hinges	
	#6 x ⅝" Flathead wood screws	
2	Locking leg braces	

CABINET OVERALL VIEW

BUILDING THE CABINET

1. Cut the cabinet parts. Cut the side panels, top, bottom, three main partitions, and the back panel to the dimensions in the Materials List.

2. Rabbet and dado the parts. Rabbet and dado the top and bottom panels as shown in *Top and Bottom Panel*

Joinery. Rabbet and dado the side panels as shown in *Side Panel Joinery.* Note that the drawing shows one side panel; be sure to make the other side panel in a mirror image. Dado the main partitions as shown in *Main Partition Joinery.* Note that both faces of the center partition have the same dado layout, but the other partitions

have different dado layouts on each face. (See "Dadoes, Grooves, and Rabbets," page 17.)

3. Assemble the cabinet. Glue and clamp the main partitions to the top and bottom panels. Install the back using glue and ⅞-inch brads. Cut the nailing cleats to fit, and attach them

TOP AND BOTTOM PANEL JOINERY

11⅛"
10¾"
10¾"
¾" × ⅜" Dados for Partitions
¼" × ⅜" Rabbet
11⅛"
3⅛"
2¾"
2¾"
2½"
¼" × ¼" Dados for Envelope Partitions in Bottom Only
2½"
2¾"
2¾"
3⅛"

SIDE PANEL JOINERY

¾" × ⅜" Rabbet for Top
¼" × ¼" Dados for Shelves
3½"
3½"
3½"
7½"
¾" × ⅜" Rabbet for Bottom
¼" × ⅜" Rabbet for Back

MAIN PARTITION JOINERY

3⅞"
7⅞"
3½"
Use these dimensions to lay out both sides of the center partition.
¼" × ¼" Dadoes for Shelves
3½"
3½"
3½"
7⅞"
3⅞"

to the back using glue and ¾-inch wood screws in counterbored holes in the back.

4. Install the cabinet. Use a stud finder to locate the studs in the wall where the unit will hang. Scribe a level line 30 inches from the floor. You'll need a helper or two and perhaps one or two temporary 2x4 braces cut to 30 inches to align the bottom edge of the unit to the line. Attach the unit to the wall by driving #10 x 3½-inch wood screws through counter-

bored holes in the nailing cleats and into each stud. (See "Installing Wall Cabinets," page 36.)

INSTALLING SHELVES, PARTITIONS & MOLDING

1. Cut the shelves and partitions. Cut the shelves and envelope partitions to the dimensions in the Materials List.

2. Install the shelves and partitions. Glue the six envelope partitions into the dadoes in the bottom panel, as shown in *Cabinet Overall View*. Glue

the two shelves that go over the envelope partitions into their dadoes in the main partitions and side panels. Make sure the envelope partitions are aligned; secure them using ½-inch brads driven through the two shelves. Glue the remaining shelves in place.

3. Cut and attach the edging. Cut edging to fit the front edges of the top and bottom panels, and attach it using glue and 1-inch brads. Cut five pieces to fit the vertical edges, and attach them the same way.

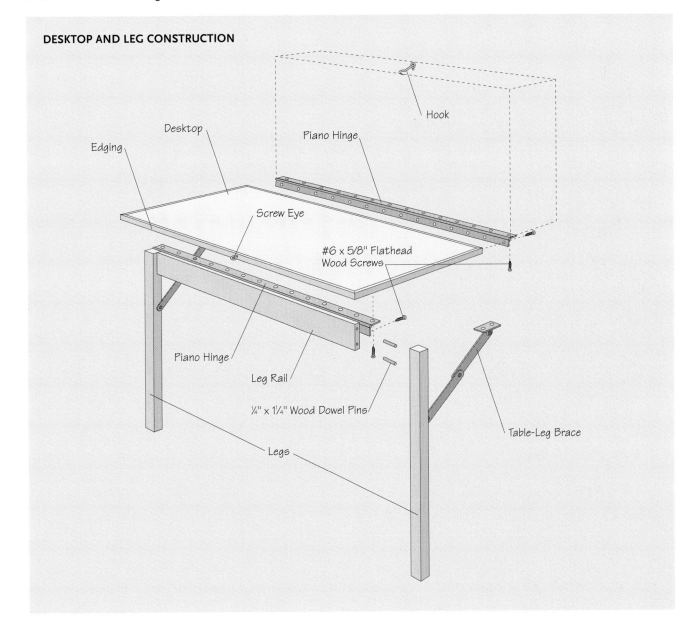

DESKTOP AND LEG CONSTRUCTION

BUILDING & INSTALLING THE DESKTOP & LEGS

1. Cut the parts. Cut the desktop, legs, and leg rail to the dimensions in the Materials List. Use clear stock for the legs and rail.

2. Cut and attach the edging. Cut pieces of solid-wood edging with 45-degree miters at each end to fit the edges of the desktop. Then attach the edging using glue and 1-inch brads.

3. Join the legs to the rail. Join the legs to the rail with glue and dowels, making the rail flush to the back of the legs. Make sure the legs remain parallel when you clamp them to the rail. If necessary, add a temporary spacer at the bottoms of the legs, and affix another clamp. Let stand until the glue sets. (See "Reinforcing Joints with Dowels," page 15.)

4. Attach the hook and eye. Install the screw eye in the center of the front edge of the desktop. Attach the hook in a corresponding spot on the top surface of the cabinet.

5. Cut and attach the piano hinges. Use a hacksaw to cut one piano hinge at 46¾ inches and the other at 43¾ inches. Attach the longer hinge to the rear edge of the desktop using seven #6 x ⅝-inch flathead wood screws and to the underside of the cabinet using seven more screws. Attach the shorter hinge to the underside of the desktop 3 inches from the front edge and centered from side to side. Then attach the hinge to the leg assembly.

6. Attach the leg braces. Following the manufacturer's directions and using the screws provided, attach a locking leg brace to the left side of the

DRAWER CONSTRUCTION

¼" x ⅜" Grooves

¾" x ⅜" Rabbet

Rear Panel

4d Finishing Nails

Finger Notch

Front Panel

Bottom Panel

Side Panel

left leg and right side of the right leg. Then attach the braces to the underside of the desktop.

BUILDING THE DRAWERS

1. Cut the parts. Cut the front, rear, and side pieces and the bottom panels to the dimensions in the Materials List. Use clear stock for the front pieces. Note that four of the side pieces and two of the bottom pieces are shorter to allow room for the nailing cleats.

2. Cut and sand the finger notches. Set a compass for a ¾-inch radius, and scribe a circle on a piece of cardboard. Cut out the circle, and cut it in half. Use this template to scribe a semicircle at the top center of each drawer front. Then cut out the notches using a saber saw, and smooth them using a drum sander or by hand.

3. Rabbet and groove the parts. Cut rabbets and grooves in the front and side pieces as shown in *Drawer Construction.*

4. Assemble the drawers. Apply glue to the rabbets in the front and side panels. Then attach the front and rear panels to the side panels using 4d finishing nails, keeping the top edges flush. Slide the bottom panels in place, and secure using three 1-inch brads driven up into each rear panel.

5. Sand and fit the drawers. Slip the two short drawers in the top-corner openings and the long drawers in the openings beneath the top corners. The drawers have been designed to have 1/16 inch gaps all around; however, if a drawer fits too tightly, adjust the sides and top edges using either sandpaper or a plane until the drawer fits and slides smoothly. Rub the bottom edges with a little paraffin (from a candle, for example) to help the drawer slide more smoothly.

file cabinet

IT'S NO LONGER BREAKING NEWS that computer technology has changed the way we live—and one of the more remarkable changes has to do with the opportunity to eliminate the vast paper trail that has followed each of us throughout our lives. Many documents, from bills to newspapers, are now delivered via computer, and the benefits of convenience, time saved, and reduced paper waste are widely enjoyed. But despite these advances, there are still plenty of records that we need to keep—insurance policies, mortgage papers, credit card and vehicle documentation, purchase receipts, and warranty information, to name some examples. And to maintain these items in an organized fashion, there is still no better tool than the reliable file cabinet.

Our file cabinet is simple in design and simple to build, using joining plates as the primary construction technique. It features two full-extension drawers with rails for lateral file storage using hanging folders—this provides easy and convenient access to all files in the drawer. The case is built of ³/₄-inch-thick plywood with solid-wood edging, and you can choose the materials to suit the type of use you plan for the case—home office, library, or basement storage. For a dressy cabinet, you can select an attractive hardwood species and apply a stained or clear finish, or you can use a less-expensive, paint-grade material (such as birch or poplar) and apply a painted finish.

Note: For best performance when constructing the tall drawers for the cabinet, we suggest ¹/₂-inch-thick Baltic birch plywood. This product differs from normal hardwood plywood in that it has thinner plies that are each one full piece, omitting the gaps that are often found in other plywood products. The panels are strong and attractive—you do not need to apply any solid-wood edging, simply leaving the edges exposed. Most home centers and lumberyards carry this product or an equivalent. If you cannot find it locally, there are mail-order suppliers that will ship cut panels to your home.

FILE CABINET MATERIALS LIST

Difficulty Level: CHALLENGING

Qty	Part	Dimensions	Qty	Part	Dimensions
Cabinet			2	Baltic birch plywood fronts (or equiv.)	½" x 10½" x 15"
2	Sides	¾" x 28" x 17¼"	2	Baltic birch plywood backs (or equiv.)	½" x 9¾" x 15"
	2 Plywood panels	¾" x 28" x 17"	2	Baltic birch plywood bottoms (or equiv.)	¼" x 15" x 15¾"
	2 Solid-wood edging	¼" x ¾" x 28"			
1	Top	¾" x 18" x 18¾"	**Hardware and Miscellaneous Supplies**		
	1 Plywood panel	¾" x 17½" x 18½"		Quick-setting epoxy	
	1 Solid-wood edging	¼" x ¾" x 18"		1" Brads	
	2 Solid-wood edging	¼" x ¾" x 18¾"		4d Finishing nails	
1	Plywood bottom	¾" x 15" x 16½"		#8 x 1" Flathead screws	
1	Solid-wood toe kick	¾" x 4" x 18"	2	⅛" x 1" x 15½" Steel or aluminum bars	
1	Plywood back	¼" x 17½" x 25¼"	2	Drawer pulls	
Drawers			2 pr.	16" Heavy-duty, full-extension, side-mount drawer slides with ½" side space	
2	Faces	¾" x 11⅞" x 18"			
	2 Plywood panels	¾" x 11⅜" x 17½"			
	4 Solid-wood edging	¼" x ¾" x 11⅞"			
	4 Solid-wood edging	¼" x ¾" x 18"			
4	Baltic birch plywood sides (or equiv.)	½" x 10½" x 16"			

BUILDING THE CABINET

1. Cut the stock. Cut ¾-inch-thick plywood to the sizes specified in the Materials List for the case side, top, and bottom panels, and cut ¼-inch-thick plywood to size for the back panel. Rip ¼-inch-thick strips of solid wood for edging the panels. Use a miter saw to cut the edging strips to length, noting the 45-degree angled cuts required for the top panel edging strips. Finally, cut the toe-kick facing board from solid stock.

2. Cut the rabbets. Next, use the router with a straight bit, or dado blades in the table saw, to cut the rabbets in the back edges of the top and side panels. (See "Dadoes, Grooves, and Rabbets," page 17.) By cutting the rabbet on the top before applying the edging, you can easily create a "stopped" rabbet for the back—this detail keeps the back panel from being exposed at the edges of the top.

OVERALL VIEW

Top Edging (Miter front corners.)

Top Panel

¼" x ½" Rabbet

Side Panel

Back

Side Edging

¼" x ½" Rabbet

No. 20 Joining Plate

Toe Kick

Bottom

2"

4"

3. Apply the edging. Spread glue on the front edges of the case side panels, and apply the edging strips. Use masking tape as a clamp to hold the strips in place while the glue sets. (See "Finishing Edges," page 12.) Spread glue on the front and side edges of the top panel, and apply those edging strips. Allow the glue to set on all parts for at least 30 minutes before removing the tape.

4. Cut the joints. Lay out the joining plates position in the cabinet side, top, and bottom panels. Use the plate joiner to cut the slots. (See "Reinforcing Joints with Biscuits," page 16.)

5. Cut the toe-kick notches. Mark the side panels to indicate the notches for the toe kick; then use a saber saw or band saw to make these cuts. Remember to keep your saw blade on the waste side of the layout line as you make the cuts.

6. Assemble the cabinet. Spread glue in the joining plate slots in case sides and in the ends of the bottom panel. Spread a small amount of glue on both sides of each joining plate before placing them in their slots; then join the sides to the bottom. Use clamps to pull the joints tight, or as an alternative, you can drive 6d finishing nails through the sides into the ends of the bottom panel to hold the parts together while the glue sets.

Next, install the top to the sides using the same techniques used for the side/bottom joints. Check that the case assembly is square by comparing opposite diagonal measurements. (See "Squaring a Carcase," page 21.) Then install the back panel using glue and 1-inch brads.

Apply glue to the front edges of the toe-kick cutout, and place the toe-kick facing board in position. Fasten the board by nailing it to the case sides using 4d finishing nails.

DRAWER DETAILS

⅛" x 1" Hanger Slot

File Hanger Bar

Side

Back

¼" x ½" Rabbet

4d Finishing Nails

Edging (Miter corners.)

#8 x 1 Screws

Drawer Slide

1" Brads

¼" x ¼" Grooves ½" from Bottom

Bottom

Pull

Front

Drawer Face

DRAWER SIDE SECTION

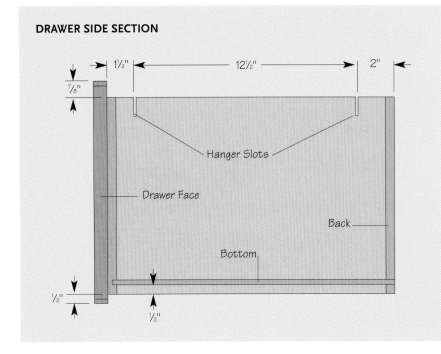

1½"   12½"   2"

⅞"

Hanger Slots

Drawer Face

Back

Bottom

½"

½"

MAKING THE DRAWERS

1. Cut the drawer box parts. Cut ½-inch-thick Baltic birch plywood to the sizes specified in the Materials List for the drawer sides and front and back panels. Cut ¼-inch-thick plywood to size for the bottom panels.

Use the table saw with dado blades or the router with a straight bit to cut the rabbets and grooves in the side and front panels as shown in the plans. (See "Building Drawers," page 28.)

2. Cut hanger rail slots. Adjust the table saw blade to a height of 1 inch. Use the miter gauge as a guide to cut the slots in the edges of the drawer side panels. Mark the position of the slots on the panels; then hold one of the panels on edge to make the cut. Simply push the panel past the blade to form the slots—repeat for each required slot.

3. Assemble the drawer boxes. Spread glue on the rabbets on drawer sides; then assemble the boxes, using

4d finishing nails to fasten the corner joints. Compare opposite diagonal measurements to check that the boxes are square, and make any necessary adjustments. Slide the bottom panels into the grooves in the side and front panels; then fasten them by nailing into the bottom edge of the back using 1-inch brads.

4. Build the drawer faces. Cut plywood panels and edging strips to the dimensions in the Materials List. Note that the end cuts on the edging strips are all 45-degree cuts—necessary for miter joints at the corners. Spread glue on the panel edges; then use masking tape to clamp the strips in place.

5. Mount the drawer faces. Drill and countersink pilot holes in the drawer front panels; then fasten the faces to the drawer boxes using #8 x 1-inch flathead screws. Take care to position the faces so that they overhang the boxes as shown in the plans.

Drill pilot holes for the drawer pulls,

and mount them to the drawers. If the mounting screws that come with the hardware are not long enough, you can either counterbore the pilot holes on the inside of the drawer or use longer screws.

6. Install the drawer slides. Follow the manufacturer's directions to install the drawer slides. Screw the slide directly to the inside wall of the cabinet side and the drawer mounting rails to the drawer sides. Use oval mounting holes for initial installation. These will allow you to adjust the position of the drawers.

Test the fit and operation of the drawers. Make any necessary adjustments, and then install the rest of the mounting screws.

7. Install the file rails. Place a small bit of epoxy into the slots in the top edges of the drawer sides; then push the rails into position. Allow the epoxy to set to lock the rails in the slots.

FINISHING THE CABINET

1. Sand all parts. Remove the drawers from the cabinet, and temporarily remove the pulls and slide hardware. Sand all cabinet and drawer parts, beginning with 120-grit sandpaper and working up to 220 grit, remembering to remove all sanding dust whenever you switch to finer grit paper.

2. Apply the finish. Apply the finish of your choice, following the specific directions supplied by the manufacturer. (For general guidelines, refer to "Wood Finishing," pages 55 to 72.)

3. Allow the final coat of finish to completely dry. Reinstall the hardware, and mount the drawers in the cabinet.

11 utility room

ORGANIZING THE HARDEST WORKING ROOM IN THE HOUSE

sewing center

SEWING is an enjoyable, creative, and money-saving pastime in many households; it's essential maintenance in most others.

This cabinet will store and organize all of your sewing tools and supplies. Best of all, setting up the sewing machine requires no more effort than opening a cabinet door and folding down a handy platform where your machine can be permanently installed.

In addition to spacious storage areas behind top and bottom cabinet doors, to the right of the handy sewing machine compartment is a convenient space divided by shelves. You can build flush-fitting drawers for this section. (See "Building Drawers," page 28.) Or buy plastic utility boxes that will stack on the shelves.

The fold-down platform provides a work surface where you can set up the machine whenever you need it, or you can permanently install the machine in the platform by following directions in your owner's manual. When the platform is in its folded-up position, the 15 inches of depth remaining behind it should accommodate most sewing machines. Nevertheless, measure the height of your machine, and make the cabinet deeper if you need to.

You can make this cabinet out of good-quality softwood plywood and then paint it. For a classier appearance, make the cabinet of hardwood plywood and apply a clear finish. If you use hardwood, and you like the slab doors shown here, cut all six doors from the same panel; then install them in the same position that they were in the panel. This will give you a continuous-grain pattern on the front of the cabinet.

SEWING CENTER MATERIALS LIST

Difficulty Level: DIFFICULT

Qty	Part	Dimensions
Cabinet		
1	Plywood top panel	¾" x 17¼" x 37¼"
2	Plywood side panels	¾" x 17¼" x 84"
3	Plywood horizontal panels	¾" x 17" x 37¼"
1	Plywood upper partition	¾" x 17" x 32"
1	Plywood lower partition	¾" x 17" x 23⅞"
3	Plywood shelves	½" x 17" x 18⅝"
1	Plywood back panel	¼" x 37¼" x 83⅝"
Face frame		
2	Solid-wood stiles	¾" x 1½" x 84"
1	Solid-wood center stile	¾" x 1½" x 79"
1	Solid-wood top rail	¾" x 1½" x 35"
1	Solid-wood bottom rail	¾" x 3½" x 35"
4	Solid-wood short rails	¾" x 1½" x 16¾"
Leg assembly & fold-down platform		
2	Solid-wood legs	1½" x 1½" x 28"
1	Solid-wood leg rail	¾" x 3½" x 11"
1	Plywood platform	¾" x 16" x 30"

Qty	Part	Dimensions
1	Platform edging	¼" x ¾" x 16½"
2	Platform edging	¼" x ¾" x 30¼"
2	Stop block pieces	¾" x 2" x 8"
Overlay-style doors		
4	Top and bottom doors	¾" x 17½" x 23⅜"
2	Center doors	¾" x 17½" x 31½"
Hardware		
	4d Finishing nails	
	⅞" Brads	
32	¼" x 1¼" Wooden dowels	
	1" Finishing nails	
1	11" Piano (continuous) hinge	
	#6 x ⅝" Flathead wood screws	
2	Locking, folding leg braces	
	#8 x 1¼" Flathead wood screws	
6	Door pulls	
6 pairs	Overlay hinges	
1	14" Piano (continuous) hinge	
2	Bullet catches	

CABINET JOINERY

BUILDING THE CABINET

1. Cut the parts. Cut the top, sides, horizontal panels, partitions, shelves, and back to the dimensions in the Materials List.

2. Cut the dadoes and rabbets. Rabbet and dado the side panels and upper partition as shown in *Cabinet Joinery*. Note that the dadoes for the shelves are ½ inch wide. (See "Dadoes, Grooves, and Rabbets," page 17.)

3. Assemble the cabinet. Assemble the top and bottom panels and the shelves to the dadoes in the side panels using glue and 4d finishing nails.

4. Install the back. Attach the back in the rabbets in the sides using glue and ⅞-inch brads.

5. Install the face frame. Cut the stiles and the top and bottom rails to the dimensions in the Materials

211

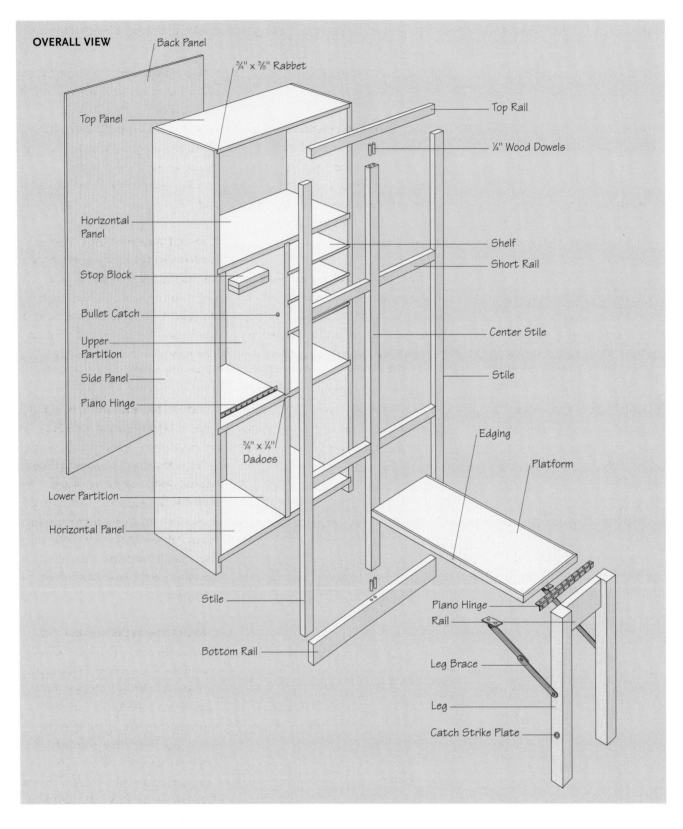

OVERALL VIEW

Back Panel

¾" x ⅜" Rabbet

Top Panel

Horizontal Panel

Stop Block

Bullet Catch

Upper Partition

Side Panel

Piano Hinge

¾" x ¼" Dadoes

Lower Partition

Horizontal Panel

Stile

Bottom Rail

Top Rail

¼" Wood Dowels

Shelf

Short Rail

Center Stile

Stile

Edging

Platform

Piano Hinge

Rail

Leg Brace

Leg

Catch Strike Plate

List. Join the center stile to the top and bottom rails using two ¼-inch wood dowels in each joint as shown in *Overall View.* (See "Reinforcing Joints with Dowels," page 15.) Attach this assembly to the cabinet using glue and 4d finishing nails. Then install the outer stiles using glue and nails. Cut the short rails to fit before installing them using glue and nails.

BUILDING THE LEGS & FOLD-DOWN PLATFORM

1. Build the leg assembly. Cut the legs and leg rail to the dimensions in the Materials List. Join the rail flush to the back of the legs using glue and two dowels at each joint as shown in *Platform and Leg Construction.*

2. Make the platform. Cut the platform to the dimensions in the Materials List. Cut platform edging to the dimensions in the Materials List. If you are making slab plywood doors, you may want to cut door edging at the same time. Miter-cut the edging to fit around the front and sides of the platform. Attach the edging using glue and 1-inch finishing nails.

3. Attach the leg assembly. Use a hacksaw to trim a piano hinge to 11 inches, and attach the hinge to the top inside of the leg rail using three #6 x

⅝-inch flathead wood screws. Then attach the hinge to the underside of the platform, centered 2¼ inches from the front edge.

4. Install the leg braces. With the platform upside down and legs fully extended, follow the manufacturer's directions to attach a locking leg brace to the outside of each leg and the underside of the platform using the screws provided.

5. Build and attach the stop block. Cut the stop block pieces to the dimensions in the Materials List. Using glue and countersunk 1¼-inch wood screws, attach one block under the top of the platform compartment, positioning it 2 inches from the cabinet face and centered side to side. Then glue and screw the other block on top of the first to create a 1½-inch thick stop.

INSTALLING DOORS & PLATFORM

1. Build the doors. The cabinet uses doors that overlay the face frame. The doors shown are flat plywood panels edged in solid wood. (See "Building a Slab Door," page 22. If you choose to make frame-and-panel doors, see "Building a Frame-and-Panel Door," page 22.)

2. Install the doors and door hardware. After applying finish to the project, attach the pulls and hinges to the doors with the screws provided. Use the screws provided to attach the doors to the cabinet face frame. (See "Installing Doors and Hinges," page 25.)

3. Install the platform. Trim a piano hinge to 14 inches using a hacksaw, and attach the hinge to the rear edge of the platform using four #6 x ⅝-inch flathead wood screws, as shown in the *Overall View.* Drill pilot holes for each screw. Then attach the hinge to the horizontal panel behind the left center door so that the hinge barrel is 2 inches inside the front edge of the face frame.

4. Attach the bullet catches. The bullet catches ensure that the platform won't flop open when you open the door. Drill holes in both sides of the compartment for the spring-loaded bullet, locating them about halfway up the compartment and ¾ inch from the front of the cabinet. Install the bullets, and fold the platform into the compartment. Mark the location of the catch strike plates on the outside of the legs. Install the strike plates.

PLATFORM AND LEG CONSTRUCTION

Piano Hinge

Platform Edging

Leg Rail

Leg Brace

¼" Wood Dowels

Leg

Platform

utility shelving

UTILITY SHELVING is a quick and simple solution to storage problems. It requires only inexpensive materials and basic tools and techniques. You can fill a wall with shelves in one easy evening.

The utility room is an obvious place to install utility shelving, but don't overlook other parts of the house where clutter tends to accumulate and where wall space is available. These shelves will also serve well in a basement, pantry, garage, or utility shed.

The accompanying plans, though specific, can also serve as general guidelines for other shelving jobs. They call for ¾-inch particleboard shelves, because this is the least expensive shelving material, usually available in lengths from 6 to 12 feet and widths from 10 to 15 inches. Nominal 1x10 and 1x12 boards are also good, as is ¾-inch plywood. Whichever material you choose, be sure to support the shelves at least every 36 inches to prevent them from sagging.

In most rooms, you'll attach the cleats using #10 x 3½-inch wood screws, driven into the studs. For masonry walls, use #10 x 2-inch screws and plastic wall anchors.

UTILITY SHELVING MATERIALS LIST

Difficulty Level: EASY

Qty	Part	Dimensions	Part
10	Solid-wood shelf cleats & ribs	¾" x 1½" x 72"	**Hardware**
3	Solid-wood shelf supports	¾" x 1½" x 80"	#10 x 3½" Wood screws
5	Particleboard shelves	¾" x 12" x 72"	#10 x 2" Screws (if attaching to a masonry wall)
1	Solid-wood temporary brace	1½" x 3½" x 15¼"	Plastic wall anchors (if attaching to a masonry wall)
			4d Finishing nails
			1¼" Drywall screws

INSTALLING THE CLEATS

1. Scribe level lines. Measure 15¼ inches up the wall from the floor, and scribe the first 72-inch-long level line. Then scribe four more, each 16 inches above the previous one.

2. Mark the studs. Using a stud finder, locate the studs that will be located behind the shelf. Drop plumb lines to indicate where the studs intersect each of the shelf lines.

3. Cut the cleats. Cut five cleats and five ribs to the dimensions in the Materials List.

4. Mark, drill, and install the cleats. Align each cleat immediately beneath a level line, and attach it using one 3½-inch wood screw driven into the middle stud. Next, mark where the other four studs cross the cleat, and predrill and attach using screws at each location. Secure the other four cleats in the same manner.

INSTALLING THE SHELVES

1. Cut the parts. Cut three vertical shelf supports to the dimensions in the Materials List. Cut the shelves to length. Cut a 15¾-inch temporary brace from a scrap of 2x4.

2. Notch the shelves, and install the ribs. Use a saber saw to cut a notch in the center of the front edge of each shelf as shown in the *Overall View.* Cut another notch at each front corner. Fasten the ribs flush to the back of the notches using glue and 4d finishing nails driven through the top of the shelves.

3. Install the shelves. Lay a shelf on the bottom cleat, and prop it up by placing the temporary brace behind the rib at the center notch. Check that the shelf is level from back to front. Put the center vertical support in place, and screw it to the rib using a 1¼-inch drywall screw. Move the prop to behind one side notch. Check the shelf for level along its length and from front to back. Attach a side vertical support using drywall screws. Repeat for the other side. Then repeat the process for all the shelves, supporting the brace on the shelf below.

OVERALL VIEW

Cleat

Shelf

Rib

#10 x 3½" Flathead Wood Screw

35¼"

Notch for Shelf Support ¾" Deep x 1½" Wide

Shelf Supports

laundry table with storage shelves

MOST OF US are not particularly enthusiastic about doing laundry—but that doesn't change the fact that it still needs to be done. While it may never be your favorite chore, it certainly will be made easier if you have a dedicated place to store supplies and fold clean items. Our laundry table features a generously sized top and plenty of storage space. You can have all of your cleaning supplies organized in one convenient place and still have shelf space to accommodate laundry baskets holding the next loads of clothes waiting to be washed. And if your laundry needs are already satisfied, this piece could serve as a general utility table for crafts or household repairs.

The table is designed to stand up to tough use, so the top is covered with plastic laminate, the same material you would find on a kitchen counter. This surface can be used for wet or dry items, without any need to worry about damaging the finish—and you can clean it easily with most nonabrasive household cleansers. In keeping with its utilitarian function, the cabinet base can be made from relatively inexpensive, paint-grade materials such as birch plywood and pine or poplar lumber.

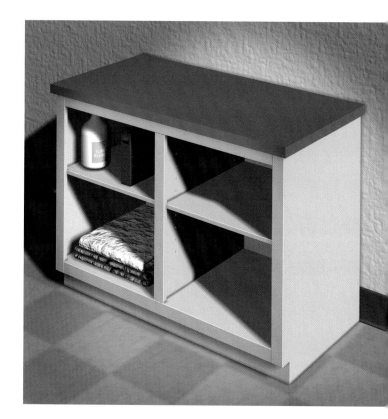

LAUNDRY TABLE WITH STORAGE SHELVES MATERIALS LIST

Difficulty Level: CHALLENGING

Qty	Part	Dimensions	Qty	Part	Dimensions
Carcase			4	Particleboard build-up strips	¾" x 4" x 15¹⁵⁄₁₆"
2	Plywood sides	¾" x 22½" x 34½"	2	Plastic laminate edging (oversized)	¹⁄₁₆" x 2" x 24½"
1	Plywood partition	¾" x 22¼" x 28¹³⁄₁₆"			
2	Plywood top and bottom	¾" x 22¼" x 45¼"	1	Laminate edging (oversized)	¹⁄₁₆" x 2" x 48½"
1	Plywood back	¼" x 29¹³⁄₁₆" x 46"			
1	Solid-wood toe-kick facing	¾" x 3½" x 46½"	1	Laminate top (oversized)	¹⁄₁₆" x 24½" x 48½"
2	Adjustable shelves	¾" x 22⅛" x 22"			
	2 Plywood shelf panels	¾" x 21⅞" x 22"	**Hardware and Miscellaneous Supplies**		
	2 Solid-wood edging	¼" x ¾" x 22"	12	¼" x 1½" wood dowels	
			8	¼" diameter shelf pins	
Face Frame				#8 x 1¼" flathead wood screws	
2	Solid-wood stiles	¾" x 2" x 31"		#8 x 1½" flathead wood screws	
2	Solid-wood rails	¾" x 2" x 42½"		6d finishing nails	
1	Solid-wood mullion	¾" x 2" x 27"		1" brads	
Countertop					
1	Particleboard core panel	¾" x 23¹⁵⁄₁₆" x 47⅞"			
2	Particleboard build-up strips	¾" x 4" x 47⅞"			

BUILDING THE CARCASE

1. Cut the parts. Cut the side, bottom, top, partition, and back panels, and the toe-kick facing board to the sizes specified in the Materials List. Mark the locations of the rabbets and dadoes in side, top, and bottom panels; then cut these grooves with either a router or the table saw and dado blades. (See "Dadoes, Grooves, and Rabbets," page 17.) Note that the rabbets in the case sides that house the back panel are ½ inch deep, while all others are only ¼ inch deep.

Lay out the toe-kick notches in the side panels; then use a saber saw or handsaw to make these cuts.

2. Drill the shelf-pin holes. Drill the holes for shelf pins in the case sides and partition using a drilling template to simplify layout and guarantee accurate placement. (See "Installing Shelf Pins," page 28.) Because the center partition is ¾ inch thick and the holes are normally ⅜ inch deep, the holes in the partition must be drilled all the way through the panel to accommodate the pins on either side. Place a scrap piece of plywood underneath the partition as you drill these holes so that the bit does not tear out the veneer on the back side when it pokes through. It is important that you use a sharp drill bit, as this will also help to prevent split-outs on the exit side of the hole.

3. Assemble the carcase. Spread glue in the dadoes in the top and bottom panels, and join them to the center partition. Use 6d finishing nails to fasten the parts. Next, spread glue in the dadoes and rabbets in the side panels, and join them to the top and bottom, nailing these joints as well. Place the carcase on its face, and

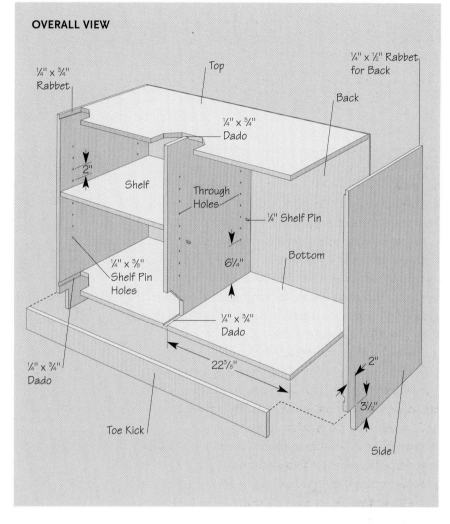

OVERALL VIEW

¼" x ¾" Rabbet

Top

¼" x ½" Rabbet for Back

Back

¼" x ¾" Dado

2"

Shelf

Through Holes

¼" Shelf Pin

Bottom

¼" x ⅜" Shelf Pin Holes

6¼"

¼" x ¾" Dado

¼" x ¾" Dado

22⅜"

2"

3½"

Toe Kick

Side

check that it is square by comparing opposite diagonal measurements. (See "Squaring a Carcase," page 21.) Make any necessary adjustments; then spread glue in the rabbets and on the back edges of the top, bottom, and partition panels before nailing the back panel in place using 1-inch brads.

Turn the carcase on its back, and apply glue to the front edges of the toe-kick cutouts in the side panels. Place the facing board in position, and fasten it by using 6d finishing nails.

BUILDING THE FACE FRAME

1. Cut the parts. Cut the stiles, rails, and mullion to the sizes specified in the Materials List. Mark the locations

of the dowel joints; then use a dowelling jig to bore the holes. (See "Reinforcing Joints with Dowels," page 15.)

2. Assemble the face frame. Apply glue to the dowel-hole joints between the mullion and top and bottom rails. Spread a small amount of glue on the dowels before inserting them in the holes; then join the rails to the mullion. Use a bar clamp to pull the joints together, and compare opposite diagonal measurements to check that the assembly is square. Adjust the clamp if necessary; then let the glue set for at least 30 minutes.

Use the same techniques to join the stiles to the ends of the top and bottom rails to complete the face frame.

3. Attach the face frame to the carcase. With the carcase on its back, spread glue on the front edges of the top, bottom, sides, and partition. Lay the face frame over the case; adjust its position; and fasten it using 6d finishing nails.

BUILDING THE COUNTERTOP

1. Cut the parts. Cut ³⁄₄-inch-thick particleboard to the sizes specified in the Materials List to form the countertop panel and build-up strips. Next, trim plastic laminate to the specified dimensions for the top and edging strips. Note: The sizes shown for the laminate are larger than finished dimensions to allow the pieces to be trimmed flush after installation. (See "Countertops," page 32.)

2. Assemble the countertop core. Spread glue on the build-up strips, and screw them to the bottom side of the countertop panel using #8 x 1¼-inch flathead screws, as shown in the plans. Drill and countersink pilot holes in the strips so that the screw heads sit flush with, or slightly below, the surface. When installing the outer build-up strips, make sure that they are perfectly flush with the edges of the top panel to provide a smooth base for the laminate edging.

3. Apply the plastic laminate. Spread contact cement on the two ends of the countertop core and also on the two short edging strips. Allow the cement to dry; then place each strip into position so that it overhangs the core on all sides. Use a laminate roller, or rolling pin, to apply pressure to the laminate; then trim it flush with a router and flush-trim bit. (See "Gluing Laminate to

FACE FRAME AND COUNTERTOP DETAIL

Core Panel

Plastic laminate cut oversized and trimmed after installation.

Build-Up Strips

³⁄₄" Overhang (Front and Sides)

#8 x 1½" Screw

Mullion

Rail

Face Frame Assembly

20¼"

¼" x 1½" Dowel

Stile

Substrate," page 33.) Repeat the process for the front edge strip.

Apply contact cement to the large piece of laminate for the countertop and also to the top of the core. When the cement is dry, place the laminate in position, overhanging on all edges, and roll it to eliminate any bubbles and create a good bond. Trim the edges flush with the router. Use a mill file to gently ease the sharp edges of the countertop.

4. Install the countertop to the carcase. Drill and countersink pilot holes in the carcase top. Place the countertop on the case, and adjust its position so that it overhangs on the ends and front by ³⁄₄ inch. Drive #8 x

1½-inch flathead screws through the top into the bottom of the countertop build-up strips to join the parts.

FINISHING THE TABLE

1. Make the adjustable shelves. Cut plywood panels and edging strips to the dimensions shown in the Materials List. Spread glue on the front edge of the shelf panels, and clamp the edging strips in place using masking tape. (See "Finishing Edges," page 12.)

2. Finish the carcase. Use a nail set to drive all nailheads below the wood surface; then fill the holes with drying wood filler. Sand the carcase parts, and apply the finish of your choice. (See "Wood Finishing," page 55.)

This list of manufacturers and associations is meant to be a general guide to additional industry and product-related sources. It is not intended as a listing of products and manufacturers represented by the photographs in this book.

APA—The Engineered Wood Association
253-565-6600
www.apawood.org
APA is a nonprofit trade association that works to promote the growth of the engineered wood industry.

Archival Methods
866-877-7050
www.archivalmethods.com
Archival Methods manufactures storage and organization products.

Ballard Design
866-863-6584
www.ballarddesigns.com
Ballard Designs is an online and catalog source for home accessories and storage solutions of all kinds.

Cabinet-Hardware.com
800-708-6649
www.cabinet-hardware.com
Cabinet-Hardware.com features a huge variety of decorative cabinet hardware.

California Closets
415-256-8501
www.californiaclosets.com
California Closets manufactures closet systems.

Easy Closets
800-910-0129
www.easyclosets.com
Easy Closets manufactures closet systems.

Elfa
888-266-8246
www.elfa.com
Elfa manufactures storage products and closet systems.

Hafele America Co.
800-423-3531
www.hafeleonline.com
Hafele manufactures cabinet hardware.

Ikea
www.ikea.com
Ikea manufacturers furniture and home-organization accessories.

Kraftmaid Cabinetry
440-632-5333
www.kraftmaid.com
Kraftmaid manufactures cabinetry and accessories.

Manhattan Cabinetry
800-626-4288
www.manhattancabinetry.com
Manhattan Cabinetry manufactures storage products, including Murphy beds.

Merillat
www.merillat.com
Merillat manufactures cabinetry and accessories.

ORG
800-562-4257
www.home-org.com
ORG manufactures home-organization and storage products, includng Murphy beds.

Organize.com
800-600-9817
www.organize.com
Organize.com sells storage and organization tools and accessories.

Schulte
800-669-3225
www.schultestorage.com
Manufactures storage systems and accessories.

Stacks and Stacks
800-761-5222
www.stacksandstacks.com
Stacks and Stacks manufactures storage and organization products.

Actual Dimensions   The exact measurements of a piece of lumber after it has been cut, surfaced, and left to dry. Example: A 2x4's actual dimensions are 1½ x 3½.

Air-Dried Wood   Lumber that is dried naturally.

Aluminum-Oxide Sandpaper   A tan-colored sandpaper that is commonly used on sanding belts and disks.

Angle Square   Often called by the brand name Speed Square. A durable triangular square used as a protractor and for scribing lines at 45 and 90 degrees.

Bevel   An edge that is angled or slanted, but not 90 degrees.

Biscuit   Pressed wood that is shaped like flat footballs. Biscuits fit into slots cut by a biscuit joiner to make wood joints.

Black Silicone-Carbide Sandpaper   A sandpaper that is made with water-resistant glue, also called "wet-or-dry" sandpaper.

Blotching   A staining problem in which wood unevenly absorbs stain, causing dark and light areas.

Brad   A finishing nail smaller than 2d with a small, cupped head.

Butt Joint   A joint with one piece of wood simply butted against the other.

Carcase   The basic case of a cabinet.

Carpenter's Wood Glue   Aliphatic resin glue used for bonding wood to wood.

Combination Square   A graduated steel blade with a sliding handle that can be tightened at any position.

Contact Cement   A rubber-based liquid glue that bonds on contact.

Corner Clamps   Clamps designed to hold two pieces of material together at a right angle.

Crosscut   A cut that is made across the grain on a piece of wood.

Dado   A type of groove that runs across the grain.

Dado Blade   A special blade used on a table saw to make dadoes.

Depth Stop   On a drill, a collar that stops the bit when it reaches a desired depth.

Drywall Screws   All-purpose screws that have aggressive threads that are designed to hold tight.

Edge-Gluing   A technique in which several boards are bonded together edge-to-edge to form a panel.

Face Frame   A frame of stiles and rails that is applied to the face of a cabinet for style and strength.

Featherboard   A single piece of wood with slots cut into one end. Featherboards are safety devices clamped to the work surface of certain power tools.

Garnet Sandpaper   An orange-colored sandpaper.

Grain   The direction and arrangement of wood fibers in a piece of wood.

Gray Silicone-Carbide Sandpaper   A sandpaper that contains zinc stearate, a soap-like lubricant.

Groove   A channel cut into a piece of wood that runs with the grain.

Hardboard   A thin, durable panel fabricated from wood fibers by using pressure, heat, and a bonding agent.

Hardwood   Wood that comes from deciduous trees (those that lose their leaves in fall).

Hollow-Wall Fastener   A type of fastener designed for use in walls made of plaster or drywall.

Jig   A device for holding a workpiece, or attached to a workpiece, that allows a tool to cut the workpiece safely and accurately.

Kickback   The dangerous action that happens when a saw suddenly jumps backward out of a cut or when a stationary power saw throws a piece of wood back at the operator.

Kiln-Dried Wood   Lumber that is dried in a kiln. Usually it is more expensive than air-dried wood, but it is less likely to shrink after it's been installed.

Knot   The high-density root of limbs that is very dense but is not connected to the surrounding wood.

Lumber Grade   A label that reflects the lumber's natural growth characteristics (such as knots) and defects that result from milling errors.

Miter Joint   A joint in which the ends of two boards are cut at equal angles (typically 45 degrees) to form a corner.

Mortise-and-Tenon Joint   A joint consisting of a mortise (a slot) and a tenon (piece that fits into the slot).

Nail Set   A pointed tool with one round or square end, used to drive nails flush with or below the surface of wood.

Nominal Dimensions   The identifying dimensions of a piece of lumber (e.g., 2x4) which are larger than the actual dimensions (1½ x 3½).

Particleboard   A term used to describe different types of sheet materials made from glue and ground-up bits of wood.

Penny (abbr. d)   Unit of measurement for nail length; e.g., a 10d nail is 3 inches long.

Plate Joiner   Also called a biscuit joiner. A tool that cuts a precise semicircular slot in which a plate or biscuit is inserted.

Plywood   Veneers of wood glued together in a sandwich. Each veneer is oriented perpendicularly to the next.

Rabbet   A ledge cut along one edge of a workpiece.

Rail   A horizontal member that is placed between stiles.

Raised Panel   A board with bevels on all four sides on one face so that stock is thicker in the center than at its perimeter.

Rip Cut   A cut made with the grain on a piece of wood.

Rip Fence   An attachment to a table saw used to guide wood through a cut.

Router   A power tool used to do such things as making grooves, dadoes, and rabbets, and mortising door hinges.

Shellac   A natural resin secreted from the lac bug.

Shim A tapered piece of wood used to level and secure a structure.

Softwood Wood that comes from coniferous trees, such as evergreens.

Stain A substance containing pigment used to color wood.

Stain Controllers Slow-evaporating, petroleum-distillate solvents that fill up the pores and less-dense parts of the wood so the stain can't penetrate.

Stile Vertical member placed perpendicular to rails.

Stud Vertical member of a frame wall, placed at both ends and usually every 16 inches on center.

T-bevel Also known as the sliding T-bevel or bevel square. A simple tool that consists of a handle or stock attached to a 6- or 8-inch slotted blade.

Table Saw A stationary power saw that can be used for crosscutting, ripping (cutting a board along the grain from end to end), grooving, and joinery.

Toggle Bolt A bolt that has spring-loaded wings and opens against the inside of the wall as you tighten the bolt.

Try Square A square with a broad blade attached to a stock at a right angle.

Varnish A type of finish that is made by cooking an oil, such as linseed oil or tung oil, with a resin.

Wood Screws Screws that are tapered so that the threads bite into the wood.

Metric Equivalents

Length

1 inch	25.4mm
1 foot	0.3048m
1 yard	0.9144m
1 mile	1.61km

Area

1 square inch	645mm^2
1 square foot	0.0929m^2
1 square yard	0.8361m^2
1 acre	4046.86m^2
1 square mile	2.59km^2

Volume

1 cubic inch	16.3870cm^3
1 cubic foot	0.03m^3
1 cubic yard	0.77m^3

Common Lumber Equivalents

Sizes: Metric cross sections are so close to their U.S. sizes, as noted below, that for most purposes they may be considered equivalents.

Dimensional lumber	1 x 2	19 x 38mm
	1 x 4	19 x 89mm
	2 x 2	38 x 38mm
	2 x 4	38 x 89mm
	2 x 6	38 x 140mm
	2 x 8	38 x 184mm
	2 x 10	38 x 235mm
	2 x 12	38 x 286mm
Sheet sizes	4 x 8 ft.	1200 x 2400mm
	4 x 10 ft.	1200 x 3000mm
Sheet thicknesses	¼ in.	6mm
	⅜ in.	9mm
	½ in.	12mm
	¾ in.	19mm
Stud/joist spacing	16 in. o.c.	400mm o.c.
	24 in. o.c.	600mm o.c.

Capacity

1 fluid ounce	29.57mL
1 pint	473.18mL
1 quart	0.95L
1 gallon	3.79L

Weight

1 ounce	28.35g
1 pound	0.45kg

Temperature

Fahrenheit = Celsius x 1.8 + 32
Celsius = Fahrenheit - 32 x ⅝

Nail Size and Length

Penny Size	Nail Length
2d	1"
3d	1¼"
4d	1½"
5d	1¾"
6d	2"
7d	2¼"
8d	2½"
9d	2¾"
10d	3"
12d	3¼"
16d	3½"

photo credits

index

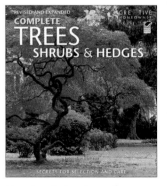